Additional Praise fo:

Witness of Tsehay Tolessa and
Gudina Tumsa, the Ethiopian Bonhoeffer

"Praise be to God for this work—as overdue as it is timely. Kudos to Samuel Yonas Deressa and Sarah Hinlicky Wilson for their research and diligence, for making this narrative of heroic faith available and accessible. Lutherans and other Christians in the Global North, where churches seem to be thinning and aging, need this model of boldness from the Global South. Gudina did not pursue martyrdom. Tsehay did not seek to be tortured. But neither did either of them recoil from their confession of the gospel in the face of terror. And the Holy Spirit bears witness, adding multitudinously to those who are saved in Ethiopia. Yes, Tertullian's timeless maxim comes alive: the blood of martyrs is indeed the seed of the church."

John Arthur Nunes, president of Concordia College-New York

"At long last this amazing story is being told. Thanks to Samuel Yonas Deressa and Sarah Hinlicky Wilson, we now have a single volume that encompasses the story of a family who endured horrific persecution to give life and vitality to the Ethiopian church and to its partners worldwide.

Every pastor, lay leader, student of theology, and congregational librarian will want to be exposed to the historical drama played out in these pages. They will discover why the church in the Global South continues to grow at such a phenomenal rate. They will also discover, in the lives of these two Oromo leaders, the spiritual and intellectual substance that carried and energized the Ethiopian Evangelical Church Mekane Yesus during a time of persecution.

This volume is a gift to the whole church. To be in the company of Tsehay Tolessa, Gudina Tumsa, and their family has been for me a profound blessing."

Paul Wee, George Washington University, Washington, DC

"This book is the compelling story of Gudina Tumsa—Ethiopian pastor, theologian, and martyr—and his beloved wife, Tsehay Tolessa. Both of these remarkable people bore witness to the gospel of Jesus Christ under the persecution of the brutal Communist regime that ruled Ethiopia in the 1970s and 1980s. Now, their story is told here through Gudina's own theological writings and, for the first time in English, the personal testimony of Tsehay. Their story, though largely unknown to the Western church, speaks of the power of faith, the cost of discipleship, and the extraordinary grace of God in the midst of unspeakable suffering. Their story is a model of what it means to heed Christ's call: 'Take up your cross and follow me.'"
Kathryn Schifferdecker, Luther Seminary, Saint Paul, Minnesota

"This couple's life has inspired people of all identities and religions. For them, Christianity wasn't only an epistemological source of eternity but also a basis for the civic and sacrosanct duty to oppose the political tyranny of the Derg. This book takes stock of the couple's lives in brisk and elegant prose to examine their unswerving ideas of liberation theology, social consciousness, and revolutionary experience that they left behind for this generation. Anyone interested in understanding the temporal and spatial interface between the spiritual and secular quests for religious freedom, political justice, and civil liberties in Oromo and beyond must know who Tsehay and Gudina are. This book is a masterfully written account of one of the most important and indomitable power couples who ever lived in Oromo."
Henok G. Gabisa, visiting faculty, Washington and Lee University School of Law, Lexington, Virginia

"Martin Luther once remarked that the gospel is like a passing shower of rain that the Holy Spirit in judgment and mercy continually relocates around the globe that people might seize it opportunistically and trust it confidently as their own good news. Ethiopia's Tsehay Tolessa and Gudina Tumsa did just that. Deressa and Wilson have made this Lutheran couple's saga accessible to a much larger share of the seventy million plus Lutherans globally, though Gudina and Tsehay's witness is surely not for Lutherans alone. On account of their Christian faith, Gudina, the 'Ethiopian Bonhoeffer' and the general secretary of the Ethiopian Evangelical Church Mekane Yesus, was murdered by the Communist Ethiopian government, which then imprisoned and tortured Tsehay for ten years. Gudina's theological writings and Tsehay's poignant memoir will surely induce you to watch and pray more eagerly for the comings and goings of the gospel shower in your part of the world."

Gary Simpson, Luther Seminary, Saint Paul, Minnesota

"The words, teaching, and life of Gudina Tumsa reach out to us from his grave. His strong confessional stance was inextricably linked to the gospel message of love and justice. His theology was holistic in the best sense of the word, calling for unity in the midst of a church divided, for justice in the midst of social and economic inequities. Now Deressa and Wilson have gathered his writings and the story of both Gudina and his wife, Tsehay Tolessa, into one book for Americans to read and cherish. Here, readers are invited to see Gudina's vision and understand the power of the gospel today for Christians in a suffering world."

Suzanne Hequet, Concordia University, Saint Paul, Minnesota

The Life, Works, and Witness
of Tsehay Tolessa
and Gudina Tumsa,
the Ethiopian Bonhoeffer

The Life, Works, and Witness of Tsehay Tolessa and Gudina Tumsa, the Ethiopian Bonhoeffer

Samuel Yonas Deressa and
Sarah Hinlicky Wilson, editors

Fortress Press
Minneapolis

THE LIFE, WORKS, AND WITNESS OF TSEHAY TOLESSA AND GUDINA
TUMSA, THE ETHIOPIAN BONHOEFFER

Cover design: Tory Herman

Print ISBN: 978-1-5064-1848-3

eBook ISBN: 978-1-5064-1849-0

The paper used in this publication meets the minimum requirements of American
National Standard for Information Sciences — Permanence of Paper for Printed
Library Materials, ANSI Z329.48-1984.

Manufactured in the U.S.A.

This book was produced using Pressbooks.com, and PDF rendering was done by
PrinceXML.

Contents

Gudina Tumsa's Life: An Overview   xiii

Foreword: xv
A Remarkable Man
and a Remarkable Woman

Introduction   xxvii
Sarah Hinlicky Wilson

Part I. Gudina Tumsa's Theological Writings

1. The Church as an Institution, or   3
   The Concept of the Church

2. Stewardship of the Gospel   11

3. Address to the Board of the   19
   Norwegian Missionary Society
   In Support of the Invitation of the Ethiopian
   Evangelical Church Mekane Yesus to the Mission for
   Assistance: Stjørdal near Trondheim in Norway,
   August 31, 1968

4. Report on Church Growth in Ethiopia   25

5. On the Interrelation between Proclamation of the   35
   Gospel and Human Development

6. Report at the Ethiopia Consultation   47

7. Serving the Whole Man: 61
   A Responsible Church Ministry and a
   Flexible International Aid Relationship

8. Pastoral Letter: 71
   The Evangelical Church Mekane Yesus
   in the Ethiopian Revolution

9. Memorandum: Some Issues Requiring Discussions   75
   and Decisions

10. The Moratorium Debate and the ECMY   97

11. Unbelief from Historical Perspective,   105
    or Kairos

12. The Responsibility of the ECMY toward Ecumenical   113
    Harmony

13. The Role of a Christian in a Given Society   121

Part II. Tsehay Tolessa's Story

Preface to *In the Fiery Furnace*   133
Lensa Gudina

In the Fiery Furnace   139
The Story of Tsehay Tolessa and Gudina Tumsa,
the Assassinated General Secretary
of the Mekane Yesus Church in Ethiopia
Aud Sæverås with Tsehay Tolessa

Conclusion: 231
The Reception and Expansion of
Gudina Tumsa's Legacy
in Ethiopia, Africa, and Beyond
Samuel Yonas Deressa

Appendix: The Church and Ideologies   243
Baro Tumsa

Bibliography   251

Subject Index 253

Scripture Index 261

Gudina Tumsa's Life: An Overview

1929 Born in Boji, Welega Province, Ethiopia

1939 Begins to attend local evangelical school in Boji

1943–47 Attends Swedish Evangelical Mission School in Najo, Welega; serves as an interpreter for missionaries and as a volunteer evangelist

1947 Employed by the Swedish Evangelical Mission's Teferi Mekonen Hospital in Nekemte, Welega; later, participates there in training course for surgeon's assistants

1951 Marries his wife, Adde Tsehay Tolessa, in Nekemte

1952 Graduates as a surgeon's assistant from Teferi Mekonen Hospital Nursing School

1952–55 Employed by Swedish Evangelical Mission as dresser in Nekemte, Bakko, and Arjo

1955–58 Studies in the second pastoral course organized in Najo by the Swedish Evangelical Mission and the German Hermannsburg Mission

1955 Attends the All-Africa Lutheran Conference, Marangu, Tanganyika, East Africa, as youth delegate from Ethiopia

1958 Ordained as one of the surgeon's assistant of the Evangelical Congregation in Nekemte

1962 Short teaching assignment to the Kambata/Hadiya area

1963 Assigned to the Kambata/Hadiya area by the EECMY officers to organize the work of the Mekane Yesus Church there

1963–66 Studies theology at Luther Seminary, Saint Paul, Minnesota, United States; receives Bachelor of Divinity degree

1966–79 Serves as executive general secretary of the Ethiopian Evangelical Church Mekane Yesus based in Addis Ababa

1968   Elected as the chairman of the Association of the Lutheran Congregations of Addis Ababa and vicinity

1970   Elected as a member of the Policy and Reference Committee of the Assembly of the Lutheran World Federation at Évian, France, where he plays a significant role by introducing an additional recommendation in the field of human rights

1972   Leads a three-man drafting committee in the production of the controversial document entitled "On the Interrelation between Proclamation of the Gospel and Human Development"

1973   Makes an official call on the government of Ethiopia to speed up work on land reform in the Ethiopian parliament

1974   Organizes the Addis Ababa Synod of the Mekane Yesus Church and is elected as the first president of the synod

1975   Initiates and takes a leading role in conducting seminars and workshops on Christianity and socialism

1976   Plays a leading role in the formation of the Council of Churches' Cooperation in Ethiopia and is elected chairman

1979   Produces a document, "On the Role of a Christian in a Given Society," his theological last will and testament

1979   Kidnapped and murdered; buried on the grounds of the former estate of Ras Kassa, Addis Ababa

1992   Reburial ceremony

1992   Establishment of Gudina Tumsa Foundation to carry on his vision

Source: Paul E. Hoffman, *Church and Society*, 267–68, alt.

Foreword:
A Remarkable Man
and a Remarkable Woman

It was November 1964 when I met a remarkable man. He was 35, married, a father, a pastor from Ethiopia, and six foot six-and-a-half. I was 23, single, a seminary student, a mere six feet in height. For the next academic year, we would share a dormitory room at Luther Seminary in Saint Paul, Minnesota. We talked at length and often laughed and joked. We spent a good deal of time together, including Christmas break with my family on the farm where I grew up. He and my father hit it off; they had long conversations, even to the point that my father uncharacteristically forgot to come out to help with a two-person task he had asked me to do.

Gudina Tumsa had been sent to the United States to study theology, funded by a scholarship from the Lutheran World Federation (LWF). Ostracized from his family at age ten for chopping down a "worship tree" where sacrifices to demonic spirits were made, he had attended a missionary school and become a trained surgeon's assistant and an evangelist before being ordained as a pastor. That first year at Luther Seminary involved a steep learning curve for someone without a college education who was also trying to master English. He would ask me to explain unfamiliar expressions and unfamiliar theological and philosophical terms, write them down, and wake up early in the morning to study those lists before he went back to his classes and assignments. The original intention had been that he would spend one year in the United States, but he did so well that he was invited to continue his studies for another two years. I was away on internship the next year. In 1965–66, he and I were both seniors, and at the end of that school year we both graduated. He returned to Ethiopia, while I went on to graduate school.

It was an exciting time to study theology. For one thing, Vatican Council II was in session from 1962 to 1965. Eastern Orthodox churches had joined the World Council of Churches in 1961. The new opportunities for conversation and cooperation between groups that had been separated for so long seemed like the dawning of a new day. One of our professors served as a Protestant observer at Vatican II, and students began to organize interseminary dialogues. For another, the civil rights movement brought a new awareness of racial injustice, and Martin Luther King Jr. offered an articulate rationale for the churches' involvement. Several members of the faculty and student body were, in one way or another, politically active. Paul Wee, a member of the LWF staff who knew Gudina after he returned to Ethiopia, has reported that Gudina was "intensely interested in the biblical rationale for the involvement of [Martin Luther] King and the churches in the civil rights movement."[1] "This movement for reform led by African-Americans affected him deeply." It affected "not only Gudina's understanding of the role of the church in society, but it also affected his understanding of ecumenism as well"[2]—the latter because it involved a variety of religious leaders working together for social change. Also, there was at Luther Seminary a good deal of attention to churches in other parts of the world. A clear sense that Christianity was a worldwide phenomenon came through, even if the full depth of the cultural differences were less well understood than they are today. And, finally, a group of newer faculty made theology engaging by dividing large classes into discussion sessions and crafting assignments that expected the assessment of theological ideas, not just their repetition. Inspired by dialectical theology and neo-orthodoxy, they invited students to rethink theology in terms of a fresh encounter with the Bible and the preached word of God. For someone like Gudina, already well versed in the Bible, this simply deepened his understanding. Students were

1. Paul Wee, "Dietrich Bonhoeffer and Gudina Tumsa: Shaping the Church's Response to the Challenges of Our Day" (speech given at the Missiological Seminar on the Life and Ministry of Rev. Gudina Tumsa, April 30–May 3, 2003, in Addis Ababa, Ethiopia), 24.
2. Paul Wee, "Ecumenical Challenges: Working in Love, Transforming Lives: The Ecumenical Legacy of Gudina Tumsa," in *Ecumenical Challenges: Working in Love, Transforming Lives*, ed. Samuel Yonas Deressa, Journal of Gudina Tumsa Theological Forum 3 (Minneapolis: Lutheran University Press, 2014), 18–19.

exposed to Reinhold Niebuhr, Dietrich Bonhoeffer, the Lundensian theologians, Emil Brunner, Rudolf Bultmann, Karl Barth, and others. These theologians criticized the earlier liberal theology for not taking sin and structural evil seriously enough, emphasized the importance of proclamation, and recommended that close attention be paid to the historical context of scriptural texts, doctrines, and contemporary listeners. While locating biblical texts in their *Sitz-im-Leben* (historical context), the focus was on the meaning of those texts, on learning to bridge the "then" and the "now" in such a way as not to lose the power of the biblical witness.

Gudina's wife, Tsehay Tolessa, stayed in Ethiopia to care for their children. Unfortunately, I never had the opportunity to meet her. From reading the memoir in this volume, I have come to appreciate what a remarkable woman she was. Born into a relatively prosperous family, by the time she was ten the Italians had taken over her father's business, and he had lost his life for refusing to transport grenades. Her mother had barely survived taking care of the family, only to have the Italians burn down the village in which they lived. After the Italians left, slavehunters had taken children from their household, never to be seen again. And then her mother died of typhus. All of this before Tsehay was ten years old. Taken in by a mission, she went to school, then worked in a home for children whose parents had leprosy. She met Gudina, and they fell deeply in love. She was a person with a faith as deep as his. Though they were sometimes separated by Gudina's work, they were very much partners.

Both came from the Oromo people of southwestern Ethiopia—a people who had endured decades of mistreatment. For them, the gospel was liberating in all senses of the word. It liberated from enslavement to fear-producing traditional spiritual practices. The gospel was accompanied by nurses and doctors and medical training that liberated from many illnesses. It brought teachers who liberated from illiteracy and ignorance. It created faith communities of mutual support, led by fellow Oromo leaders. The message of love affirmed their God-given dignity, on the basis of which they could confront the economic and political consequences of being treated as feudal vassals by more well-connected Ethiopians.

The one thing this good news did not bring was immunity from suffering. Both Gudina and Tsehay would experience a good deal of it. Their first son would die as a toddler after ingesting a hard kernel of corn that blocked his breathing. Two decades later, when the militant

Marxists were in power, another son would die after being beaten by an anti-government group of youths. Still another son would escape a similar fate by fleeing to Kenya and then to Germany. Two daughters would win scholarships that sent them to East Germany and Czechoslovakia, only to be in danger there and need to flee to West Germany. And their youngest daughter would be imprisoned for a time at age sixteen and then soon left on her own, with one parent "disappeared" and the other in prison.

For reasons that will soon become clear, Gudina has become a potent symbol for the Ethiopian Evangelical Church Mekane Yesus and for the Oromo people. Clergy forums continue to pass on and assess his theological legacy, and large numbers of people hold him up as a model of faith and wise leadership.

Let us go back to 1966. Following graduation, Gudina returned to Ethiopia to become the general secretary of the Ethiopian Evangelical Church Mekane Yesus, a church that had been formed in 1957 by combining several Lutheran missions and some congregations of Presbyterian background. Its theological identity and international affiliations were Lutheran. As is clear from what Gudina told me while he was at Luther Seminary and from Tsehay's memoir, the position of general secretary was not something he sought or even wanted but, after repeated requests, he accepted it as a calling.

In that position, he articulated a theology that was both deeply rooted in core Lutheran ideas and deeply contextual. It was a triune theology that gave attention to creation, redemption, and the work of the Spirit. It was a holistic theology that explored the implications of the gospel for all of life, not just for individual spirituality (as important as that may be).

His accomplishments were remarkable.

For example, in the 1970s, as the emperor was replaced by a highly nationalistic Marxist-Leninist government and the country went from feudalism to socialism, he was one of the first to comprehend the significance of what was happening. He was in favor of reform, but the official atheism and totalitarian character of the regime concerned him. His leadership helped the church adjust to its new political situation. He organized workshops on Christianity and socialism. As part of this adjustment, he recognized the need for the church to move away from its heavy dependence on overseas assistance. With 70 percent of the church's budget coming from Europe and North America, revolutionaries in the government could easily accuse it of disloyalty or of foreign influence. He also objected to the restrictions Europeans and Americans were placing on the use of their contributions to the Ethiopian church. He preferred that Ethiopians identify the priorities for their own church and avoid the false dichotomy between evangelization and social development. Some voices were calling for a boycott of those funds. He resisted this call, because the goal of church relations was not independence but a respectful interdependence. "The various parts of the universal church are and should be interdependent. Independence is a legitimate national aim; it can never be an acceptable theological aim for a church."[3] The diverse traditions of the different missions (Swedish, German, American, Norwegian, and Danish) were also reflected in the church, so he worked to unite it. His task was to bring this young church to maturity.

His leadership also helped to form an ecumenical alliance, the Council for Cooperation of Churches in Ethiopia. It included, at first, even the Ethiopian Orthodox Church that had caused the Protestants so many problems. He was elected its first chairman. The council grew, in part, out of his recognition that the churches, when faced with a government suspicious of religion and of anything other than its own influence, needed a united voice. For this and other reasons, he also led his own church to join the World Council of Churches and the Lutheran World Federation.

Serving as chairman of an ecumenical organization helped to make him a target for the new government. Unless he could be co-opted, the totalitarian leaders regarded anyone with his visibility and influence to be a threat.

His leadership kept the church focused on the gospel, on human dignity (growing out of the biblical view of men and women created in the image of God[4]), and on social justice. His was a Christ-centered, triune theology concerned about the whole person. God "is busy and active in this world, creating ever new. And Jesus, the Son of God, came with this same creative power." God is at work in all creation, "constantly bringing good out of evil."[5] His leadership reflected the best of the African mission tradition, with education, medical care, microdevelopment, a strong sense of community, and Christian piety all rolled into

---

3. See chapter 9 of this volume: Gudina Tumsa and Paul E. Hofmann, "The Moratorium Debate and the ECMY (August 1975)," 116. The document was jointly written, but the quotation is from the part written by Gudina.

4. Øyvind M. Eide, *Revolution and Religion in Ethiopia* (Oxford: J. Currey, 2000), 126.

5. See chapter 10 of this volume: Gudina Tumsa, "Unbelief from Historical Perspective or, Kairos," 129.

one. Beholden to no political ideology "invented by men throughout the centuries," he also saw that in Africa, "politics decides who should die and who should live."[6] Early on, he was one of the few willing to criticize the stratified society of the emperor, and later, one of the few willing to say "no" to the revolutionary government. His theology was not overtly political, but he did not back away from criticizing the policies of the emperor, and after the emperor was succeeded by a Marxist regime, he was able to give it only qualified support. He endorsed the new regime's economic reforms but objected to its overt materialism. A particularly poignant moment occurred during a church assembly in 1975 when his own brother gave a speech lauding the benefits of a socialist dictatorship. Gudina took the floor and responded, "It must be understood that there can be no reconciliation and no compromise between what the church believes and materialism. . . . Materialism thinks and lives from below, from matter, and the church lives from the Spirit of God, who comes from above."[7] As the new government consolidated its power and began to seek to control the churches, Gudina saw what was in store. That same year, 1975, he told a group of pastors, "I see it as my duty to prepare the church for the persecution that will surely come. I'm afraid it will prove fatal to me one day."[8]

His leadership did not falter. In 1978, he was arrested and held without charge for a month. The government wanted to make a deal with him. They wanted him to go abroad and raise money for government projects. He refused, saying he served the church. In 1979, he was again arrested and held for three weeks, this time charged with preaching against the ideals of the revolution and fostering dissent among the youth. His captors interrogated him intensely and threatened him with execution. They also imprisoned his sixteen-year-old daughter and threatened to kill her and his wife. His captors were shocked to hear him say that torture would make no difference. He could only tell the truth.[9] International pressure prompted the government to release him. Responding to the request of church leaders, the government of Tanzania agreed to let him live there in safety. He knew that a third arrest would be his last, but when told by Christian Krause

6. See chapter 8 of this volume: Gudina Tumsa, "Memorandum: Some Issues Requiring Discussion and Decisions," 101.
7. Gunnar Hasselblatt, *Gespräch mit Gudina*, ed. Wolfgang Erk (Stuttgart: Radius, 1980), 43, as quoted in Eide, *Revolution and Religion*, 127.
8. Interview with Gudina Tumsa, September 9, 1975, quoted in Eide, *Revolution and Religion*, 125.
9. Interview with Gudina's daughter, Lensa Gudina, March 30, 1995, quoted in Eide, *Revolution and Religion*, 176.

of the arrangement worked out with Tanzania, Gudina, with a totally uncharacteristic burst of anger, refused. "'Here is my church and my congregation. How can I, as a church leader, leave my flock at this moment of trial? I have again and again pleaded with my pastors to stay on.' He then quoted [from what had become a key passage for him in prison] 2 Corinthians 5:15, 'Christ died so all that those who live should no longer live for themselves but for him who died for them and was raised again.'"[10] In Krause's words, Gudina "drew all his motivation from Scripture. In my opinion he is only comparable to Bonhoeffer!"[11] (Dietrich Bonhoeffer had refused the safety of staying in the United States and returned to Nazi Germany shortly before the outbreak of World War II.) Following Krause's lead, many others have called Gudina "the Bonhoeffer of Africa."

On July 28, 1979, while leaving a church service, Gudina and Tsehay were stopped. He was taken away, she was allowed to return home.

For a long time after Gudina's abduction, no one knew what had happened to him. All attempts to find out yielded no information. Only years later, after the regime fell, did a guard reveal that Gudina had been killed that same night. The guard also shared where the bodies of Gudina and thirty-eight other victims had been buried. His remains were located in April 1992, and a funeral was held on June 27 of that year, almost thirteen years after his execution.

On February 2, 1980, roughly six months after Gudina's death, Tsehay was arrested. She was hung upside down and badly beaten. With broken bones and open wounds, she was put into a prison so crowded that the prisoners had to take turns sleeping. Her wounds received no attention. Three months later she was tortured again, this time sustaining wounds from which she never fully recovered. She was kept in prison for ten years, sometimes receiving assistance from Christians "on the outside" and inspiring many of her fellow prisoners by her deep faith. The mistreatment was awful. Prisoner after prisoner "disappeared." For reasons unknown, she was released after ten years. She lived until 2014.

In 1979, days before his death, Gudina had written these words: "As someone [Bonhoeffer] has said, when a person is called to follow Christ, that person is called to die. It means a redirection of the purpose of life, that is death to one's own wishes and personal desires and finding the greatest satisfaction in living for and serving the one who died for us

10. Interview with Christian Krause, February 13, 1991, quoted in Eide, *Revolution and Religion*, 177.
11. Ibid.

and was raised from death (2 Cor 5:13–14)."[12] He continued, "A responsible Christian does *not aggravate any situation and thereby court martyrdom. . . . To be a Christian is not to be a hero to make a history for oneself.* A Christian goes as a lamb to be slaughtered only when they know that this is in complete accord with the will of God who has called them to his service."[13]

Much of what Gudina accomplished was a reflection of what kind of person he was.

He was a man of deep faith. This was the core. Everything about him was related to it. As a result, he was a deeply grounded person.

Gudina was a wise man. He paid close attention to human beings and understood them. He also understood himself. He had absorbed a biblical vision of what contributed to human well-being and to a healthy community, and he was ready to act on this vision. His wisdom stemmed from a kind of humility, not the artificial nor the self-effacing kind, but the kind that saw himself as clearly as it saw others, not thinking of himself more highly than he ought.

Gudina was not afraid to have an independent voice. This courage was a product of his deep faith and his wisdom, and he exhibited it even before studying theology. But his theological studies further equipped him to speak the language of church leaders in Europe and the United States, just as it equipped him with the confidence that there were good theological reasons for resisting the political leaders when they attempted to control him or his people.

Gudina felt a deep calling to serve the church in which he grew up. As I have already said, he had no ambition to become its leader, but when called to do so, he accepted the position graciously and took the responsibility very seriously.

As was already evident while he was studying theology, Gudina was a man of keen intelligence who thought deeply about things theological. Everything he did was informed by careful theological reflection. This kept his attention to his church's context from becoming a mere endorsement of that context. It enabled him to keep growing. And it prevented him from adopting religious or political ideologies.

Gudina loved life. He had a wonderful sense of humor. The martyrdom that came his way was not something he sought.

So, why is Gudina's story important?

My first answer is that it invites us to celebrate the love of God and

---

12. See chapter 12 of this volume: Gudina Tumsa, "The Role of a Christian in a Given Society," 152.
13. Ibid., 150. Italics added.

to take our calling very seriously. The depth of Gudina's faith and the integrity with which he lived it are both challenging and inspiring. What is wonderful is how generous a faith it was, how committed it was to the well-being of others. It was enlarging, not diminishing—ethically serious without being legalistic, theologically informed without being dogmatic. His faith and the theology that grew out of it were relational and communal.

The importance of this generous faith is related to what is happening in America. According to Pew Research, some 30 percent of persons under thirty identify themselves as "unaffiliated." What often prompts this self-designation is the unattractive portrait of Christianity they have gained through the media. What is portrayed there is so often harsh, judgmental, and not at all generous. What has affected the "nones" has also affected many others. They long to find a Christianity that is more authentic, one that quite evidently makes a positive difference in people's lives. In the stories of both Gudina and Tsehay, we find portraits of authenticity and integrity. The way they lived exhibited the depth of their faith. This was true from one corner of their lives to another—from refusing to cease their work in the church even when their lives were in danger to insisting that Gudina's salary as general secretary be reduced along with the salaries of other pastors in the church, from welcoming into their new home Gudina's sister and two brothers after their parents' death to refusing to be co-opted by those in power.

My second answer is that it is good for non-Africans to appreciate the leadership provided by Gudina—leadership that reached beyond Ethiopia to worldwide Christianity. It challenges the expectation, buried deep within many Americans or Europeans, that Africans are less capable. This image assumes that Westerners are the ones with economic or intellectual or medical resources, and that with these resources comes a right to lead. The implication is that Westerners are to not only provide the resources that are lacking but also decide how to use them. Gudina's impressive leadership abilities challenge this less-than-fully-conscious assumption. To be sure, Gudina did benefit from the education he received in the United States and from the Western theological tradition to which he was exposed, but he did not merely absorb something and take it back to Ethiopia unchanged. He engaged with it, assessed it, and worked with it creatively. He was already a recognized leader before he came. His education did not change who he was. It deepened his understanding and refined his skills. This was quite a different kind of benefit than is suggested by the model of carrying back knowledge from "the enlightened" to "the unenlightened."

My third answer is to call attention to the importance of context in any theological thinking. Christianity is not a complete package of ideas and practices that can be adopted without modification anywhere or anytime. The calling or vocation of Christianity is to foster shalom—whole, healthy relationships among God, humans, and the rest of creation. What this entails must be worked out in each context. It cannot be imported from another part of the world or from another historical period. Gudina was deeply rooted in his own setting. This does not mean that he endorsed everything about it—only that he was deeply aware of what it offered and what it needed. He learned from the civil rights movement but applied these learnings to a different set of problems in his own country. He learned from the ecumenical movement that was gaining momentum in the United States but applied these learnings to quite a different situation in his own land. Cooperation in the face of a hostile government was an undertaking quite different from the ecumenical task in the United States of overcoming ethnic isolation and denominational misunderstanding. To the degree that we appreciate how creatively he engaged his context, we will see more clearly the shape of our own setting and the need to think carefully about what to do in our own time and place.

Allow me one example. Racial injustice has reemerged as a significant problem in American society. In the 1960s, Martin Luther King Jr. identified the ways countless Christians could work together to end the overt forms of segregation present in that day. Today, Christians need to rethink the issue, understand the subtler forms of white privilege, and identify the ways we can end the injustices that persist today. All of this calls for careful thinking. The question to be addressed is: What does it mean for believers to advance racial justice today?

My fourth answer is that Gudina mistrusted ideologies. In a document that came out of a discussion following a seminar on Christianity and socialism, he said, "We aspire for justice, respect for human rights, and the rule of law. Ideologies cannot be considered as absolute. Complete allegiance is due to God and God alone."[14] An ideology claims to have the complete truth along with an invincibly correct outline of mandated behavior. In retrospect, we can see that ideology under-

---

14. See chapter 7 of this volume: "Pastoral Letter: The Evangelical Church Mekane Yesus in the Ethiopian Revolution," 85.

mined the aspirations released by the overthrow of the empire in Ethiopia. In the United States today, rival ideologies are currently creating paralyzing polarization. When ideologies are endorsed by religious leaders, the situation is even worse. A theology that recognizes the gap between our knowledge and wisdom and God's knowledge and wisdom challenges such ideologies. It keeps us open to new insights. It keeps us focused on the common good. It keeps us involved in respectful deliberations. It does all of this while still standing for something important.

We see quite clearly in Gudina's life and writings how Christianity is political without being partisan. The kingdom of God has implications for our common life as well as for our personal lives. Our calling as citizens is to identify and advance what benefits all. Christianity offers insights for envisioning the common good, even though it has no prescribed program of how to advance it. Human wisdom and wide-ranging deliberation produce political programs that serve the common good.

My fifth answer is that, in academia at least, "missions" have come to be associated with Western imperialism. I expect that in some cases this linkage is deserved, but in others it is not. The story of Gudina, Tsehay, and the Ethiopian Evangelical Church Mekane Yesus is evidence of how beneficial the work of missionaries, when done well, can be. For a number of reasons, in this setting it was Ethiopians who spread the message and, when isolated by World War II, it was Ethiopians who assumed leadership. Gudina stands as a symbol of that Ethiopian church. In addition to ending the fear associated with demonic spirits, in addition to providing medical care and education, it has given its members a new sense of their dignity as creatures created and loved by God. The remarkable growth it experienced in the twentieth century and on into the twenty-first came about because of its many important contributions to the lives of its people.

After 1966, I never saw Gudina again. But I treasure the opportunity to have known him and the opportunity that has come my way more recently to learn more about his accomplishments and his continued influence. And I am grateful for the even more recent opportunity to learn more about Tsehay's life, what she was like, and what she experienced.

This book invites us to ponder the lives of Gudina Tumsa and Tsehay Tolessa. Theirs is an instructive, inspiring, challenging, and sometimes sobering story. Tsehay's memoir describes the childhood of Gudina as well as her own, their life together, and Tsehay's imprisonment. The memoir follows the extant writings of Gudina. I commend to you all that this book has to offer.

Darrell Jodock
August 2016

Introduction

Sarah Hinlicky Wilson

It would have been so easy for Gudina Tumsa to escape. His friends had made all the arrangements. Christian Krause, a German pastor friend with long experience helping refugees from east Africa, brought news of the offer. They would spirit him over the Ethiopian border, through Kenya, and into Tanzania, where he would be offered asylum. Gudina's son had already fled the country, and it would be the best thing for Gudina, too, not to mention his wife Tsehay and their daughters. All he had to do was say yes.

But he did not say yes. Far from accepting his friend's best intentions with relief and gratitude, Gudina seized Christian by the lapels, shook him violently, and cried out, "Don't tempt me! Here is my church and my congregation. How can I, as a church leader, leave my flock at this moment of trial? I have again and again pleaded with my pastors to stay on." Then he quoted 2 Corinthians 5:15: "Christ died for all, that those who live might no longer live for themselves but for him who for their sake died and was raised." He concluded, "Never ever will I escape."

Gudina remained true to his word. Twice he was arrested by the secret police of the Communist Derg regime in Ethiopia under the violent leadership of Mengistu Haile Mariam. The third and final arrest came on the night of July 28, 1979. Gudina was abducted off the street on the way home from teaching a Bible study. He was brutally murdered, his body dumped in an unmarked grave near the occupied emperor's palace. But no news was given to the family or the church. For the next thirteen years, they were caught between fear and hope, never knowing if Gudina still lived in a wretched cell somewhere or had been put to death. Only after the fall of the regime in 1991 were they able to put the clues together and finally locate Gudina's remains. He received a Christian burial on June 27, 1992.

In many ways, Gudina the martyr might be considered the lucky one. The same night of his abduction, his wife Tsehay Tolessa was arrested as well. Initially released, the day soon came when she was thrown into prison—without accusation, trial, or sentence—and there she stayed for ten years. At the beginning of her imprisonment, she was subjected to unimaginable torture, which had already by then become routine procedure in that evil system. Even when the worst of the torture was over, the conditions in which she spent the next decade were appalling: overcrowding, substandard sanitation, inadequate food, no heat in the winter or fresh air in the summer, infestations of insects and rodents, not to mention the pervasive air of fear and death. It is astonishing that she even survived after what they had done to her body.

What made these two people, a loving couple who had given life to six children, such a threat to the Communist government of Ethiopia? Why did the Derg need to silence Gudina's voice forever and lock Tsehay away for a decade?

Gudina's crime was being an outspoken Christian. It didn't matter that, in theory, many of Gudina's efforts on behalf of the people of Ethiopia dovetailed with the ideals of the revolutionary party. It didn't matter that he had been an outspoken critic of Emperor Haile Selassie's tacit blessing of landowners' abuse of peasants and farmers or exorbitant taxation. It didn't matter that Gudina continually strove to gain for his people better education, land reform, or health care, even to the point of becoming a trained surgeon's assistant himself. It didn't matter that in a historically hierarchical and ethnically divided country, Gudina shepherded a lay-led, democratically structured church body that refused to impose a single language or church culture but struggled through the hard work of becoming truly multilingual and multicultural.

Gudina was dangerous: dangerous because, however much he opposed the tyranny of the emperor and the old ecclesiastical regime, he was not deceived by the true spirit of the new atheist regime. He insisted on care for the human body, but he would not accept the materialist conviction that humans are *only* body. His holistic approach to Christian ministry had even brought him into conflict with European mission agencies, who tended to support either evangelization or social-diaconal development but not both at the same time. In his years as general secretary of the Ethiopian Evangelical Church Mekane Yesus (EECMY), Gudina articulated together with his colleagues a vision of caring for "the whole man," body and soul alike, individual and community alike. He would not accept false dichotomies no matter where they came from. And he certainly would not keep silent in the face of atrocities, even if they were rubber-stamped by the supposedly progressive revolutionary party.

And Tsehay? Tsehay's crime was being Gudina's wife and a faithful Christian herself. She was not a political activist, not a troublemaker, not a subversive, only a pious woman of prayer and service. That was enough. Enough to be locked away and forgotten for ten years.

***

The following pages will open a window into the lives and extraordinary witness of this Christian couple. They contain two distinctly different sets of records from their lives.

The extant writings of Gudina Tumsa are collected in part 1. They start with presentations from early in his career as general secretary on the nature of the church as both body of Christ and institution, and on the stewardship of the gospel, which Gudina understands as the call to bring the good news to all the people of the world, communicating the love of God in the cross of Jesus Christ. It is a task for all Christian people, not just clergy or missionaries. Such concerns continue in his "Address to the Board of the Norwegian Missionary Society" and "Report on Church Growth in Ethiopia."

By the early 1970s, Gudina's writings reveal a more conscious articulation of holistic ministry, integrating service to the body with mission to the soul—if speaking in such dichotomous terms is not already an error. In "On the Interrelation between Proclamation of the Gospel and Human Development," Gudina challenges some old missionary verities, going so far as to critique Western notions of what constitutes a good life and how such notions affect the flow of funds to Ethiopian projects. Tension with missionary agencies surfaces again in the "Report at the Ethiopia Consultation" and "Serving the Whole Man," reaching an apex in "The Moratorium Debate and the ECMY," in which the prospect of stopping missionary funding and personnel altogether is entertained.

Political circumstances claimed more of Gudina's attention by the mid- to late 1970s. His "Pastoral Letter" attempts to delineate how the church might remain faithful to its calling amidst the upheavals of revolution, and the "Memorandum" distinguishes between the kind of service the church renders and that which can be expected or demanded of the government or businesses. His presentation "Unbelief from Historical Perspective or, Kairos," though apparently an academic recitation in genre, bespeaks an impassioned struggle with the overt atheism of the new regime, embodied in Gudina's own brother Baro Tumsa, whose response to the church on behalf of Marxist ideology is included in the appendix of this book.

Gudina's penultimate writing is "The Responsibility of the ECMY toward Ecumenical Harmony." Much of the evidence points to the fact that it was the ideas contained herein that ultimately earned Gudina the death sentence. Alone he was problematic enough, but when his efforts led to the creation of a Council for Cooperation of Churches in Ethiopia, he became intolerable. Christians speaking in one voice would have been too much for the unstable and violent regime to keep down.

His final writing, "The Role of a Christian in a Given Society," penned just weeks before his death, speaks boldly of the atoning salvation of Jesus Christ, the forgiveness of sin it confers, and the victory awarded to those who believe in him. In the strength of the gospel, human beings can take their place as responsible, contributing, transforming members of their societies, supporting the good and opposing the evil but never confusing historical or political movements with the kingdom of God. Christians ultimately lead two lives at once: the crucified and risen life they share with Jesus Christ and the common life of a given society and culture. It is no sin to be faithful to the latter as long as it does not demand a foreswearing of the former. But a regime that aspires to be absolute will not tolerate such a dual life, and for that reason it had to put Gudina to death.

Part 2 shifts from theological and ecclesiastical documents to a much more personal account. Here, the voice of Tsehay Tolessa takes the lead, narrating her own childhood as well as Gudina's, how they met and married, the birth of their children and the death of two of them, and the life of ministry they shared. Tsehay was an evangelist herself, at times traveling with Gudina to corners of Ethiopia far from their

Oromo homeland and, much later, in prison, smuggling Bibles and teaching the word to people desperate for freedom and hope in a place rife with oppression and violence. She tells of Gudina's studies, his pastorates, and his service as general secretary alongside her own struggles, worries, and small victories.

The largest portion of Tsehay's story is also the most difficult. It describes in detail the arbitrary injustice of the regime, the hideous torture inflicted upon her, and the years of unremitting suffering in prison. The reader is warned that these are painful pages to read. Yet no one can fail to be impressed at the faith that sustained Tsehay through the darkest days—indeed, and even more so, at the way Christ himself comforted and sustained Tsehay in the valley of the shadow of death.

Despite the loss of her beloved husband, Tsehay's story had a happy ending. For no apparent reason, ten years after she was put behind bars she was let back out again. She reunited with her family and lived another quarter of a century free and at peace, continuing to minister the gospel that had found her and held her through the years. She died quietly at the age of eighty-four on October 12, 2014, as mourned by her community as her martyred husband had been so many years before.

***

A few notes to the reader are in order for this first North American edition of Gudina's writings and Tsehay's account of their lives.

The fate of Gudina's writings is little less than a tragedy. After his three-year stay in Saint Paul, Minnesota, from 1963 to 1966 to earn a Bachelor of Divinity degree at Luther Seminary, he shipped his belongings home by boat. As it turns out, the boat was torpedoed and sank in the Red Sea as a casualty of the tensions in the Middle East in the late 1960s. That eliminated all of his written work from the first part of his life. Then in 1980, one year after his abduction and murder, the Derg regime repossessed the EECMY's property in Addis Ababa and confiscated all that it contained—including all of Gudina's writings. As far as anyone knows, every last one of these papers was destroyed, presumably burned. Add to this the fact that Gudina, like all good evangelists, preached most of his sermons extemporaneously, and it is miraculous that we have any written record of his thoughts at all.

The thirteen essays contained in this volume all come from the period of Gudina's career as general secretary of the EECMY. They were first collected and printed in a small volume produced by the Gudina Tumsa Foundation in Ethiopia, entitled *Witness and Discipleship: Leadership of the Church in Multi-Ethnic Ethiopia in a Time of Revolution: The Essential Writings of Gudina Tumsa*. Not all of them claim Gudina as the sole author. As general secretary, he encouraged and regularly participated in communal efforts to articulate a vision for his church. At the same time, the clarity and power of his vision meant that even communal documents bore his distinctive stamp, and in any event, they required his approval as general secretary before going to the public. The original introductions to each essay were written by Paul E. Hoffman, an American pastor who had married a German woman and, on behalf of the Berlin Mission, served as a teacher at Mekane Yesus Seminary. He became a good friend of Gudina's. His introductory notes have been rewritten and expanded for the present volume.

Tsehay's memoir, appearing here as *In the Fiery Furnace*, was entitled *The Long Shadow of Power* in the original Norwegian by Aud Sæverås and in the German translation by Antje and Ralph Meier. I discovered the German translation through Samuel Yonas Deressa, my co-editor on this volume, and was so moved by the story that I thought it needed to be translated into English, which I went on to do myself, with Lensa Gudina and Aster Gudina's blessing. This turned out to be the first time that either of them read the story for themselves, as Lensa explains in her preface. The translation also came in time for them to review it with Tsehay herself before her death. In the process, they discovered that some minor errors had crept into the Norwegian (and thus also the German) version. These were probably due to the fact that Sæverås, the "ghost writer" of sorts, and Tsehay had communicated in Amharic, which was a second language for both of them, before Sæverås wrote the story down in Norwegian. Thus, the resulting version that we offer here is somewhat, though not drastically, different from the Norwegian and German versions, but this English edition should be considered the "authorized" one approved by Tsehay and her daughters. Lensa Gudina and Samuel Yonas Deressa also helped to standardize the spelling of Ethiopian names for this book, which have gone through many versions in the history of English transliteration, a process that will no doubt continue.

Two final matters of terminology should be mentioned.

Ethiopian "surnames" are generally the father's first name; thus, Gudina's surname of "Tumsa" was his father's first name, and his children's names are Lensa Gudina, Aster Gudina, Kulani Gudina, and

Amanti Gudina. For this reason, it is more appropriate to refer to Ethiopians by their first names than by their last.

The name of Gudina's church has varied over the years. It was known as the Ethiopian Evangelical Church Mekane Yesus (EECMY)—the last two words mean "the dwelling place of Jesus"—from its recognition by the imperial Ethiopian state as an independent, self-governed church in 1959 until 1968, when, under pressure from the Ethiopian Orthodox Church, the government mandated the omission of the word "Ethiopian." From then on, it was simply the Evangelical Church Mekane Yesus (ECMY), until 1978, at which point the word "Ethiopian" was restored. In keeping with European usage, the word "evangelical" most closely approximates the American English term "Protestant," with connotations of continental Reformation heritage rather than British or American evangelicalism. Though largely derived from Lutheran missions in Europe, the EECMY also has a sizeable portion of churches descending from Presbyterian missions, and today it is a member of both the Lutheran World Federation and the World Communion of Reformed Churches. Already experiencing extraordinary growth in Gudina's time, today it counts more than 7.8 million members.

***

While Christianity has for several centuries now been bursting the old boundary lines of Christendom, only in the past several decades have the full implications of that reality caught the attention of North American and European churches. The balance has shifted: there are now more Christians in the "Global South" than in the historic territories of the North, and the level of commitment to and evangelistic fervor for the Christian faith is markedly stronger in these young churches. Yet Northern Christians dealing with secularism, disestablishment, pluralism, and the legacy of old divisions are often at a loss to imagine another way.

Gudina and Tsehay's story, it is hoped, will begin to spark the North Atlantic imagination in new directions. Their story is a fascinating intersection of a two-thousand-year-old faith with a five-hundred-year-old confessional shape taking root in a cultural setting profoundly different from what it had known before. It is a story of critiques and affirmations of Lutheran Christianity; of cultural overhaul, conservation, and adaptation; of the collision between Africa and foreign missionaries of both religious and political visions. It would be a mistake to treat their story as a handbook for immediate solutions in old Christendom. Rather, it is an opportunity to start seeing the gospel in a new light and, even more so, to see the church that emerges in response to the gospel in a new light. It is only in the mirror of another (church) culture that we truly begin to understand our own.

Gudina and Tsehay's is not the only story of remarkable Christian fidelity and witness among the younger churches of the earth. In the African Lutheran realm alone, they take their place among other great lights like Bishop Manas Buthelezi in South Africa, Bishop Josiah Kibira in Tanzania, and the prophetess Nenilava in Madagascar. Their stories also need to be told and heard beyond the boundaries of Africa. It is the hope of all the people who have worked to bring this volume together that the readers will be as moved as we are by the many astounding stories of the gospel's movement around the world and in Africa especially.

PART I

Gudina Tumsa's Theological Writings

1

The Church as an Institution, or
The Concept of the Church

At an executive committee meeting of the EECMY in January 1968, a little over a year after he had been named executive secretary (later renamed general secretary), Gudina Tumsa was asked to give a paper on the church and the practical issues that the EECMY was or should be facing. He presented "The Church as an Institution," to which on his own personal copy he later added, as an alternative or supplementary title, "The Concept of the Church." This retrospective double designation for the title of his paper is significant. The two parts of his presentation stand in a certain tension with one another. The first part examines the New Testament view of the church, while the second part goes on to look at the church more specifically as an institution. Only a decade old at that point in time, the EECMY had to face concrete institutional challenges in a biblical light. The thread between the two sections is the emphasis on the church as the people, the assembly of saints. Those who are called out to experience the salvation offered in Jesus Christ and who dwell in the hope offered by the Holy Spirit are also those who form and regulate the institutional church, which has implications for practical matters like the salary scale of the clergy, ecumenical contacts, and relations with the (at this time, still imperial) government.[1]

The Concept of the Church[2]

It is normal to turn to Article VII of the Augsburg Confession to show that one is orthodox Lutheran in one's understanding of the concept of the church, where "the church" is defined as "the assembly of saints in which the Gospel is taught purely and the sacraments are administered rightly." The term "church" is customarily used, at least by some people, to designate a building or house dedicated to the service of the Lord, rather than to refer to the people, as defined in the confession. Thus, I prefer the term "ecclesia" to the term "church," which to my understanding seems a proper description of the Lutheran concept of the church as the people of God.

The church-defined-as-building denotes the idea of static inactivity and something motionless, thereby implying self-sufficiency and laziness. That this was far from the mind of Christ when he founded the church is clear to the casual reader of the New Testament.

The church-defined-as-people denotes an idea of dynamic character, activity, process, movement, involvement, and a living organism. A right description for the latter is "ecclesia."

Ecclesia is not a simple designation for the gathering assembly. Primarily it denotes the one summoning the assembly and his purpose for the summoning. We have to remind ourselves again that "ecclesia" connotes the assembly second. Whether the term "ecclesia" or the familiar word "church" is used in this paper, the intention is to designate the one calling the assembly, his purpose, and the called ones at the same time. The ecclesia belongs to God because he has called it into being, dwells within it, rules over it, and realizes his purpose through it. The church is constituted by the community of believers who are called by God and call upon him as their Lord and Savior (1 Cor 1:2).

Jesus Christ is the founder of the church (Matt 16:18) and its head (Eph 5:23). The church is the new community he created (Eph 2:9) in time and history, making his abode in our midst (John 1:14). Certainly it is not necessary to look for individual texts to argue for Jesus's founding of the church of whom he is the head.

A look at the whole of the life of the Savior, in my opinion, will sufficiently express that he (the Messiah) intended to create a community

---

1. See the discussion in Paul E. Hoffman, "Gudina Tumsa's Ecclesiology—His Understanding and Vision of the Church," in *Church and Society: Lectures and Responses: Second Missiological Seminar 2003 on the Life and Ministry of Gudina Tumsa* (Hamburg: WDL-Publishers, 2010), 231–65.
2. Ed. note: The supplementary title, "The Concept of the Church," should be understood as applying to the *first* section of this paper.

of believers to continue the mission work (an assignment of heaven to be fulfilled on earth) that he has begun for the salvation of mankind. Through the coming of the Messiah (the anointed one of God), the new age has been inaugurated. In the life, death, and resurrection of Jesus Christ, as the promised Messiah, all the promises of God to the old Israel have found their fulfillment. In him, God's purpose for humanity's salvation finds its realization in time and history. The inauguration of the new age is evidenced by the powers of the kingdom of God at work in our midst (Luke 11:20). Thus, the New Testament church is seen as the eschatological people of God placed in a new order of existence, created by God through Jesus Christ, the instrument of God's salvation.

The coming of Jesus Christ is, from beginning to end, a reconciling work of God embracing the whole of his life in incarnation, teaching, death, resurrection, and ascension. This extends to the consummation of all things. In him, the church has its ontology (being) in Christ on the cross. The ecclesia has the fabric of its personal existence in the "once-for-allness" of the atonement that was wrought by the blood of Christ; thus, the solidarity of the new community (the church) is in him who created a peculiar people unto himself from all nations. The apostle of the gentiles urges his readers to underline that the church they should minister to was "that which he (the Lord) has obtained with his blood" (Acts 20:28).

The church of God exists by reliving the past, experiencing the finished work of reconciliation comprising the life, death, and resurrection of the Son of God with its climax on the day of Pentecost, the outpouring of the third person of the Holy Trinity, that the life of the new community constituted by Christ may be possessed by him. The outpouring of the Holy Spirit presupposes the atonement wrought by Christ, reconciling man to God and man to man (2 Cor 2:16–21). He is the Spirit of truth who leads the new community in Christ to all the truth that the historical Jesus taught during his earthly life (John 16:13), the Counselor of the ecclesia, who proceeds from the Father (John 15:26). He is the one who empowers the new humanity in Christ to bear witness to the living Lord (Acts 1–8). The Holy Spirit is the life-giving, creating power of God who is actively engaged in calling, sanctifying, and making holy the church of God.

Another characteristic of the people of God is expectation. What characterizes the life of the church is hope. Faith is a relational life with God, for what he did in the past and will do in the future (Rom

5:1–6). The church is a community looking forward to the final consummation, raising its head and awaiting its final redemption (Luke 21:25–28). The concept of the church, the eschatological people of God, is defined in the New Testament not only in relation to what it already is but also in relation to the future, in relation to what it is intended to be at the parousia, the second coming of its Lord. The ecclesia is the people living by expectation, having "tasted the goodness of the word of God and the powers of the age to come" (Heb 6:5) and called to hope (Eph 1:18). Though we now live in the world as a community whose Lord is Christ, yet "our commonwealth is in heaven, and from it we await a Saviour, the Lord Jesus Christ, who will change our lowly body to be like his glorious body by the power which enables him even to subject all things to himself" (Phil 3:20–21).

Expecting, recollecting, and worshipping, the church is formed in response to what God has done, does now, and will do, which are held together in the unity of God's time. The past and present of the church are brought together by God's act. Since the past and present of the church are present in Christ (Heb 13:8), the future meets us in him. Seen in these two dimensions, the church is a being-in-becoming (1 John 3:2). This is to say that the ontology of the church is determined by its eschatology. (The future is interpretative of the present.) Defined in this sense, the church of God is a movement, where the indicative and the imperative are intertwined (Rom 12:1–2).

The church as the people of God is in a new order of existence, where the law of love is determinative for life. The church remains faithful to its Lord, Jesus Christ, as it fulfills its missionary commission to the world. The gracious God who vindicates himself in righteousness has moved toward us for our salvation in Christ, who commands his church to raise its eyes to see the readiness of the time for harvest (John 4:35). The church is alive only when it fulfills its God-given commission—the evangelization of the world, the sole purpose for which it exists—after the pattern of the life of its Lord, in the form of a suffering servant. A missionary-minded church is the body of Christ in action—the kingdom of God in the making, hastening the coming of the Savior. We must state that, according to the New Testament, the concept of the church cannot be fully measured without taking into consideration the missionary character of Christianity. To belong to the body of Christ is to live for others, to labor for the salvation of the sheep that are not of this fold (John 10:16).

To be in Christ is a dedication to life in prayer for those who are "helpless" (Matt 9:35–38). If this statement is biblically correct, there cannot be "self-supporting" congregations (churches) while millions are facing a tragic death, death without having tasted salvation in Christ.

The EECMY as an Institution[3]

A) In the short, oversimplified definition of the church as stated above, nothing of the nature of its organizational structure was implied. The New Testament interest is not in organizational structures in whatever form they may be but in people, people created in the image of the God of the Bible, reconciled through the blood of the redeemer, Jesus Christ on the cross.

The church as an organization is a human institution. The gracious God condescends to use this human institution for the furtherance of his purpose. As a human institution, the organizational setup of the church must always be subject to critical evaluations. The ever-undesirable ecclesiasticism lurking behind the organizational structures of the church must be checked and rooted out at any moment in our church life. In the case of the EECMY, a question mark was placed on its organizational setup. In his report to the Fifth General Assembly of the church, the President of the EECMY has urged the Assembly to scrutinize whether the structure of the church in its present form is serving in a way that is satisfying the needs of its synods.

The same principle must apply to the institutional setup of the synods as well. The organizational structure of the EECMY must be judged on the quality of service it is rendering to the people of God. The New Testament concern is with the world,[4] people (believers and unbelievers), the world for whom Christ has died, not with organizational structures of the church. This must ever be kept before our eyes if we are to remain faithful to our call.

B) What is stated above on the organizational structure of the church must be said also of the administration of the church. The administration of a church should not be run for its own sake or for the sake of the upkeep of the organizational setup. The administration of the EECMY must use its organizational structure as an effective tool and be itself an effective means whereby the gospel proclamation is

---

3. Ed. note: From the content of what follows, this would have been the appropriate heading for this second section of this paper.

4. Ed. note: The mimeographed copy in the EC minutes has "word," which, from the context, must be considered a typing error.

accelerated. A unified administration is a visible sign of the unity of the EECMY, the church that God has constituted in Ethiopia. A unified administration is a *must* for the EECMY, but the form of its administration shall be subject to change from time to time, to meet the requirements of the various needs that arise with emerging situations.

The present administration of the church aims at fulfilling its threefold task, which is relation to the synods and to the Imperial Ethiopian Government as well as to international relationships, as laid down in the constitution of the EECMY. Whether this contributes to the proclamatory character of the church is open to discussion and judgment.

Before concluding this paragraph, if I may say something out of my experience during this short time in the EECMY headquarters: I find the dialectical theology of the law and the gospel, in a restricted sense, to be an analogy to the church as an institution and the church as proclaiming Christ. The church-as-institution, with its routine administrative tasks, strives to dominate us after the fashion of the law. There also is the danger of being mechanical. The church-as-proclaiming is the assembly of saints where the gospel is preached in its fullness and the sacraments are administered, whereby the risen Christ presents himself with the forgiveness of sins. The proclaiming church is the local congregation in action, the right place for investing manpower as well as funds.

It must be obvious by now that the organizational structure as well as the central administration of the EECMY are seen to be of secondary importance to the life of the church. Thus, the central administration must be kept to the minimum.

C) In a brief paper submitted to the Fifth Assembly of the EECMY, at Bako, I referred to the undesirable consequences that the different liturgical practices may have in the life of the EECMY. In the four synods of the church, there are four types of order of services imported by the cooperating Lutheran Missionary Societies. We may say that one of the hindrances of the coordination of the Mekane Yesus Seminary and the Sidamo Seminary (Tabor Seminary) was the difference in liturgical practices. The EECMY is a layman's church; we are very thankful for that, and it must remain a layman's church. The ever-present danger of ecclesiastical structure must be eradicated before it sends roots. I am not contending for any one liturgical practice. The point I am trying to make is this: for the sake of the unity of the church that was constituted by the four synods of the EECMY, a common order of service should be adopted. To achieve this, the full cooperation of the Lutheran Missions is required if they would like to see the EECMY growing in unity. The nationals are urged to see that the difference in liturgical practice was one of the dividing factors in the life of the Western churches.

D) We should like clear guidelines to be laid down for the Scriptures in matters pertaining to discipline, to which we can refer as challenging problems arise. The difficulty that a particular synod is confronted with in one area is sometimes the same as that of another synod. I am thinking of a particular question, that of polygamy. The question of polygamy, given different interpretations, may be a threat to the unity of the EECMY. To avoid such consequences, it is high time that the church adopts a common policy that will be a sort of guideline for the synods.

E) Complaints are heard from graduates of the Mekane Yesus Seminary who are serving in the various synods of the EECMY. The cause of the complaints is the differences in salary scale from one synod to the other. The synods are free to decide matters in their respective jurisdictions. There is no question about that. However, as the church is aiming to serve the same cause, there must be a mutual understanding among the synods of the EECMY to ease the situation. It may be that different conditions in different areas can stand in the way, but the EECMY cannot rule out the possibility of adopting a basic common salary scale. Copies of employment contracts can be obtained from the EECMY headquarters. Of course, they are to be modified to suit conditions in the synods.

Ecumenical

Whenever "ecumenical" is mentioned, our minds start to travel to Geneva where the World Council of Churches (WCC) is situated, comprising major Orthodox churches and Protestant families throughout the world. Nowadays, a negative attitude toward "ecumenical" is regarded as being narrow-minded about, and having a lack of understanding of, the international situation. It is not necessary here to go into the history of the two movements called "Life and Work" and "Faith and Order," which formed the first ecumenical assembly at Amsterdam in 1948. Nor is it necessary to evaluate contributions that are made to theological studies and social developments by the WCC. The question we are concerned with is "What is the policy of the EECMY with regard to ecumenical relationships?" If we think of "ecumenical" as making the WCC *more* ecumenical, the EECMY has not, as yet, adopted a policy demonstrating its views with regard to the matter.

But if this inclusive term "ecumenical" is taken in a narrower sense, as negotiation with Christians of other denominations, the EECMY has been open, or rather has been making attempts to engage itself in matters of an ecumenical nature. This was true even ten years ago, before the formation of the EECMY. A history of the Lutheran church in Ethiopia cannot be complete without recording the efforts the Lutherans were making, beginning right after the war, to form a federation (or, may we say, a union) with Christians of other confessions. It is hoped that the negotiation between the EECMY and the Evangelical Church Bethel will attain a visible form in the near future. Lutheranism has not denied the incorporation of other Christian denominations into the body of Christ. The Lutheran World Federation (LWF), of which the EECMY is a member, is talking on ecumenical issues with Orthodox churches (*LWF Information* No. 44–67, p. 7). A statement issued after talks held between Lutherans and Catholics says, "Both sides agreed that the death and resurrection of Jesus Christ as the eschatological saving deed of God is the Center of the Gospel" (Ps, No. 42, p. 2).

Ecumenicity, as demonstrated unity of the household of God, is given in Jesus Christ our high priest (John 17). A letter from the LWF is asking if the EECMY is considering membership in the WCC. A letter reached our office some time ago from the All Africa Conference of Churches that raises the same question. In view of these, the position of the EECMY will have to be clear with regard to ecumenical relationships.

Source: EECMY, Thirty-Fifth Executive Committee, January 18–20, 1968.

2

———

Stewardship of the Gospel

On May 13-17, 1968, Rev. Gunnar Østenstad hosted a stewardship workshop on behalf of the Lutheran World Federation's Secretariat on Stewardship and Congregational Life for the EECMY, the Evangelical Church in Eritrea, and the Lutheran Church-Friends of the Bible. The workshop took place at the EECMY headquarters in Addis Ababa, and Gudina Tumsa delivered the following paper. His emphasis is not primarily on money, the more common association with the concept of "stewardship," but the extraordinary grace given in the gospel and the call of Christians to share it through evangelism.

Addis Ababa, May 15, 1968

Introductory Remarks

Before coming to the main point of this paper, I would like to express that it is now about six years since the EECMY expressed its desire that a workshop of this type should be held in Ethiopia. This was clearly stated in resolutions passed by the church leaders at their various meetings. In a sense, it may be concluded from the resolutions of the church that the church is interested in looking for ways and means of utilizing all the possible potential resources of its members. But it may be truer to say that the idea of conducting such a workshop on stewardship has not just grown out of desire but has originated out of a concrete situation with which this young, developing national church is confronted as it has made attempts to understand itself in the responsibility that was laid upon its shoulders by the God who has founded it in this country.

No doubt the word "stewardship," if not defined, has been described by those who have undertaken to prepare papers for presentation and discussion. Already before this workshop began—because of scanty materials on the vital subject—we must have found ourselves, if not at a loss, at least fumbling in our customary ways of doing things. In my opinion, it seems to be valid to say that this workshop has already done part of its work by making us aware of the lack of material on the subject. My hope is that through exchange of views and ideas during this workshop, we will come to understand our lack of a working knowledge on the subject of stewardship, which in itself, as I see it, will incite interest in studying the subject.

Generally speaking, it is a well-known fact that anyone placed in charge of money ought to handle it properly if one wants to get the members interested in continuing to contribute what they have earned through their sweat, to achieve the objective that they have set for themselves.

Definition of the Word *Gospel*

Coming to our topic, as this is the first workshop on stewardship to be conducted in our church, it seems to me to be necessary to define the two terms that comprise our topic, "stewardship" and "the gospel," to remind ourselves what these two pregnant words are trying to communicate to us.

The gospel is usually defined as good news.

Certainly it is good news. Although our world is distorted by the power of sin, it cannot be denied that much good news can be found in our planet. But to define the gospel simply as ordinary good news only indicates the weakness of the language that we are using. This may be one of the reasons why many theologians spend their time on etymological study (study of the history and original meaning of a word), and it is proper that we sympathize with them since something helpful does result from such endeavors.

Our interest in this workshop, I am sure, is not in etymological theories but in the religious meaning of the term, and for that we turn to the apostle of the gentiles, who declares, "For I not ashamed of the

Gospel; it is the power of God for salvation to everyone who has faith" (Rom 1:16). When the gospel is defined as Paul does it, as "the power of God," then we agree that it is nothing less than the presence of the living Jesus Christ, our Lord: "Through him we have obtained access to this grace in which we stand" (Rom 5:2). This grace in which we stand is the privilege of being stewards of the gospel of Christ.

Stewardship

The Greek term *oikonomos* primarily refers to the relationship to material things, and it is defined in the Oxford English Dictionary as the "official who controls the domestic affairs of the household, supervising the service of his master's table, directing the domestics, and regulating the household expenditures." This aspect of the idea of stewardship, with its theological roots in the Old Testament and the New Testament, I think will come out in other papers for discussion.

In this paper, attempts are made to describe our relationship not to the material things that have been entrusted to us by our Creator but to that by which we are possessed. Since the gospel is "the power of God," we are possessed by it and placed in a world where the new law of love regulates our life, directing our mind, thoughts, and emotions to the service of the gospel of the living Jesus Christ. A man can never remain in the same situation where he was born of the flesh after his heart has been touched by the gospel of God's salvation in Jesus Christ. The description of stewardship, therefore, should not be confined to a narrow area of life, describing only the relationship to property, which is a common notion. Stewardship must be understood in its broader sense, as the New Testament presents it, including all areas of Christian responsibility and the whole response of love. The steward is an apostle, the one commissioned by Jesus Christ, to make him known by proclaiming the gospel message to the world, for whom it was intended in God's plan of salvation.

R. M. Olson puts it this way,

Most clearly the Christian is a steward of the Gospel. This is the greatest treasure with which he is entrusted. It must be his concern so to use all he is and has that the Christian message will be kept clear and will be sent forth greatly and actively among men. It will be his purpose to cultivate the desire of others to share generously in such a concern. This is part of the accounting due to his Lord in the stewardship which he holds. ("Stewards Appointed," 6)

Olson also quotes Kantonen and Heman as saying, "The stewardship life is a life completely dedicated to God through faith in Christ Jesus. Martin Luther said, 'If anyone should rap at the door of my heart and ask, who lives here? I would answer, Martin Luther once lived here, but Martin Luther has moved out, and Jesus Christ moved in.'" Paul's first words after his conversion were, "Lord, what wilt thou have me do?" He gave his whole life to God.

David Livingstone expressed the complete dedication of his life to the King in these immortal words. "I will place no value on anything I have or may possess in relation to the kingdom of Christ. If anything I have will advance the interest of that kingdom, it shall be given away to promote the glory of Him to whom I owe all my hope and faith in life and eternity" ("Stewards Appointed," 10).

"In the Pauline epistles, 'oikonomia' becomes a definite religious concept." Paul uses it in defining his commission as a preacher of the gospel. He speaks of himself as a steward of the grace of God and of the mysteries of God. He even resorts to this term to define Christ's administration of God's redemptive love for the world. Stewardship obtains its highest meaning and strongest theological foundation when the apostle relates it to God's purpose that he set forth in Christ, "to unite all things in him, things in heaven and things on earth" (Eph 1:10) (p. 11). Christ made it possible for men, through his death, to be stewards of his gospel.

The preacher of the gospel has to put the great things in the front. God's love in Christ, by its magnitude, wins the heart of sinful man and evokes responses in faith. Love is that which is willing to take upon itself the responsibility of sin for the sinner's sake. God's love as demonstrated in the finished work of Christ is the central message of the New Testament, and this must be presupposed in our proclamation and teaching, if we are to remain faithful stewards of the mystery of God (Eph 3:2). The mystery of God is that Christ took the responsibility of sinful men and its consequences upon himself. This is the atonement, the finished work of the Son of God. The atonement, therefore, is the presupposition of our ministry as it is the inspiring and controlling love in our corporate and individual witness for Christ. Death was our due. It was not his. Because it is ours, he made it his own. He made the atonement. "He bore our sins." What constitutes the death of Christ is the demonstration of divine love for sinful men. This is to be grasped as the New Testament presents it, if our witness for Christ is apostolic in character. Christ, who accepted the responsibility of our sins, stands in our midst as the pledge of God's love. Without grasping the meaning of sin, what sin means in our experience, and how God has dealt with it in the death of his Son, Jesus Christ, our witness lacks its constraining motive in the human will.

As the apostle grew in the grace and knowledge of our Savior, his vision was broadened, and he declared that God was pleased to reconcile to himself all things, whether on earth or in heaven, "making peace by the blood of his [Christ's] cross" (Col 1:20).

The Commission

The motive for the commission of the apostle was the cross of Christ. The commission is to go to the utmost part of the world, but it has to begin at Jerusalem, at home. The coming of the power of the Holy Spirit is antecedent to the beginning of the task (Acts 1:8). The outpouring of the Third Person of the blessed Trinity, in power and in fullness, is dependent on the death and resurrection of Christ. Thus, death is not the last word that we should transmit to others. Jesus Christ was raised from the dead. Paul writes, "For I delivered to you as of first importance what I also received, that Christ died for our sins in accordance with the Scriptures, that he was buried, that he was raised on the third day in accordance with the Scriptures" (1 Cor 15:3–4). As stewards, our responsibility is to transmit that which was delivered to us.

Difficulties Involved in Fulfilling the Commission

Looking at this vast planet and the population explosion, very often our vision is frustrated and the power of our imagination is weakened. The field is so vast and the task of evangelism is at its beginning. We try to locate sources of manpower and funds to carry out this unfinished task.

We are not shown a permanent source from where to get all that we need to discharge the responsibility that was laid upon our shoulders. Our prospects seem to be bleak. Our uncertainty as to what to depend on to carry out plans for the task of evangelism contributes to the frustration of our vision. The "unfinishedness" of the task and the limitation of our resources in all areas added to our shortcomings, which are inseparably connected with our sinful nature, lead us to the point of losing hope. Paul writes, "We do not lose heart." In the view of Paul of Tarsus, our discouragement springs from looking in the wrong direction.

Our Source of Sufficiency

What we are and what we have cannot be a determining factor for carrying out the commission, "Go therefore and make disciples of all nations." The "God" of the commission is inseparably connected with the promise: "And I am with you always, to the close of the age" (Matt 28:20). "I am with you always." This is eternally valid, and without it no one can dare think of the mission of the church. Ability in its various forms is not required from us; what is required is that we acknowledge our inadequacy. The apostle writes, "Such is the confidence that we have through Christ toward God. Not that we are sufficient of ourselves to claim anything as coming from us. Our sufficiency is from God, who qualified us to be ministers of a new covenant" (2 Cor 3:4–6). "Without me," says Jesus, "you can do nothing" (John 15:5). When we work with him, nothing is too great to undertake for his sake. Someone has said, "To plan should be a venture. Faith is nothing less than a relational life with the Savior. To walk by faith is to let the Holy Spirit guide our ways as we claim the world for Christ." To plan and work by faith is to allow the God of revelation to fulfill, through us, his purpose for the salvation of mankind.

The Congregation Lives to Evangelize

There is a tendency that should be attacked. This is the idea of establishing self-supporting congregations to take care of themselves.

The concept of establishing self-supporting congregations came up in connection with our discussion on the Integration Policy of the EECMY. According to this view, congregations are to be set up to mind their own congregational business. In my opinion, a congregation without an evangelistic outreach will become ingrown, and sooner or later will become a sort of social club. That Christ did not intend to found such congregations (churches) must be clear to all of us. If our preaching does not invite interest in our congregations for the task of evangelistic outreach, then our preaching is not apostolic in force. We may ask, what is the purpose of establishing congregations, if not for evangelistic outreach? What is the purpose of nurture, if not to evangelize the world? No one is saved unto himself.

An apostolic church is a missionary church. Salvation is to be involved in making Christ known in our congregational life and our individual life. The command of Christ, "Go and make disciples," is directed to us as congregations—not to someone else. If this fundamental biblical teaching is not guiding our minds, something must be wrong in our relationship with the Lord who will come to judge "the quick and the dead."

Source: Archives of the Gudina Tumsa Foundation, Addis Ababa, Ethiopia.

3

Address to the Board of the
Norwegian Missionary Society

In Support of the Invitation of the Ethiopian
Evangelical Church Mekane Yesus to the Mission for
Assistance: Stjørdal near Trondheim in Norway,
August 31, 1968

On August 31, 1968, Gudina Tumsa met with the board of the Norwegian Missionary Society to discuss, for the first time, the prospect of cooperation. His original oral address was later written down at the board's request, which is what is presented here. Noteworthy already are his integration of evangelistic, diaconal, and political concerns, and on behalf of a different people group from his own, namely the Shanqellas.[1] It is even more extraordinary on realizing that a Shanqella had poisoned Gudina's father, leading to his death.

Minor corrections to the wording, punctuation, and paragraphing have been made.

---

1. Ed. note: "Shanqella" is sometimes also spelled "Shangalla," and today often carries a derogatory connotation, though such was not intended by Gudina himself.

Mr. Chairman, members of the Board of the Norwegian Missionary Society, may I first of all express my sincere and deep thanks to you for offering me this opportunity to give you more explanation on the invitation extended to your mission by the EECMY.

I would prefer standing while presenting this matter. In my country if a man is serious, he should be standing when he presents his case. What counts is the treatment the case presented receives. Here I am standing as your poor brother, begging you to come out and help us in our evangelistic outreach. You know that no one prides himself in begging; however, I am not ashamed of it, because I know that I am appealing to my brothers. Believing in Jesus Christ, we are taken into his church and are members of his body. As members of that body, we work for the same cause, striving to reach the same goal—to make our Lord Jesus Christ known to the world. My appeal may be emotional, but I cannot help it, because I feel that this is the chance given to me to discharge my responsibility.

Let me tell you briefly how the question of inviting the NMS was started. In connection with the nineteenth annual meeting of LWF/CWM [Lutheran World Federation/Commission on World Mission] at Baden near Vienna, Austria, 1967, I was offered a study tour to Norway by the Secretariat of Stewardship and Evangelism of the LWF [Rev. Østenstad]. During my stay in Stavanger, I got in touch with Rev. G. Gjelsten, whom I had known in Ethiopia when he was working at RVOG ["Radio Voice of the Gospel," the LWF radio station in Addis Ababa]. Rev. Gjelsten told me that, if I wish, I should take up the matter [of an invitation to the NMS] with the leaders of the missions [with which] we are directly involved.

On my way back to Ethiopia, I stopped over in Geneva and talked with Dr. S. Aske [of the LWF Department of World Mission and director of RVOG] about a possible invitation to the NMS by the EECMY. As Dr. Aske had a plan to come to Ethiopia, he told me to make arrangements for a meeting with H. E. Ato Emmanuel Abraham, president of our church. Upon his arrival in Addis Ababa in July of 1967, Dr. Aske had a meeting with the president of the EECMY. Since then, the officers of the EECMY have been exploring to get more information on your society. In December of the same year, our president had the opportunity to take up the matter with Rev. J. Skauge [of the NMS], who stopped over in Addis Ababa on his way home from Madagascar. Prior to my visit to Norway in May 1967, my church had not had any idea of a possible invitation to your missionary society.

When Rev. Skauge stopped over in Addis Ababa, I was on a visit to one of the synods. Our president called a meeting of the church officers at which the treasurer of our church, Mr. Magnar Magerøy [of the Norwegian Lutheran Mission in Oslo], was present. After that, our president addressed a preliminary letter to your missionary society. The executive committee of the EECMY at its sixteenth semiannual meeting in January of this year extended an invitation to you, and our invitation is still standing.

Now, in connection with the twentieth annual meeting of LWF/ CWM, I met the board members of the Danish Ethiopia Mission and requested them to redouble their assistance to the Bale Province in South Ethiopia. I also stopped over in Helsinki to discuss with the leaders of the Finnish Missionary Society [FMS] matters pertaining to their coming out to Ethiopia to assist us in our evangelistic outreach in the Kambata District (south of Addis Ababa).

In response to an invitation by the Norwegian Lutheran Mission, I come to this country to discuss matters related to our common interest. In Oslo, I had a very good discussion with Mr. T. Vagen, Mr. Brevik, and Mr. Lindtjom. At Hurdal, I had a meeting with the board members of the NLM. At both meetings, one of the points discussed was our invitation to the NMS. There was a frank exchange of views and understanding among us, and my impression is that the difficulty raised can be overcome if sufficient explanations are given from both the NLM and NMS. Our invitation to you does not indicate in the slightest sense that the cooperation and assistance of the NLM is minimized. The NLM is one of the missions who constituted the EECMY in its present form. They cooperate and supply the need of our church. The EECMY has appreciated this spirit of understanding and is turning more and more to the NLM. The NLM is in the policy-making body of our church. Our treasurer is from the NLM. Our accountant is offered through the NLM. We have requested the NLM for a professor for our seminary in Addis Ababa, and our request has been met with a favorable reply. The director of our hostel for university students [in Addis Ababa] is from the NLM. I hope that this can give you an idea of the attitude that the EECMY has toward the NLM.

The EECMY has repeatedly requested the Lutheran missions in Ethiopia to extend their support to the areas where evangelistic work is badly needed. All of them replied that they could not extend their assistance beyond the present areas where they are working. The church therefore started exploring possibilities for assistance elsewhere. Your society is not the first to be approached. I was in contact with churches and agencies in the United States of America that I knew when I was studying there. So far, I have not found something on which the church could base its invitation.

Tremendous opportunities are presenting themselves in Ethiopia, and we want to make the best use of these opportunities. There is a people movement, and hundreds of people are racing for evangelists and teachers. Although we want our church to be missionary-minded and our congregations to be missionary, for the time being, as our resources are limited, we feel that we cannot do as much as we wish without assistance from our Christian brethren abroad. You know that the EECMY is the outgrowth of the activities of the Lutheran missions in Ethiopia. Certainly we want our church to remain true to its heritage, a missionary movement.

Before I left for the LWF/CWM meeting in Hillerød [Denmark], I was instructed by our president to make contact with the delegates of the NMS to the CWM meeting, to give them any information needed with regard to our invitation to your society, and report on my return. Those of you who were at Hillerød know the efforts I was making to explain the situation to you as a group as well as individually. As I had nothing concrete to report on my return, upon my arrival in Helsinki, I wrote to Rev. Skauge requesting him to give me some idea. Now it gives me great pleasure to be able to stand here, hoping to get something to report when I go back.

We have requested your assistance to the Shanqellas along the Blue Nile. The Shanqellas are nomadic tribes who have not had the opportunity to hear the gospel of our Savior. Fifty percent of the Shanqellas under twenty-five years of age die of malaria. They are in need of spiritual and physical help. We are concerned for them because they die without the opportunity of hearing the saving gospel. Shanqella means "very black." They are called Shanqellas in contempt; they are despised tribes. Since my first visit to the Shanqellas, I could not forget them; I have them on my heart.

Your coming out to assist us in our concern for the Shanqellas along the Blue Nile will open new avenues of assistance to the Shanqellas. First, it will enable the EECMY to approach the Ethiopian government for assistance for the Shanqellas. Our church has made a great impact upon the Ethiopian society through its radio and literacy programs. At the beginning of this month, we received a letter from the prime minister's office inviting the EECMY to membership in the Advisory

Committee on National Adult Education, signed between the imperial Ethiopian government and UNESCO. This is to give you some idea of what attitude the government has toward our church.

Second, your assistance will enable us to work out a resettlement project for the Shanqellas. For such a project, the EECMY will also approach the LWF for assistance. You know that if our negotiations with the Ethiopian government and our request to the LWF for such a project are to appeal forcefully, something must be done before we start negotiations with them.

Allow me, friends in Christ, to give you general information, which I think will be new to you, on the Ethiopian situation in connection with her neighboring countries. The Ethiopian boundaries between Somaliland and the Sudan are not marked. As you know, those countries are Muslim countries. On the eastern border, the Somali Muslims are infiltrating into Ethiopia. On the western border, the Sudanese are flocking into our country. I heard a sheikh (Muslim priest) who claimed to have converted six thousand primitive animists in a period of one year. About half (if not more) of the twenty-five million people of Ethiopia are Mohammedans. This is very dangerous to our existence as Christians. The Mohammedans have easy missionary methods. One of their missionary methods is polygamy. They practice polygamy and get as many children as possible. Through this easy method, they propagate their religion. Another easy method is this: in Ethiopian tradition, anyone who has eaten meat slaughtered by a Mohammedan is automatically a Muslim. Giving such food in areas where a crop has been destroyed, they convert people through such easy methods. The Muslim creed is also very easy to learn. "There is no God but Allah, and Mohammed is his prophet." What is required of the neophytes is that they should recite the creed while shaking hands with a sheikh.

It is required of a Muslim to do all that he can to make a country of which he is a citizen a Muslim country. This may sound strange to the Western mind, which sees politics and religion as separate things. For the Muslim mind, religion and politics are one and the same thing. In their thinking, separation of religion and politics invites a curse from Allah. In the Biafran war, it is not only tribalism, economic, and political factors, but religion is playing its role.

When the Sudan was a British colony, Catholic, Baptist, and Presbyterian missions were working in the southern part of the country. Most of the southern Sudanese became Christian. In the southern part of the Sudan, there were about 4.5 million Sudanese where the Christian missions were working. Right after independence, the Sudanese government adopted a policy of transferring Christians from the south to the north. In the north, there are about eight million Arab Muslims. Muslim teachers were placed in Christian missions after independence. Now the Christians in the southern part of the Sudan are under brutal persecution. They are coming to Ethiopia in hundreds. I am a member in the Ad Hoc Council for Sudanese Refugees. For political reasons, refugees from the Sudan are not recognized as refugees in my country. The Ad Hoc Council is channeling the refugees to Uganda, Kenya, and Tanzania. About one million southern Sudanese were killed. This was written in *Newsweek*. Counseling sixteen refugee students from the Sudan, I came to know the situation very well. Muslims are infiltrating into the western part of Ethiopia. The Shanqellas are exposed to such an influence.

From this general description, you will understand the situation out of which we are crying for help. No one can understand us unless one places himself in our situation. We are struggling for existence. We need assistance today. God has given us a wonderful opportunity today. We do not know about tomorrow. Tomorrow may be too late. Your assistance at this time may be one of the determining factors in our future history. We are in need of support today. Today is ours to assist and to receive assistance. It all depends on whether you would like to see me after some ten or fifteen years. I am concerned for the future of my children, whom I am bringing up in the Christian faith; I am concerned for the future of the people to whom I am preaching Jesus Christ.

This week I have been reading the book of Acts and came across chapter 17, verse 30, in the address of the apostle of the gentiles to the Athenian philosophers, where he says "the time of ignorance God overlooked, but now he commands all men everywhere to repent." I asked myself, will repentance and forgiveness in his name be a reality for the Shanqellas along the Blue Nile? It is for you to reply.

Source: Archives of the Norwegian Missionary Society (NMS), Stavanger, Norway.

$$4$$

_____

Report on Church Growth in Ethiopia

The Lutheran World Federation established a Commission on Church Cooperation (CCO) at its assembly in Évian in 1970. The first meeting under the auspices of the CCO took place in Tokyo from April 29 to May 4, 1971. LWF member churches from Asia, Africa, Latin America, and the Pacific all sent representatives, with Gudina Tumsa representing the ECMY. While his topic is "church growth," he begins with an outline of Ethiopian church history, from the ancient Orthodox church to the departure of Protestant missions during World War II, observing the startling growth that followed upon this otherwise unhappy event. He highlights the prerogative taken by the laity to evangelize and the power of the message that "Jesus saves," while openly acknowledging other factors contributing to conversions like social prestige and the hope for a better quality of life. It is worth noting that this report comes well before the exponential growth of the ECMY that began in the late 1970s.

Slight modifications have been made to the report's wording and punctuation.

Speaking about church growth in Ethiopia, one has to say something about the Ethiopian situation to which the Protestant missions went during the second half of the last century. This is to say that any discussion of church growth in Ethiopia has to touch upon the situation of the Ethiopian Orthodox Church, without which the situation of the country as a whole cannot be described properly. I therefore wish to state in a few lines the position of the Ethiopian Orthodox Church at the time when the Protestant missions entered Ethiopia. This, in my opinion, is necessary for an understanding of the reasons for the existence of Protestant churches in Ethiopia, a country in which Christianity was preached in the early years of the Christian era. Ethiopia has a history that sets her apart from the rest of the African countries, not only in her political life but also in her religious history. That Christianity was preached in Ethiopia in the first years of the Christian era is evident from what is recorded in the book of Acts. During the fourth century, a group of people organized themselves in the northern part of the country as a church, which has continued to this day. Until the last century, the western and the southwestern parts of present-day Ethiopia were not known as integral parts of the country, although some areas paid tribute to the emperors periodically.

During the second half of the nineteenth century, the Christian kingdom of the north extended its rule to the western and southwestern parts of the country, and by the end of the century, these were considered integral parts of modern Ethiopia. Since the thirteenth century, the Ethiopian government and the Ethiopian Orthodox Church have not been considered separate entities. They were considered to be one and the same, and there is a slogan to the effect that "there is no church without the state and no state without the church," a slogan that is still heard in daily conversation. When governors were appointed to rule the new areas annexed to the kingdom, they took Orthodox priests with them, and Orthodox churches were established in the centers of administration. It therefore should be clear that there was no real effort to evangelize or Christianize the southern and southwestern parts of the country until the arrival of Protestant missions about the beginning of the twentieth century. Orthodox churches were built in the various districts to show the faithfulness of those appointed to important positions in the government rather than to proclaim Christ to the people in those areas.

The argument of this brief report on church growth in Ethiopia is supported by regulations by the imperial Ethiopian government on the establishment of missions, issued in 1944. The regulations defined areas in which missions might operate and those from which they were barred as "Open Areas" and "Ethiopian Church Areas," respectively:

1. "Ethiopian Church Areas consist of those areas in which the inhabitants adhere predominantly to the Ethiopian Church Faith."

2. "Open Areas consist of those areas whose inhabitants are predominantly non-Christians."

The regulations of 1944 on the establishment of foreign missions may be seen as a recognition on the part of the imperial Ethiopian government of the existence of about half of the population who were non-Christians. Furthermore, it indicates the positive policy that the government maintained as regards the social services provided by the foreign missions.

There was no intention of establishing a Lutheran Church in Ethiopia when the Protestant missions (especially the *Evangeliska Fosterlandsstiftelsen* [from Sweden]) arrived in Ethiopia during the second half of the last century. The goal was rather to cooperate with the Ethiopian Orthodox Church in order to spread the gospel of Jesus Christ to the pagan Oromos (commonly called "Galla"), many of whom had embraced Islam. However, the situation at that time was not such as to allow cooperation, and Protestant congregations were therefore established in the southern and southwestern parts of the country before World War II.

In the preceding paragraphs, I have made an attempt to describe the general situation in Ethiopia at the time when Protestant missions entered the country. It will be impossible to give a fair picture of the situation in Ethiopia into which Protestant missions came in the introductory remark of a short report on church growth in a country like Ethiopia, with her particular characteristics in the continent of Africa. Please note that I originally used as title for this paper, "A Short Report on Church Growth in Ethiopia." This is to imply that this paper is not a research paper on church growth in Ethiopia, which would require a considerable length of time to expound. Due to lack of publications on church growth in Ethiopia, too great a shortage of time, and some other reasons, I find it impossible to present a research paper on church growth in a country often called "an island of Christianity in a sea of paganism."

The following factors are assumed, in my opinion, to contribute to church growth (mass movement evangelism) in Ethiopia.

1. The departure of foreign missions due to World War II may be considered one of the contributing factors to the spread of the gospel in the country. The insignificant number of believers in the western and southwestern parts of the country took upon themselves the responsibility of witnessing to the gospel of the risen Christ. There was thus a revival, during the five-year period of occupation by Italy, among

the Christians left behind around the mission stations. Many Christian groups had nowhere to look for guidance and decided to depend on the reading of the Scriptures. The missionaries, to whom they used to look to draw advice, counseling, and assistance, were, so to speak, replaced by the Bible. The only authority to appeal to on ethical questions in the absence of missionaries was the Bible. The Bible being the only source to turn to, Bible study and reading played a vital role in bringing about a revival among the groups of believers. It is to be noted that these groups of believers had a minimal knowledge of Christian doctrines. One may even say that, in many respects, their knowledge of basic Christian teaching was almost nil. The reading of the Scriptures, combined with prayer, was the main cause of the revival movement, which sent deep roots in the life of the groups of believers left by the missions.

2. If a revival movement is described as requiring a certain knowledge of Christian teaching for its dynamism, then it should be said that this had taken place and should be seen as one of the contributory causes for the rapid growth of the evangelical churches in Ethiopia. The revival among the groups was directed by or took as its motto the great commission of the living Savior, "Go therefore and make disciples of all nations. . . . Lo, I am with you always." The revival preachers were unaware of what was geographically implied by the "nations." "Nations" meant to them their neighbors next door, and the theological impact of the words of Jesus, "Lo, I am with you always," perhaps, did not play a greater role than the psychological comfort they drew from these words in the absence of the missionaries in whom they had confidence prior to their departure due to World War II.

3. In the process of their activity during this period, when the missions were out of the country because of the war, it is significant to note that the revival movements developed some type of indigenous pattern. The missions used to teach Western melodies. Now that was seen as a matter of the past, and the revival movements started making use of primitive indigenous melodies, whereby the believers were helped to feel at home with the message proclaimed to them—forms [i.e., orders] of service, music, and songs were made indigenous, without working out such a plan. It should be added that the ethical line developed was, in some cases, somewhat different from the mainstream of Christianity, due to a lack of theological education and a very literal understanding of the Bible. In some cases, this created difficulties when the movements at a later stage were forced into a more

usual church pattern. This was not the case in the southwestern part of the country, where the leaders had relatively well-trained people. In the southern provinces, Sidamo and Gamu Gofa, the mass movement toward Christianity was related to independent movements in Wallamo and Kambata. However, the movements coincided with the arrival of the Norwegian Lutheran Mission in 1948 in Sidamo and Gamu Gofa provinces.

4. The Second World War period may be considered "bitter days" when viewed from one point, but it served to produce faithful laborers in the vineyard of the Master. Furthermore, it created an atmosphere for an ecumenical movement of evangelical groups, which was weakened after the return of the missions.

5. Independent movements were channeled into church patterns through the assistance of the Bible schools established by the missions upon their return to the country after World War II. The South Ethiopia Synod may be cited as an example. The Norwegian Lutheran Mission undertook extensive Bible training programs, though the movements in Sidamo and Gamu Gofa provinces did not show the typical signs of independent churches. The South Ethiopia Synod has twelve Bible schools, with the enrollment running from ten to seventy-five students in each school. In most cases, the schools give courses on a yearly basis. Very few of the students are employed as evangelists. Mostly they are trained with a view that at least one in every group will have basic Bible knowledge, in order that he or she may be a leader locally. In some cases, they become living witnesses for the gospel of the Savior in their neighborhood or in their family. I have several times witnessed the influence that these young students from Bible schools exerted upon their communities, preventing the danger of neophytes returning to paganism due to lack of biblical knowledge. Funds granted by the missions enabled evangelists employed full-time to move at will to reach new areas. And the danger of considering the preaching of the gospel of the living Christ as the sole responsibility of the missions has been kept to the minimum, in view of the experience of World War II.

6. Another factor to be seen as contributory to the fast growth of the evangelical churches in Ethiopia is the right understanding of laymen (the people of God) of their responsibility as Christians in their congregations. The revival movements during the war were started by laymen, and they still continue to have their roots in laymen. Evangelical congregations do not allow professional pastors and evangelists to monopolize the ministry of preaching; lay preachers and pastors

have equal access to the pulpit, and there is not too much difference between preaching in churches and personal witness in ordinary life. It may be said that the professional ministry is playing its role in nurture, but the rapid growth of the evangelical churches at a high rate is through the normal witness of the lay Christians in common daily life. It's true that the biblical knowledge of the lay Christians is very minimal, even today. In spite of that, there is a general feeling of urgency to reach those who have not had the opportunity of hearing the gospel of the risen Christ.

7. In describing a mass movement, its complex social factors—its religious, sociological, anthropological, and political character—have to be dealt with in a satisfactory manner. In order, however, to give a vivid picture of the situation, this brief report on mass movements in Ethiopia, as was indicated earlier, does not attempt to do this, due to various reasons. As indicated in the previous paragraphs, central to the proclamation and witness of the believers is the idea that Jesus saves. This is repeated very often, and one can never miss it in one form or another. There is no distinction between curing malaria or pneumonia and saving from sin. "Jesus Christ saves" means that he literally cures physical diseases, as well as the burden of sin. The simple preaching of the gospel was very often accompanied by healing, exorcism, or by some other signs that were interpreted to be the new God demonstrating his power. The following striking example indicates what role the religious factor plays in the mass movements, as they have been seen in Ethiopia. In a certain area of Gamu Gofa (a southern province), a big tree played an important role in the primitive cult. At a certain time of the year, the people would come together there from a wide area to make sacrifices to the spirit in the tree. Just before one of the annual festivals, two school boys who had accepted the gospel of Christ went to the village and started to witness to the people. The people laughed at the boys and scorned them, saying that the spirit residing in the tree was the most powerful god and that they believed in it. The boys said that they would pray to their God that he would reveal his power. On the day of the festival, while several hundred people were gathered for the sacrifice, the tree suddenly fell down. The whole crowd said that this was the new God. From that day on, they said they would believe in the new God. Similar things have happened in many other places. A sick person was healed, a demon-possessed person was made free, and so on, and the crowds took these as divine signs and decided to become Christians.

8. Socially, to have religion has been given a kind of prestige. It is usual to divide people into two categories in daily conversation, those who have religion and those who have not. I once heard a truck driver, who was a Muslim himself, talking about people in a certain area who were partly Christians, partly Muslim, and partly animists. In this classification, Christians and Muslims were considered as those who have religion and the animistic sector of the society as those who have no religion. This is one of the factors to be considered seriously. An ethnic group or a clan in an area can today add something important to their social prestige by becoming Christians. From this point of view, becoming a Christian means acceptance by society at large.

9. Looking at the mass movements from a political angle, it cannot be denied that people who have been under landowners have found strength in turning to Christianity. They understand their true humanity in a new way. Of course, they are limited—but they are strong enough to make the best of what can be done under the present system in fighting for their rights. It made a great impression on the people of the Konso area in Gamu Gofa when the evangelical Christians united and, through one of their leaders, filed a case against a certain official who had taken a large portion of their land. They fought to the High Court and won the case. Politically, this is but the beginning (Matt 24:8). It is no wonder that their revival songs are hymns of praise to God, who made it possible for them to get back their land.

10. Anthropologically, their general dissatisfaction with the existing conditions of life is noticeable. The ethnic groups and clans want change. They are not quite sure as to what they want, but a desire for something new and better is discernible. In such a situation, our duty is to sell our goods. The people themselves have started to change, looking for better ways of life, for something new to satisfy their inner longings. Leaders of a group of people recently came to one of our evangelists and asked him to go with them to teach them a way of life. When asked why they wanted to be taught, they said they were not satisfied with their living conditions. Old forms of social life are disintegrating and something has to replace it.

11. Even if the social and political factors cannot be overlooked, one would misunderstand the mass movements if one does not put the main emphasis on the religious aspect as indicated in point 7 of this report. People are tormented with fear of spirits, and they want to accept the new religion of love and justice. Although a mass movement will not automatically lead the masses to the church, it will create

fertile soil for tremendous possibilities to sow the seed of the gospel, to proclaim the risen Christ who makes man free from fear. Where the church understands the mass movement, it becomes a tremendous opening, but still it is a stream that must be led in the right direction, and if in the right direction, it is a tremendous factor in the harvest of the Heavenly Father. This is to say that the evangelical churches have been working in a situation that mass movements have created, and the importance of the teaching ministry cannot be overlooked in Ethiopia, where this has been successfully tried, in particular, in the southern part of the country.

12. It would be unfair not to mention the role the vernaculars have played in contributing to church growth in Ethiopia, where about seventy languages and dialects are spoken. Portions of the Bible had been translated into the Kambata, Wallamo, and Sidamo languages before the Protestant missions had to leave the country because of the Second World War. Although it is somewhat difficult to estimate how much influence the use of vernaculars has had in paving the way for the mass movements in the southwestern part of the country, the use of the Oromo Bible published in 1899 has had a considerable impact upon the people, who have no other literature in the language they understand.

13. In concluding this brief report on church growth in Ethiopia, it would not be out of place to mention how the Evangelical Church Mekane Yesus visualizes herself to be, as outlined in the first five-year plan, from 1971 to 1975.

Alarmed at the high growth rate, the General Assembly decided in 1969 that a plan, whereby the church could be able to know where she stands, be worked out. During the two-year period 1969–70, the necessary data were collected for assessment. In the process of working out the plan, it became clear that in the past three years, 1968–70, the average growth was calculated to be about 15 percent. Membership growth for 1970 was 27 percent. The membership will be about doubled by the end of the first five-year plan, which means that the ECMY will have a membership of about 285,000 by the end of 1975.

To make proper use of this expansion, according to the plan, about 137 pastors must be trained during this period, as well as about 1,000 evangelists. By January 1970, our statistics show that 420 evangelists and 82 pastors will be serving full-time the 143,000 members of the ECMY, with 831 congregations and 258 preaching places. There are also about 159 working missionaries at present in the ECMY, and it is our earnest and sincere hope that there will be more expatriate personnel during the period of the plan. In view of the present general trends in the world, it may seem out of place to call for more missionary personnel, but our church needs increased resources in personnel and finances to meet her manifold tasks in Ethiopia.

Realizing the urgency of making use of the present opportunity in Ethiopia, our Seventh General Assembly [Debre Zeit, January 1971] passed a resolution requesting the LWF to approach the donor agencies in Europe and the United States to reconsider their criteria for aid and include direct support for congregational work and leadership training, so that the ECMY may be able to cope with the rapid growth taking place at present. The earnest wish of the ECMY is that this request be passed on to the member churches of the LWF to be communicated to the congregations, in order that they know our problems and desires. And it is our sincere and earnest hope that the LWF will do its utmost, in the first place, in passing on and making known our concern to the churches, and, secondly, that the LWF may influence the present donor agencies to review their criteria for allocation of assistance, thereby giving due consideration to our evangelistic outreach plan. Our hope is that our sister churches do not judge our needs solely on their own criteria and on the conditions that they have stipulated. We want to proclaim Christ, because people are hungering for him and want us to introduce him to them.

Connected with this rapid growth is the question of self-support. Church growth has to be commensurate with economic growth; in our case, this is far from being realized as yet. It is a well-known fact that the economic life of any church is tied up with the economic life of the country where the church is placed. As national product, our per capita income is considered to be one of the lowest in the world. The matter of self-support does not appear to be an easy one; it requires a careful and nationalized study to be tackled from a realistic standpoint. What one can say at the moment is that this subject will be thoroughly studied. We hope it will be possible to predict the time when the ECMY will be able to stand on her own.

The ECMY was organized in her present form in 1958. This is to say that she is a teenager and needs all the care that tender age demands so that her mind and spirit may be molded by sound teaching, which will determine her future. The role Bible studies play in her life will determine whether this young church will fall into the danger of being some sort of social club under the guise of Christ, the danger that this age, characterized by uncertainty, is running. For us, this is not the question of being a conservative church or something else one may call it; it is a matter of life and death. This is so because, as far as I understand, nothing can bring a man to a living faith in the risen Christ except proclamation and teaching of the living word as "delivered to 'us,'" namely, "that Christ died for our sins in accordance with the Scriptures . . . and that he was raised on the third day in accordance with the Scriptures" (1 Cor 15:3–4).

Source: EECMY Archives, Addis Ababa; LWF Archives, Geneva, Switzerland.

5

On the Interrelation between Proclamation of the Gospel and Human Development

Complaints had been raised by the ECMY to Northern partners concerning the lopsided availability of mission funds: those for development projects were quickly granted, those for evangelism work much less willingly. This was coupled with a widespread displeasure, shared by young churches across the Global South, with the criteria established by mission agencies for the use of their funds, on the grounds that the criteria reflected Northern bias rather than Southern needs and priorities. A good percentage of the funds sent to the ECMY came through the LWF's departments of Church Cooperation and World Service, so it was suggested that the ECMY set forth in detail its point of view and address its concerns in a letter to the LWF.

Here as elsewhere in official ECMY statements, Gudina Tumsa played a major role in formulating both the ECMY's concerns and its resulting document. The ECMY's leaders affirmed Gudina's work as chairman of the committee appointed for this purpose, whose other members were Rev. Olaf Sæveras of the Norwegian Lutheran Mission and associate general secretary of the ECMY at the time—he did the actual writing—and Rev. Manfred Lundgren of the Swedish Evangelical Mission.

This statement, drafted in May 1972 and sent to the LWF along with various other mission agencies and development agencies, gives voice to Gudina

Tumsa's theological foundation and embodies much of ECMY and, more broadly, African theological thought. It stresses "integral human development" and the fact that human beings are always agents in their own development, not merely passive recipients of others' efforts. It led to an "Ethiopia Consultation" convened by the LWF Commission on Church Cooperation in Villach, Austria, on November 4, 1972, and a jointly sponsored World Council of Churches/ Division on World Mission and Evangelism and LWF/Commission of Church Cooperation consultation called "Education in Mission" at Hothorpe Hall, England, on November 17–20, 1972.

In January 1971, the Seventh General Assembly of the Evangelical Church Mekane Yesus passed a resolution requesting the Lutheran World Federation to approach the donor agencies in Germany and other countries to reconsider their criteria for aid and include direct support for congregational work, leadership training, and church buildings.

The action was prompted, on the one hand, by the fact that the church realized her own inability to cope with the fast-growing congregational work and the opportunities for evangelistic outreach in this country. On the other hand, the church had become more and more concerned about the prevailing imbalance in the assistance given to the church by its overseas partners. It is true that the church had become more and more aware of her obligation to serve our fellow men and society by engaging herself in community and social development projects. The church could not responsibly let the opportunities to get funds for development projects go by without making the fullest possible use of them. Over a number of years, the church has therefore considered it her responsibility and privilege to work out project requests that would meet the criteria decided by the donor agencies. It is also with great gratitude that the church acknowledges the generosity on the part of the donor agencies in granting funds for so many development projects presented by the ECMY.

At the same time, the church, in faithfulness to her Lord, realized her obligation to proclaim the gospel to the ever-growing crowds expecting more than bread. The church cannot possibly remain silent where a genuine spiritual need is prevailing and people in thousands are flocking to newly established churches, and in places where there are no churches, to hear the good news. Finding that her own resources are insufficient both in personnel and funds, the church has called on a number of churches and mission organizations in the West to come and help. In spite of the encouraging response received, the church is not able to cope with the situation.

In turning to her overseas partners and sister churches in the West for assistance in the work that has been regarded as the prime responsibility of the church both in the field of development and the proclamation of the faith, it has become evident over the last few years that the churches and agencies in the West are readily prepared to assist in material development, while there seems to be little interest in helping the church meet her primary obligation to proclaim the gospel. From the African point of view, it is hard to understand this division and the dichotomy created in the West and reflected in the criteria for assistance laid down by the donor agencies.

The ECMY therefore felt that it was her responsibility as well as her duty to call the attention of the Lutheran World Federation to this, in our opinion, most vital issue. In consequence, the president of the ECMY, H. E. Emmanuel Abraham, addressed a letter to the General Secretary of the LWF, Dr. André Appel, on March 9, 1971, enclosing the above-mentioned resolution of the Seventh General Assembly of the ECMY.

It is with satisfaction that the ECMY has come to understand that the concern of the church, expressed in the Assembly resolution, has been taken seriously by the LWF and that consideration is being given to it. We are sufficiently encouraged by this to reiterate the request outlined in the resolution and in the letter from the president, as well as to give the request more substance by presenting a brief supporting document explaining in more detail the reasons for our concern. In doing this we should like to refer to three issues:

1. our understanding of man and his needs;
2. the old and new imbalance in assistance from the West; and
3. the present situation in Ethiopia and its challenge to the church.

Our Understanding of Man and His Needs

It is generally known and admitted that we live in a divided and terribly unjust world, where some people have more than enough and others do not have enough even to survive. We talk today about "rich" and "poor" nations, about "developed" and "underdeveloped" or "developing" societies, and even of the "Third World." In doing this, we are using only generally adopted socioeconomic measurements to determine which society is rich or poor, developed or underdeveloped. The standard of human life and that of society is normally evaluated in terms of economic growth and material wealth, or in technology and production. Based on this materialistic Western concept of development, and in an effort to find a remedy, at least two things seem to have been largely overlooked, namely:

1. That there are values in life beyond those of modern technology and economic betterment, without which man's development will never be meaningful and lasting.
2. That man is not only the suffering creature who needs help but that he is also the most important development agent.

In our view, a one-sided material development is not only self-deceiving, in the sense that man needs more than that, but it is also a threat to the very values that make life meaningful, if carried out without due attention to a simultaneous provision to meet spiritual needs.

We know that we need more of modern technology. We need more equipment and know-how to use it. We need to learn more effective methods to replace the primitive ones in agriculture and other production. We have still to learn and gain much from the Western world, from the experiences and discoveries they have made in various fields, and we hope that the Western churches and agencies will continue to share with us their wealth of knowledge, skill, and funds.

However, when we in effect are told, by virtue of criteria unilaterally decided by the donor agencies, what we need and what we do not need, what is good for us and what is not good, then we feel uncomfortable and become concerned about our own future.

Looking at the so-called developed societies, we realize that in the midst of their affluence, man is still suffering from all kinds of evil. The values that make life meaningful seem to be in danger of being lost in these societies. It seems to us that what is happening in the affluent part of the world today points to the fact that technology and economic growth, beyond the ability of people to control and responsibly use, is leading to development in reverse, where man has to suffer new evils. The present ecological or environmental crisis in the form of physical and moral pollution indicates the danger of this one-dimensional development.

We therefore see the development of the inner man as a prerequisite for a healthy and lasting development of our society. Unless our people are helped to the spiritual freedom and maturity that enables them to responsibly handle material development, we are afraid that what was intended to be a means of enhancing the well-being of man can have the opposite effect and create new forms of evil to destroy him.

We believe that an integral human development, where the spiritual and material needs are seen together, is the only right approach to the development question in our society. The WCC Central Committee also pointed to this when it was stated in the meeting in Addis Ababa in January 1971 that from the Christian point of view, development should be understood as a process of liberation by which individuals and societies realized their human possibilities in accordance with God's purpose. Charles Elliott, in his book *The Development Debate*, goes as far as to say that "humanism closed in on itself and not open to the values of the spirit and to God who is their source could achieve apparent success. True, man can organize the world apart from God, but without God he can organize it, in the end, only against man. An exclusive humanism is an inhuman humanism. There is no true humanism but that which is open to the Absolute and is conscious of a vocation that gives human life its true meaning. Far from being the ultimate measure of all things, man can only realize himself by reaching beyond himself. As Pascal has said so well: "Man infinitely surpasses man." The spiritual is thus easily linked to the secular vision, indeed the two merge.

Throughout man's civilized history, he has been plagued by the dilemma that even though he may know what is good and right and even want to do the right things, yet he fails to achieve it. It has therefore rightly been said that: "Our problem is not primarily to know what is good. Our problem is to find something which will make a man do good when he knows the good" (Dr. Alvin N. Rogness, *Lutheran Standard*, February 1, 1972). St. Paul spoke of this in Romans 7:15–20. There is, however, for many today a struggle to accept this rather depraved view of man. Man is still seen as the most noble of all creatures, with a power within him to be guided by his higher intellect. Man is capable of reasoned response. If he knows what is right, he will do it. "Knowledge is virtue" is the motto of this appealing humanism. Can history support such a view of man? Obviously not. Though certain flagrant abuses of justice have been removed from the affairs of man, unjust practices like racism, oppression, and corruption continue wherever man is found. Thus, man's basic need is not simply to be informed of what is good and right. Man's primary need is to be set free from his own self-centered greed. Here is where the gospel of Lord Jesus Christ comes in as the liberating power.

The other aspect, which in our opinion has been overlooked and for which there is very little room within the present framework of the criteria of the donor agencies, is the question of man as an agent in the development process. The basic question that is asked is: How many will benefit from this project? The community that the project is supposed to serve is seen more as an object than as an agent for betterment. This basic approach has resulted in two problems:

1. Too narrow and well-defined projects, which require professional experts and, in turn, are bound to be remote from those who should be involved.
2. Too few possibilities of long-term support by way of broad training at the grassroots level.

In order to get the ordinary man involved with a view to becoming an agent in the development process, provision must be made to work with unimportant groups over long periods of time. Within the church structure, this brings us down to the congregational level, where, in our view, this potential is available. In the SODEPAX report from the Driebergen Consultation in March 1970, it is pointed out that the church provides a unique possibility to carry out development ideas. It says: "Each pastor working in a rural community could potentially be a change agent in favor of development; each Christian women's or youth group could be a center for the diffusion of innovations. Equally important, because of its grassroots penetration, the church could provide one avenue for the democratization of development by allowing scope for participation and expression by the local rural population." Here again the artificial division between church work and development is an obstacle in the attempt of the church to develop the manpower potential it has within its congregational structure.

We submit that a fresh approach to development aid through church channels would be to consider man and his needs as a totality. This would mean that the present artificial division between spiritual and physical needs would be done away with, and provision would be made for an integral development of man in order to enable him to play his role as an agent in the development process. In our view, the most urgent and the most important investment needed at the present time in the ECMY is in manpower development, and here we see no division between congregational work and development projects. They must go together, because the Creator made man that way.

We also maintain very strongly that it is the need that should determine where assistance should be given and not criteria laid down by the donor agencies, which reflect trends in the Western societies and churches. It is the need in a given local situation that should be the guiding principle for assistance, and therefore there ought to be more flexibility in order to meet extraordinary opportunities in an African church that does not necessarily share all the views of Western churches and agencies.

Old and New Imbalance in Assistance

The old emphasis in the mission of the church had been on the verbal proclamation of the gospel. All other activities in the educational, medical, or technical fields were regarded as being of secondary importance, or even as "means to an end," namely, avenues by which the message would reach people. In the promotion of the mission work, social responsibility, or help toward material betterment of the living conditions among the people, was usually mentioned only as a side issue of expressions of Christian charity.

The new emphasis is on social action, community development, liberation from dehumanizing structures, and involvement in nation building. Proclamation of the gospel has become a side issue, which should be referred to those who may have a special concern for the spiritual welfare of people. The two should be kept apart. It has been said that Christian service is "an end in itself." These two extreme positions are equally harmful to the local churches in developing countries, which see it as their obligation to serve the whole man. It has been suggested that "false piety" is responsible for the old imbalance in assistance and "a sense of guilt" is responsible for the new imbalance in the assistance to the work of the church. It seems as though the prevailing view in the West assumes that the evangelical missions have not in the past paid due attention to the material and physical needs of man, and that they were only concerned about the salvation of souls, doing very little to bring about change in society, that they called themselves "evangelicals" and declared wherever they went that they were there to evangelize non-Christians. By this attitude of a false piety, they created an image of mission work as being only, or, at best, mainly, verbal proclamation of the gospel.

This, however, is not the true picture. The Western churches and the Western world at large had been misinformed by the missions themselves. Although they spent a larger portion of their total resources on social activities, the missions never reported it, or reported it in a distorted form, due to false humility and false piety. It would seem that they operated on the principle, "your left hand should not know what your right hand is doing." We must therefore hold the missions themselves largely responsible for the situation that has developed and the misunderstanding that has resulted in the breakdown of the relationships between development and proclamation, or between witness and service, which from the biblical and theological point of view are inseparable. Here is, in our opinion, a field where a proper study of the foreign mission era could bring about a new understanding of the integral development approach that, in fact, was a significant part of mission work, although it was not admitted, nor rightly understood, by all involved.

The false piety we have mentioned resulted not only in distorted information about mission work but also in a distorted understanding of social activities as "means to an end." The gospel was not understood as the good news for the whole man, and salvation was given a narrow individual interpretation, which was foreign to our understanding of the God-man relationship. God is concerned about the whole man, and this concern is demonstrated in the gospel. The imbalance in assistance created by some missionary attitudes has been harmful to the church in its consequences.

The new extreme position taken by more recently formed donor agencies has drawn a line between mission and development that is completely artificial. The new emphasis is reflected in the criteria laid down for the distribution of funds.

It has been suggested that the prevailing understanding that the church had largely failed to carry out its mandate in the world resulted in a feeling of shame and guilt, which resulted in a reaction to make up for this "failure." When the motto "We must minister to the whole man" was adopted, it was implied that the church had not been ministering to the whole man in the past. There was dismay and a feeling of guilt that gripped the church when, about twenty years ago, the injustice and exploitation of colonialism began to come to the surface. Somehow, the church felt that she had to defend her actions in those "colonized" countries. The church was faced with the questions and often the accusations: "Has the church been an instrument of oppression? Has the church been so busy saving souls that the physical and political needs of man were ignored? Has this not led to an indoctrination of passive subservience as the ideal Christian conduct, which left colonialism almost unopposed?"

As the church rocked under the impact of such guilt (this was always implied as a sin of omission), the cry went up, "Ministry to the whole man." As the emerging nation-states began to exercise control over the influences that they admitted into their countries, the church was forced suddenly to make explicit in all her activities that which had always been implicit. Certainly, the church had always emphasized medical work, education, and other community improvements, but in the early sixties it was necessary to make all such work all the more visible to accommodate the new nationalism and refurnish the "mission" image in the sending countries. This led to an undefendable (from the theological stance) division of ministry and witness. The "real" ministry of the church was seen as service, and this service as an end in itself. The ulterior motives of conversion, evangelistic outreach, and spiritual nurture should be done away with. These matters should be dealt with separately and in a different context.

This overreaction to the church's failure to engage in social and economic matters in the past, and the sense of guilt on the part of the wealthy Western churches, led to a new imbalance in assistance to the younger churches. All this happened in the West, but why should this historical and theological development in the West be the only determining factor in the aid relationship between the older and the younger churches? The national churchman in Africa today is unencumbered by an "image" that has to be maintained for the benefit of a guilt-ridden constituency "back home." He is free to interpret the commands of his Lord in the context of his brother's situation (which he shares intimately) without having to apologize for the power of the gospel.

Thus, it was providential and foreordained that we, the national churchmen today, should begin to question the hesitancy and the equivocation in the proclamation of the gospel that we witness in some of the agencies that support our work.

When the ECMY felt the time had come to call the attention of the LWF to this issue, she did it with the conviction that something could be done to bring assistance into balance. It is our firm belief that Christian service is neither "a means to an end" nor "an end in itself," but an integral part of the total responsibility of the church. The division between witness and service, or between proclamation and development, which has been imposed on us, is, in our view, harmful to the church and will ultimately result in a distorted Christianity.

Having made this, our concern, clear, we hear some people say: "Why should we change the criteria because of wrongs done in the past?" Others say: "The present arrangement is only a division of labor. One cannot do everything, and therefore this division must be there for practical reasons." In our opinion, such remarks are only meant to avoid this issue, which is the artificial division of things that belong together.

The Present Situation and Its Challenge to the Church

Among the many remarkable things that happen in Africa today, the rapid growth of the Christian church is probably one of the most surprising. The phenomenal expansion of Christianity across Africa in the last few decades is simply frightening for the responsible church leaders. Dr. David Barrett[1] in his thorough analysis of the situation has, on the basis of available statistics, suggested that within the next thirty years the center of gravity of the Christian world will have shifted southwards from Europe and North America to the developing continents of Africa and South America. He points out that while the Western churches will have doubled their membership in the twentieth century, the younger churches will have multiplied seventeen times. If we take this development seriously, it puts a tremendous responsibility on the whole Christian world. If the historically young churches will represent the "center of gravity" in the Christian world in three decades, they must be prepared.

Dr. Barrett points out some of the consequences of the present expansion of the Christian church in Africa and one of them is an urgent and massive help [needed] in order to prevent a widespread breakdown of the church. So far, very little planning has been done both among Roman Catholics and Protestants. The growth rate indicates that "the construction of four times more physical plants, such as Church buildings, religious education for children, mass production of Christian literature, literacy programs and so on are urgently needed."

What is happening in this respect in our continent at large is also happening in the ECMY. The problems that Dr. Barrett has pointed out

---

1. "AD 2000: 350 Million Christians in Africa," *International Review of Missions* 59, no. 233 (January 1970): 39–54.

for Africa as a whole are also our problem today. We are alarmed by the development and challenged by the opportunities to such a degree that we must share our concern with the sister churches in the West, which, we believe, have both the desire and the means to help us. Here we should like to quote some parts of the ECMY general secretary Rev. Gudina Tumsa's report ["Report on Church Growth in Ethiopia"] at the LWF/CCC Meeting in Tokyo last year [1971].

Alarmed by the high growth rate, the General Assembly decided in 1969 that a plan whereby the church could be able to know where she stands be worked out. During the two-year period 1969–70, the necessary data were collected for assessment. In the process of working out a plan, it became clear that in the past three years, 1968–70, the average growth was calculated to be 15 percent. Membership growth in 1970 alone was 27 percent. However, if we stick to the more moderate growth figure of 15 percent, the membership of the ECMY will be about doubled by the end of 1975, which means that the ECMY will then have a membership of about 285,000.

To meet this expansion, about 137 pastors must be trained during this period, as well as about 1,000 evangelists. Realizing the urgency of making use of the present opportunities in Ethiopia, our Seventh General Assembly passed a resolution requesting the LWF to approach the donor agencies in Europe and the United States to reconsider their criteria for aid and include direct support for congregational work and leadership training, so that the ECMY will be able to cope with the rapid growth taking place at present. The earnest wish of the ECMY is that this request be passed on to the member churches of the LWF to be communicated to the congregations in order that they may know our problems and desires, and it is our sincere and earnest hope that the LWF will do its utmost—in the first place, in passing and making known our concern to the churches and secondly, that the LWF may influence the present donor agencies to review their criteria for allocation of assistance, thereby giving due consideration to our evangelistic outreach plan.

Our hope is that sister churches do not judge our needs solely on their own criteria and on the conditions that they have stipulated. We want to proclaim Christ because we believe it is our responsibility. We want to proclaim Christ because our people are hungering for him.

We trust that in this document, we have made the reasons for our concern clear, and that the current theological and missiological trends in the West will not be the sole determining factors for aid, but that African views will be taken more seriously and considered against the background of the present situation.

Addis Ababa, May 9, 1972

Source: The 358th Church Officers' Meeting, Minutes C0-72-63.

6

Report at the Ethiopia Consultation

A second Ethiopia Consultation (the first took place in Austria in 1972; see the introduction to the previous document) took place in Hannover, Germany, on November 22 and 23, 1973. Its purpose was to discuss the disagreement between the administration of the Hermannsburg Mission (Missionsanstalt Hermannsburg, MAH) and the ECMY regarding the latter's relation to mission and development agencies on both the national and synodical level.

The MAH had signed a general agreement with the Western Synod under the expiring presidency of the late Rev. Daffa Jarmo, setting the terms of the relationship between the MAH and the synod. The general manager of the MAH, a Mr. Welge, had defended the right of the mission to do so by appealing to the "federal" character of the ECMY. This elicited fierce resistance from the ECMY's leaders and the following vigorous rebuttal in defense of the unity and integrity of the ECMY as a national church. At issue was also the interpretation of the Integration of Church and Mission, which was officially completed in 1971 when the ECMY assumed full responsibility, as an independent church, for all mission-initiated projects within the country.

As general secretary, Gudina Tumsa orally presented the ECMY's position at the consultation, which was subsequently transcribed from tape and edited for publication. It illuminates Gudina Tumsa's ecclesiological thinking, as he puts forth his understanding of the nature and structure of the ECMY in its particular historical setting. Familiar themes from "On Proclamation of the Gospel

and Human Development" (1972) and "Report on Church Growth in Ethiopia"
(1971) also make their appearance.

Mr. Chairman, Christian Friends:

I have been very much delighted to see many familiar faces so that I can relax among friends and express my views on the present situation in Ethiopia, for which we are all here. I am very grateful for this invitation.

When the invitation letter by Mr. J. Gotthardt [of the *Evangelisches Missionswerk* in Hamburg] reached our office, I did not quite know what it was that we were expected to come together to discuss. After serious consideration, I came to realize that we have come to a stage where we have to face realities, which historical development of our time has placed before us. Although this consultation is dealing with the Ethiopian situation, problems of the nature that we will be discussing are not peculiar to the Ethiopian situation; they are somewhat international or worldwide, if we think in terms of the Third World. What we may talk about here, I hope, will not only lay a foundation for future better relationships between the Evangelical Church Mekane Yesus and the organizations here in Germany, but also may give some hints for finding solutions to problems of relationships with others as well. Because of the nature of the problem we are dealing with, and since the questions we were supposed to find solutions for during this consultation were not clearly indicated, I am not going to present a written lecture but simply take up some points that I consider to be relevant for consideration by this consultation. To these points, which I will raise from the viewpoint of the ECMY, I would like to invite questions so that a monologue may be avoided and an atmosphere for real dialogue prevail, where we may exchange views and ideas in our common interest.

In case interest is expressed in getting in written form what I am now presenting orally, I would be ready to make it available to you.

Let me just try, then, to describe how the situation stands in Ethiopia today. The ECMY is one of the national churches emerging in the Third World. This has not come about suddenly but is the natural growth of the activities of Lutheran missions in Ethiopia. The Lutheran missions have been laboring in Ethiopia since about the start of the present century, and groups of Christians were formed in almost all parts of our country. For their past labor, I must say, we give full credit to the missionary societies who worked in Ethiopia, regardless of where they came from. They served, and their ministry was blessed with the establishment of the Evangelical Church Mekane Yesus, one of the fast-growing national churches in the Third World.

After making such statements, when I now come with some critical points, I hope that nobody may take this as an attack against a particular mission organization, thereby misinterpreting the interest of the ECMY in the task of proclaiming the gospel of Jesus Christ in our country. The interest of the ECMY, let me say, stands as it is. We are interested in using whatever resources we may find to preach the gospel and to serve those who are around us in that particular society, where we believe we have been placed by God and been given a responsibility to carry it out, as we understand it from our point of view.

The Swedish Evangelical Mission and the German Hermannsburg Mission started preaching the gospel in the western part of Ethiopia before World War II, or roughly put, about the beginning of this century. Because of World War II, the Lutheran missions were forced out of the country. The Ethiopians, who had nowhere to go, took upon themselves the responsibility of spreading the gospel in the areas where they lived. This is the beginning for the spreading of the gospel by indigenous groups of believers in our country, in spite of those bitter days. This is to say that indigenous groups of believers formed themselves during World War II. After the war, other Lutheran missions started working in various areas in Ethiopia. For the first time, in 1957, indigenous groups of believers came together from different parts of Ethiopia to form the Evangelical Church Mekane Yesus. At the second meeting, in 1958, the Constitution of the ECMY was signed. The Constitution of the ECMY was registered by the Imperial Ethiopian Government and the ECMY was recognized as a national church. At this point, the task that the Lutheran missions were carrying out in the various parts of the country was shared by the ECMY, and the two, the Lutheran missions on the one hand and the ECMY on the other, continued alongside each other. Since it was understood that the Lutheran missions and the ECMY work for identical purposes, the church and the Lutheran missions signed an Integration Policy in 1969, the ECMY thereby taking over the various activities of the Lutheran missions in Ethiopia. In April 1969, when the Integration Policy was signed and registered at the Imperial Ethiopian High Court, the Lutheran missions ceased to exist as foreign organizations in our country.

Now comes the crucial point: in our opinion, integration means that foreign organizations on Ethiopian soil have ceased to exist and that the church is responsible for any type of activity in the country. Whatever assistance we may get we thought would be assistance on a temporary basis, because we are in need of resources in personnel and finances to discharge our responsibility. Our understanding is that the responsibility of preaching the gospel of Jesus Christ and serving the Ethiopian people rests with the Evangelical Church Mekane Yesus, and any assistance, in whatever form it may be, is assistance given to the church to help her to discharge her responsibility in the country. Now the Integration Policy became some sort of a test case in our situation. The way we understood it is different from the way cooperating missions understood it.

I think this is one of the points to be discussed here. Being a national church is neither for the sake of prestige, nor for having institutions to impress the society at large. A national character, identity, and integrity are a must for a church in a given society if she is to fulfill the commission of her Lord.

The ECMY has to realize her selfhood and identity, which we feel is very important if this church is to exist in the future on Ethiopian soil. This is to say that the ECMY can never be an agent for rich mission organizations, donor agencies, and churches.

What has caused the present discussion is what is called by the *Missionsanstalt Hermannsburg* the "General Agreement," signed with the Western Synod. Neither the so-called General Agreement, nor the letter of Mr. Welge, has created any new situation. Both these documents have accelerated a process that was bound to come about any time. Unfortunately, I am very much limited as to information, as far as the letter of Mr. Welge goes. The letter is a reply to a report which was given by Mr. J. Gotthardt on his visit to Ethiopia.

I really dislike seeing the two Germans fighting, but now that seems to be the situation. As the report was not made available to me in English, any statement I make in reply to some of the points raised in Mr. Welge's letter should be understood on that limited background information, since an official translation of his letter is lacking. Mr. Gotthardt's report, with which I am not familiar, Mr. Welge's letter, and the so-called General Agreement, these unfortunate documents, let me say again, have not created any new situation but have accelerated the development of problems that were bound to come about any time in the course of historical development of this church. The so-called General Agreement, signed between the *Missionsanstalt Hermannsburg* and the Western Synod, was submitted to our office, and it has been expressed in writing to the synod, with copies to the *Missionsanstalt Hermannsburg* in Germany and the Evangelical Lutheran Church of Hannover, that the document was illegal. The reasons for considering the document to be illegal, I should indicate in the following lines:

1. As I have just stated, when groups of believers came together from various parts of Ethiopia to form the Evangelical Church Mekane Yesus in 1958, her constitution was accepted by the Imperial Ethiopian Government, and the law of the country recognizes the ECMY as one legal entity in Ethiopia. The synods are understood by her constitution as integral parts of the ECMY. Since in the constitution, the law of the country recognizes one national church, the ECMY as a legal entity, the so-called General Agreement concluded between the MAH and the Western Synod is illegal before the law of Ethiopia. This is to say that according to the law of the country, one can never deal with an organization that the government has not accepted and registered as a national organization in the country. Unless one represents an organization recognized by the law, one has nothing to represent but himself. Before the law of the country there is no organization called the Western Synod. What the law of the country recognizes is a legal entity called "The Evangelical Church Mekane Yesus" with her synods. Whether the synods of the ECMY are five or six or ten, or whether they are big or small, is a different matter, but the law recognizes one national church. Therefore, if this illegal document called the General Agreement comes to light, it may implicate the ECMY in matters of an illegal nature, contrary to the law of the country, when one of her synods concludes an agreement with an organization that does not exist in the country.

2. The MAH did not act only against the law of the country; the MAH acted contrary to the letter and the spirit of the constitution of the ECMY. We are criticizing the MAH for making all efforts to divide the church by applying "the Machiavellian philosophy of divide and rule," influencing one section of the church to maintain her own interest—domination.

3. There are universal trends in ecumenical movements toward church unity in today's world. Desire for unity is strong everywhere, regardless of denominational loyalties. In spite of this, the MAH is working for a division of a national church, which is legally one, constitutionally one. This is morally wrong in our opinion. This is our reply to the General Agreement, and the General Agreement is, in our opinion illegal, unconstitutional, and immoral.

I should say something about the letter that Mr. Welge has written:

First: Mr. Welge argues that the Western Synod is "related to the ECMY." He doesn't say the Western Synod of the ECMY, but "related." (That is the phrase he is using. If I am misquoting him, then it is due to the translation and let him defend himself. At least this is the way we understand him.) In the course of his argument, Mr. Welge states that the ECMY has some kind of federalist structure, which he sees as loopholes to strengthen his contention. In another place in his letter, he speaks about a federation of churches. To say that the ECMY is a federation of churches is not true. This is because, according to the law of Ethiopia, to form a federation there must be legal entities to come together. One can never form a federation unless there are legal entities to come together and form another organization. This is impossible. The Mekane Yesus Church is not a federation of churches but one church, established on democratic principles. But the ECMY is not trying to dictate what her synods are doing. The task of the ECMY is divided in such a way that international relationships and ecumenical affairs, which have been clearly stated in our constitution, as well as policy matters with regard to the Imperial Ethiopian Government, are taken care of by the Central Office of the Church. Now, this is completely misunderstood. Rather than taking the democratic principles on which the church was established, stating that our synods are free and have the freedom to act in their own areas, to develop their work, to preach the gospel, to establish hospitals, to establish Bible schools, to undertake community development projects, as provided in the constitution, our church is defined by Mr. Welge as a federation of Lutheran churches, which does not exist in the country.

Mr. Welge disregards Article IV of the Constitution, where it is stated clearly that international relationships, ecumenical affairs, and governmental questions are taken care of by the church. This article of the constitution has no place in the argument of Mr. Welge. Mr. Welge finds in Article V of the Constitution of the Church statements that declare that the synods of the ECMY can run hospitals and schools and institutions. From this Article V, he contends that the Western Synod can act as if there is nothing in the constitution. This I consider to be unfair. It is not only unfair but also unchristian to find loopholes where there are clear-cut statements to divide the ECMY.

Second: The second argument for Mr. Welge is found in the Integration Document that he sees as a replacement for the Constitution of the Church. He maintains that the relationships between the synods of the

ECMY and the former mission organizations in Ethiopia were provided for in this document of legal character.

Let me tell you briefly how we understand the Integration Document. The Integration Document was drafted and signed in April 1969. Article III in the Integration Document deals with the interim period of time from the date of signature of the document until all programs are taken over by the various synods of the church from their respective supporting Lutheran missions, from mission organizations in Ethiopia. This is how we understand the document. Since the last institutions and programs have been integrated about the beginning of this year, the programs having been taken over by our synods, we consider the Integration Document as having fulfilled its purpose. It has no bearing any longer; it has served its purpose. From a legal point of view, as far as we are concerned, relationships between the church and international organizations are taken care of by the Central Office of the Church.

Even if I am not a lawyer but a theologian, this is so clear as far as the law of our country is concerned. Before the law of the country, if there is a document contrary to a document by which an organization is guided, the second document, in this case the Integration Document, contradicting the Constitution of the Church, must be adjusted. This is to say, any document of legal character must be changed to be in conformity with the Constitution of the Church, otherwise it would not be valid. I hope you understand the points of my argument in this case.

Third: The ECMY has a constitution that is recognized by the Imperial Ethiopian Government as a legal document not for a certain period of time but, we believe, as long as the church is interested in the present structures, or as long as the present law in the country exists. Looked at from this point of view, the contention of Mr. Welge has no basis, is invalid.

Fourth: Mr. Welge refers to what he calls "Minutes from the Board Committee." Let me just blindly say that we are not aware of what he called a board committee. The ECMY does not recognize any board committee formed by missions anywhere. A letter was addressed to us some time ago by the LWF, Department of Church Cooperation, suggesting to us to set up some kind of an organization similar to that of the Evangelical Lutheran Church in Tanzania, the Joint Board Committee, and so on. You are all familiar with that structure. We replied to the LWF stating that we already have enough problems with the existing organizations. It is not in our best interest to set up another structure in Geneva, in Sweden, in Norway, or in Germany. We want to deal with the organizations who are interested in working in Ethiopia individually. This, I think, is not very important, but I am trying to show that some kind of board committee, or whatever it may be, has no place in our opinion. We are not even aware of what it is, the document to which Mr. Welge refers. I think one can contend a full day on the logic that Mr. Welge has followed in his argument.

Fifth: Mr. Welge states in one paragraph of his letter that the *Missionsanstalt Hermannsburg* would not want to interfere in the internal matters of the ECMY. He sees the position of MAH as neutral in what he calls a "struggle for power" between the Western Synod and the Central Office of the Church. Having stated that the MAH is neutral in what he alleges is a "conflict for centralization," he contradicts himself by trying to justify the involvement of the MAH in an illegal way in the affairs of the ECMY. He argues that since about 50 percent of the constituency of the ECMY is from the Western Synod, what the Western Synod says should have more weight. As you see then, he departs, as far as I understand, from the strictly legal point, wishing to put us under pressure so that he can argue from a strong position. This is how an Ethiopian understands the argument of the letter. But now to say that the MAH is neutral, is not involved in the internal affairs of the church, is, I think, not true. The MAH is not only involved in the present problem but has laid the foundation for it. As I have stated earlier, the MAH is interested in dividing the ECMY, thereby strengthening their domination. Mr. Welge alleges that there is a tension or conflict for centralization or decentralization. Our interest is in implementing our constitution. Anyone who has taken a look at the constitution of the ECMY may see that there is no indication for centralization. We have no interest for it. I would not like to state this here. We are tired of centralization. We are not interested in it. We have enough experience with what centralization means. My contention is that there is no indication or justification for what Mr. Welge has written, as far as our dealings with our synods or with international organizations go.

What we are trying to do, gentlemen, is to implement our constitution, which Mr. Welge is striving to avoid. This is the way we understand it. We are contending that the Integration Document has placed the MAH on the international level, as far as we are concerned. The MAH is here in Germany, the Swedish Evangelical Mission is in Stockholm. What we are saying is that these missions are international organizations, and the Constitution of the Church applies. To avoid the main issue, Mr. Welge concentrates on the relationships between the Western Synod and the Central Office of the ECMY. From his argument, you get the impression that the ECMY has been formed by someone else other than the congregations of the church. The present structure of the ECMY has been established by the General Assembly of the Church, which meets biannually, where all the congregations of the church are represented, in accordance with the constitution, by which we are bound to be guided. In the constitution, areas of responsibility have been defined as regard the present setup.

Sixth: In light of this, the way we are understood from abroad is mistaken. This mistaken view is maintained not only by MAH but by others. What Mr. Welge is interested in is a Federation of Lutheran Churches in Ethiopia. I wouldn't like to dwell on this point, but Mr. Welge's argument falls to pieces when he wants to create a neutral position for MAH, while quoting all these documents to justify the involvement of the MAH in the affairs of the ECMY in an unconstitutional manner. This is to say that his argument that the synods are reacting against centralization is neither convincing nor justifiable. Not at all.

We have come to this point in the historical development of the ECMY. What is the crucial point here? What is at stake in the life of the ECMY? At present, what is at stake in the life of the ECMY is the identity of a national church. As I have stated already, we would not like to be, we can never be, an agent for rich mission organizations, donor agencies, and churches. Let it be clear to all that the ECMY is not an agent to carry out policies and decisions made in Europe or America, nor is the ECMY willing to fulfill the purpose of international organizations, which appears to be contrary to what she holds to be right. We want to be ourselves. We have come to this stage in our historical development where as a national church we have to maintain integrity and assert maturity. The ECMY has come of age; we are not children to be told how to behave. We are not ready to accept a statement that we are too immature to understand the constitution by which we are guided, that somebody in Germany interprets our constitution for us and says to us: Now you are mistaken, boy, go and behave yourself well. This kind of paternalistic, colonial attitude can never be tolerated, can never be accepted. This is to be understood clearly, that the ECMY, as I have just stated, is not an agent for the organizations you are representing, there is no doubt about that.

The ECMY is a national church. Whether we get assistance from you or not, we are determined to sacrifice in serving our people. We are ready to discuss, argue, and exchange views and ideas as mature people, on an equal level with you. If our interests happen to coincide, we would be ready to work together, to serve the Ethiopian people as we understand it. But never as an agent, like some people who work for German or American companies in Ethiopia. The church of Jesus Christ can never be used as an agent by anyone except for the One who has died for her. Using the church as an agent is not in agreement with our theological understanding. What makes the church is not the funds she has. No, what makes the church is the faith that she has, the gospel of Jesus Christ, her confession of Jesus as her Lord and Savior, which liberates man, this is what we believe. In spite of this, we are told that we cannot understand our constitution by which we are being guided, and we are warned to behave ourselves. We are told that whatever agreements are signed with nonexistent organizations are valid for us. We are told that we cannot manage our affairs on the international level. We are told that we cannot take care of our own activities on the international level. We are told that we cannot take care of our own activities in our country and therefore need advice from abroad, specially from MAH.

Seventh: The MAH claims to represent the interest of the ECMY before German organizations. This is an attack upon our maturity, integrity, and identity. We are mature enough not only to take care of our own business but also mature enough to contribute to international efforts in finding solutions to the problems of our day. The paper that we have sent out ["On the Interrelation between Proclamation of the Gospel and Human Development"] is calling you to take a fresh look at what you are practicing, your structures. The division that you have made between what you call body and soul is unfair to man. Now, we are telling you that there is a contradiction in your thinking. I am sorry to say this, but I think it is just when I make such a statement that you take the matter seriously. Criticism is healthy when taken in a right way. I hope you will understand me. On Sundays you confess that you believe in the resurrection of the body; during the rest of the week you tell the world that the body is of secondary importance—what matters is the soul. Therefore, preach the gospel, the most important thing in the world! For us it is very difficult to dissect human life into various parts, ministering to one aspect while neglecting the other. Man is created by God as a totality. What we confess on Sundays as the resurrection of the body should be practiced during the week and must be in conformity with the biblical understanding of man. What we confess and what we believe in our daily life should be in conformity.

We must be considered as mature people. To consider the ECMY as an immature church, which cannot handle her own affairs, cannot be justified at all. I would be happy to listen to anyone here, whether from MAH or the Swedish Evangelical Mission, or all of you here, address any sort of criticism that you may have as far as my church is concerned. As I have just stated, taking criticism, arguing, establishing reasoned policy are signs of maturity, and my church is mature enough for such reasoning. The statement I have made on behalf of my church will be justified on this basis. To say that people from the Third World will be offended if criticism is addressed to them is, in my opinion, an unfounded emotional expression—contrary to maturity based on reasonable discussions. We are mature enough to accept criticism in case it is justifiable, we are mature enough to stand criticism, to correct our mistakes, and ready to reach an agreement with anyone who is interested in cooperating with our church. Let me say it again, no one can embarrass or offend us as far as our church is concerned, even if strong criticism is addressed to us. This should be considered to be a sign of maturity. I must emphasize this again and again: we would not like to be considered children. Paul said to the Corinthians, now I have to feed you strong food, not only milk. Now let me assure you we have passed that stage of being fed with milk; what we need now is strong food. I would not like to take more time on this.

The ECMY has come of age. I have touched on the Document of the ECMY ["On the Interrelation between Proclamation of the Gospel and Human Development"], which is being studied by various groups in this country as well as in others. I wanted to accentuate the points raised in the document. According to the information received from the Lutheran World Federation, there are groups who interpret the document according to their own taste—to strengthen their own positions. Reaction papers and letters to the ECMY Document forwarded to us by the LWF show that some of the groups say, now come back to the saving of the souls, which you have forgotten! The Mekane Yesus Church is calling your attention to this important task. Others say: Now you have to serve. Development is the most important thing under heaven; what Africans need is development. We are interpreted in four or five ways, and perhaps in many more ways, because the Western mind is good at interpreting documents, including the Mekane Yesus Paper. Of course this is good, not bad at all. What we are calling your attention to, ladies and gentlemen, is to reconsider your criteria, your views, and we are asking you to reconsider your whole assumptions. One of the points in the questionnaire of the LWF circulated to the member churches of the federation defines "proclamation" as spiritual activity. When I read this, I said this is ridiculous, I should have been consulted by Geneva people before the questionnaires were sent out. "Proclamation," as we understand it, is based on Luke 4, where it states the blind receive sight, the poor hear good news, the oppressed are given liberty, prisoners are set free. You know that text. Now to us, proclamation is not some kind of spiritual activity as understood by the Western mind. But it is a saving power to release man from whatever conditions he finds himself in. It involves the total human personality. To this, I assume we will have the chance of replying, making our position clear at the forthcoming [LWF] Consultation. Although I am not informed of the month, the consultation may be called in the course of the coming summer.[1]

At this time, I wish to point out something as far as development programs go. I know that we are just exchanging views, ideas, and a lot of questions are going to be raised in the course of this consultation. As I stated already before we went for lunch, the ECMY is receiving a substantial amount of funds from the Western churches and organizations to serve the Ethiopian people. These have been tremendous contributions, certainly, in improving the living conditions of our people, and to lay a foundation for a higher future development we have to think in terms of a longer period of time. Of this I have to remind you. During the last LWF Assembly in 1970, the president of the ECMY presented a very short paper in which he indicated that development projects for the Third World—and particularly, let us say, for Ethiopia—must be planned from the grassroots level. The second point raised in the president's paper is that development cannot take place overnight. It needs a longer period of time. It is a painful undertaking. In many cases you have to change the attitude of many people. You need a certain period of time to talk to people, to explain that poverty is not a natural phenomenon but a historical condition that can be changed, if the people concerned are willing. There was someone in the assembly who paid serious attention to the point raised by the president of the ECMY, and as a result now we are running what we call a "Rural Development Project"—the Henna pilot project. Of course, this does not mean from

---

1. Ed. note: For Gudina's contribution to that consultation, see "Serving the Whole Man," the seventh document in Part I of this volume.

our side bigger projects, which will require bigger amounts of grants for development projects. What I am saying is this, that the time element involved is very important. Let us say that terms of three or four years for projects may not achieve the desired result. Let us say half a million *Deutschmarks* planned for a period of ten years may achieve a better result than the one planned for five years. When we know that we deal with people in Ethiopia, not with advanced people in Germany, but people who cannot read and write in many cases, who are not informed, who have no background, the time element deserves our serious attention.

Mr. Chairman, we all have a common interest in Ethiopia. As a church body we want to contribute to the cause of the promotion of the gospel of Jesus Christ in my country, which means, from our point of view, liberating Ethiopian society from their living conditions. It is through such a total service to the total man that a just society may evolve in Ethiopia.

I would invite questions. Any questions will not embarrass or offend me. I will try to justify the statements I have made here. If I cannot justify them I would admit that I am mistaken. In the course of this consultation, my statements will be justified by argument. Thank you, Mr. Chairman.

7

Serving the Whole Man:
A Responsible Church Ministry and a
Flexible International Aid Relationship

The Lutheran World Federation convened a special consultation in Nairobi, Kenya, in October 1974 to discuss the issues raised by "On the Interrelation between Proclamation of the Gospel and Human Development." As in that document, so in this one: Gudina Tumsa delivered the address—the first of five at the consultation—which he had a major role in formulating in cooperation with other ECMY church leaders, clarifying, explaining, and amplifying the position of their church.

Corresponding to the views stated here is this excerpt from a letter Gudina Tumsa wrote to Dr. Carl-J. Hellberg, Director of the LWF's Department of Church Cooperation, on December 12, 1972: "I would like to say something about the questions raised in [the] Mekane Yesus Paper [of May 1972]. Some people who talked with me in Sweden and Germany, the countries I visited prior to the Villach Consultation [the first "Ethiopia Consultation," November 4, 1972], were surprised that the Mekane Yesus Church raised such a question, that an African view assumes the totality of man which is not in line with the Western ways of thinking. During the Consultation also quite a number of people who talked with me . . . said that they were surprised such a theologi-

cal issue was raised by the Mekane Yesus. On my part I am surprised at their surprise, because it is, in my opinion, just time to raise such questions by the African churches. I believe that an African theology will be developed along the line that has been defined in the Mekane Yesus Document. . . . In my opinion, reconsideration of criteria and review of policies by the Western churches require a theological rethinking which has led to the laying down of the criteria. In Africa there are some thinkers who are interested neither in the Western nor the Eastern ways of thinking. The one divides man into various parts, while the other denies the reality of the religious dimension of human existence. In Africa we are not interested in this. We have [to], if we are to develop healthy societies, look at life as a total unit and try to cater to its needs."

When the Evangelical Church Mekane Yesus in March 1971 communicated to the Lutheran World Federation its concern about existing criteria and the imbalance in the present aid relationships with its overseas supporters, and when the church a year later repeated the concern in an explicit document, the underlying issue has not been more financial aid, as some have interpreted it, but a more responsible church ministry.

The ECMY found itself in a situation where its conscience and Christian conviction called for maximum engagement in social development activities and where, at the same time, it was faced with both the responsibility for a massive spiritual nurture of its rapidly growing membership and unusual opportunities for evangelistic outreach in unevangelized areas of the country.

Considering its responsibility in this situation and trying to work out a strategy for its ministry, the church realized that its hands were tied. It was not in a position to set its own priorities and, at the same time, engage in development activities for which funds were available from abroad and that it was convinced were part of its total ministry at this particular time. Although available, the funds approved were fenced in by criteria set by the donor agencies and were earmarked for specific activities.

The church was thus faced with a painful dilemma. Should it cut down on its social development involvement in order to maintain the inner balance of its ministry, or should it continue to make maximum use of development aid within established criteria and put aside the question of imbalance? To do the former would mean a retarded development program and continued suffering for those of our fellow men the church would have been able to help, to some degree, in their poverty, sickness, and ignorance. To do the latter would have been to weaken the spiritual life of the church and turn away those who long for the gospel.

It was only within these limitations that the church was able to make its decisions. It was not in a position to work out a comprehensive strategy for what it felt was a responsible church ministry in the cultural, social, and political setting of this particular age.

As we struggled with these problems, the question arose whether it was responsible of the church to let its ministry be governed by earmarked funds and by aid criteria that, in effect, arbitrarily determined what was needed and what was not needed. The church concluded that the time had come when this whole issue should be discussed on the international level. The main purpose of the document submitted by the ECMY in May 1972 was to initiate such a discussion, which eventually and hopefully would bring about a new and more healthy aid relationship between the rich and the poor churches.

We appreciate the efforts made by the Lutheran World Federation to facilitate an open and frank exchange of views on the issues involved, and we only hope that this consultation will pave the way for a new understanding of responsible church ministry and provide for more flexible aid relationships with a view to meeting the challenges of the immediate and more distant future.

Against this background and within the framework of the main topic of this consultation, the Evangelical Church Mekane Yesus would like to comment briefly on these two issues: a more responsible church ministry and a more flexible international aid relationship.

A More Responsible Church Ministry

We deliberately use the expression "more responsible" because we feel that, on one hand, the churches in Africa have so far not sufficiently taken upon themselves the task of seriously reviewing their ministry in the light of their cultural, social, and political setting. It is urgent that a fresh initiative for such a review be taken by the churches themselves. On the other hand, as long as the ministry of a given church is governed to a greater or lesser degree by earmarked funds or by aid criteria arbitrarily determining what should be done and what should not be done, that church is handicapped. We need to establish aid relationships that allow planning and implementation of a fully responsible ministry in a given situation.

Let us first take up the controversial question of church involvement in activities other than worship, administration of the sacraments, and direct proclamation of the gospel. We are here referring to church involvement in public and social affairs and in community development efforts. This question has a direct bearing on the issues we are here to discuss.

We have to ask ourselves the question: What is a responsible ministry of the Christian church in today's world and in a given cultural, social, and political situation? Where and to what extent should the church involve itself and employ its resources?

By a narrow definition of its ministry, some are reducing the church to an insignificant factor in society, alienated from and to modern man. It is a church for God and for a selected few, but not for the world. Others want the church to identify itself fully with the world and actively to engage in the struggle for social justice, removal of dehumanizing structures, and the liberation of the oppressed. They hold that only by doing this can the church be true to its Lord, who identified himself with the world even unto death on the cross. In between these extremes are those who represent more moderate positions with regard to the understanding of what a responsible church ministry should be in this day and age.

A debate on this issue is useful insofar as it keeps the church alert, but it becomes harmful as soon as it is claimed that certain concepts and definitions must be universally applied, and that any church that does not meet them cannot be considered a true Christian church. It is here that the paternalistic attitude of a supporting church or agency becomes inimical.

In our opinion, there is no universal and simple answer to the question of what constitutes a responsible church ministry. We believe that the gospel itself, when faithfully proclaimed and faithfully lived, gives the necessary guidelines for a responsible church ministry. A true theological definition of a responsible church must always grow out of an "action situation," or, to go even one step further, true biblical and evangelical theology must always allow for a contextual interpretation of the gospel and the action strategy of the church, and priorities must be decided upon in faithfulness to this interpretation.

It is true a contextual definition of a responsible church ministry is always a risky undertaking because in every situation and in every event both divine and demonic elements are at work, and, as has rightly been said, one can easily be carried away with the wind of the times and allow the church to become a tool of other powers than the Lord.

Canon Burgess Carr, the general secretary of the All-Africa Conference of Churches, has warned the African churches of this very risk when, at a meeting in Ibadan last year, he said: "The churches run a real risk of being used by independent African governments in very much the same way as missionaries were used by the colonial exploiters. The consequence is obvious: a surrender of our prophetic vocation over against our nations. Both the credibility and the integrity of the churches in Africa are placed in desperate jeopardy."

On the other hand, it has also been said:

> A church which always wants to do everything correctly and which therefore tries to stay out of anything which is risky, i.e. a church which itself does not really want to live for the justification of the sinner, will also not be able to preach the Gospel of gracious affirmation and the liberation of the real sinner. Only a church which dares to go out into the world recognizes secular man's problems and can learn by listening to his hopes and hopelessnesses, his illusions and resignations, and how the Gospel would have to be phrased if it is to relate to him (Dr. W. Krusche).

A responsible church ministry in a given cultural, social, and political setting can only be defined by the interpretation of the gospel into the action situation of the church concerned. For this to be possible, relationships with supporting churches and donor agencies must be such that the church concerned is really free to act according to its Christian conviction.

The other important question to be taken up here is the question of the objectives of a responsible church ministry. We would like to mention three basic objectives that, in our opinion, constitute the biblical mandate given to the church by its Lord. These objectives are inseparable, but emphasis on each one of them will have to be changed in accordance with the contextual interpretation of the gospel. Any attempt to separate the three objectives will immediately have implications for the quality of the total ministry of the church.

The church is first of all commissioned to preach the gospel of Jesus Christ to all nations (Matt 28:19–20). This is the evangelistic outreach of the church and the missionary obligation that it can never withdraw from or delegate. There is always something wrong when the missionary dimension of the church is reduced to groups and societies organized within or outside the church to carry on the responsibility that belongs to the church at large. We are thankful to God for what the missionary societies have done in Africa, but we are also concerned that a church that resulted from their work should have inherited a concept of mission that is something different from the church. This has been further reinforced by the artificial division between mission and development aid. We are concerned with this situation because the missionary dimension of the church suffers. In our opinion, a responsible church ministry must have a strong mission emphasis.

The other objective is the healing of brokenness and making man whole. The church has a healing ministry to carry out, which is more than medical care for the physically ill. It has to do with the restoration of man to liberty and wholeness. Here the church simply has to follow its Lord and Savior, who during his ministry here on earth cared for the whole man.

The ministry of our Lord Jesus Christ can be summarized under three aspects, which together fulfill one purpose—namely, to restore man to what he should be according to God's plan in creation. He was seeking those who were lost to bring them back to fellowship with God (Luke 19:10; Luke 15:1–32). He involved himself in all genuine human suffering to heal and make people whole (Luke 4:18–21; Matt 4:23). He gave his life to redeem sinners and offer forgiveness on the basis of his redemptive death on the cross and his victorious resurrection (Matt 20:28).

In his ministry, we note that forgiveness of sins and healing of the body, feeding the hungry and spiritual nurture, opposing dehumanizing structures, and identifying himself with the weak were never at any time divided or departmentalized. He saw man as a whole and was always ready to give help where the need was most obvious.

The brokenness of man and of the world at large has its real root in the sinful nature of man. Sin is not only situational or an act that destroys the relationships between man and man and between man and God, it is a reality itself within the individual. The healing of the brokenness in human life can therefore never be accomplished without the gospel message of forgiveness, which has in itself the power to liberate man from the most dehumanizing power in his own life and in his relationships with other men and God. This aspect of a responsible church ministry has been largely overlooked not only in interchurch aid programs but also in the recent study on "Salvation Today."

The third objective of a responsible church ministry must be to engage in the betterment of human existence wherever needed. This includes any lawful activity, from being a prophetic voice in condemning injustice and oppression to involvement in social and community development.

So much has been said about the social responsibility of the church that there is no need to say more about it in the context of this paper. We only want to repeat again that it is the prerogative of the local church to determine those activities in which it should be involved and to what extent.

In concluding this section of our presentation, we should like to call attention to the traditional African concept of life and the Western concept, which has created a credibility gap between the recipient churches in Africa and the supporting churches and donor agencies in the West.

Already in our original document (of May 1972) we emphasized that from the African point of view, it was difficult to understand the artificial division in the West between mission and development. We pointed out that, in our opinion, an "integral human development, where spiritual and material needs are seen together, is the only right approach to the development question in our society." We should here like only briefly to substantiate further this opinion.

Dr. Manas Buthelezi, who is a well-known African theologian, said at a recent consultation in Arusha, Tanzania, September 1973, that religion was so integrated in the traditional African society that there was not even an institutional symbol that marked it off from daily life. To exclude religion from any sector of life was inconceivable. He continued: "There was no separate society of religious people in contrast to those who had opted out of faith. To opt out of faith was to opt out of life itself." In conclusion, Dr. Buthelezi noted: "It is a well-known fact that when Christianity was brought to Africa this wholeness of life was disrupted. This is mainly because the brand of Christianity which was introduced in Africa was heavily influenced by Pietism. Pietism paved the way for a total secularization of the natural, namely, the spheres of work, politics, economics and as a matter of fact all that gave concrete meaning to daily life. It set the inner life rather than the social as the place where God and man may enter into relationship with each other."

At the same consultation, the Rev. Judah Kiwovele pointed out that the traditional life setting in Africa is inclusive and that the spiritual cannot be separated from other life values. He went on to say that "this inclusiveness of the African life setting is being disrupted by the horizontal dimension of the church which is exclusive and atomistic." He said further:

> The horizontal dimension of the church in its relation to other parts of the church is weakened by the interchurch aid and support that has no flexibility for the supported, which does not leave them free to decide matters pertaining to the life of the church. As long as man, community and nation continue to be divided into body and spirit by church supporters, theology in the church in Africa will remain foreign to Africa, no matter how far it is still accepted blindly by that church. Theology grows from the local situation as a result of God's encounter with existence as such.

In order to plan and implement a more responsible church ministry, all that has been briefly mentioned above must be taken into consideration. Here we address ourselves both to the African church leaders and to our overseas partners.

A More Flexible Aid Relationship

We should like to say here first of all that we have already come a long way in mutual understanding between the ECMY and its overseas partners. We are grateful for the generosity our supporters have demonstrated, for the change that has taken place, and for the willingness they have expressed to discuss further improvements.

In the process of integrating the administrative structures of foreign missions into the Evangelical Church Mekane Yesus, we have over the past few years experienced two things that we should like to mention as introductory remarks in this section of our presentation.

The first is the communication problem. Here we are referring to both internal and external communication. The church was not well equipped to handle this delicate and important matter, and adequate provisions were not made to remedy this weakness from which the church is still suffering. The second is the coordination problem on the administrative level. Traditions established over decades are not easily uprooted and replaced by new procedures and new policies. Communication and coordination are, in our opinion, also the most crucial issues in our international aid relationships. Unless we are able to communicate intelligibly, and unless we can establish more effective coordination in the employment of our total manpower and financial resources, we cannot expect much improvement.

There are two main issues we should like to bring up for discussion with regard to aid structures and relationships.

The first is the neo-paternalism in aid relationships reflected both in established criteria and in administrative procedures. The other is the distribution of resources within the world Christian community.

Paternalism in its traditional forms is a phenomenon of the past, but it tends to linger on in new forms, which are both directly hampering the work and humiliating for the recipient. This is not a unique problem for interchurch aid and mission support. It is a universal problem with which international development aid has been confronted for quite some time. Dr. Emilio Castro, in his editorial in the October 1973 issue of *International Review of Mission*, has pointed out:

> We cannot forget that the church lives amid today's human tensions; the growing disparity between the so-called developed and under-developed countries, and the factors of prestige and power which accompany the relationships between churches. Called to obedience to the Lord, who transcends political and economic frontiers, how can we express this situation in our relationships? Pious phrases and good intentions abound, but we do not know how to implement them, submitting ourselves to the discipline of the Christian community—the brotherhood of the faith—which demands of us a common responsibility. But if we do not find adequate structures, we shall destroy relationships. . . . We must find the means to express mature relationships appropriate to the present time, seeking new possibilities for mission boldly and fearlessly.

Whether we like it or not, there is a neo-paternalistic tendency reflected in both aid criteria and procedures of screening requests and controlling implementation. While donor countries and secular agencies are well on their way to solving these problems, the churches and church-related agencies are rather late in seeking solutions. The old mission boards have been heavily criticized for their paternalistic attitude, but unless the present decision-makers take a serious look at their criteria and procedures, they will soon be given the same label.

The ECMY has suggested an "integral human development" approach, which requires more flexibility and less structured projects. Examples of what we have in mind and the problems we are facing will be clarified in the course of the consultation.

The other issue has to do with distribution of resources. Here we are thinking of the total resources within the Christian community. It has been argued that, for the sake of identity and selfhood, the quantity of aid should be gradually reduced. It has even been suggested that it should be drastically cut off by way of a voluntary moratorium. (Report of the Bangkok meeting on "Salvation Today.")

We believe that the economy of the Christian community should be seen in a global perspective and the aim should be to arrange for a more fair distribution of resources. Here the church should even lead the way toward this goal.

We have now, according to official information, a maldistribution of the world's resources on a scale where the developed countries are consuming about twenty-five times more of the resources per capita than the developing countries. Similar figures are probably also true for the churches within the Christian community. The over-consumption of spiritual care in the affluent parts of the world can be compared with the over-consumption of medical care and excessive material standard of living. And the tragic thing is that church members consider it their right to use the resources in this way in spite of all the zeal for mission and development.

In our opinion, it is irresponsible to just accept this maldistribution of resources for God's mission in this world. We should therefore like to advocate for completely new criteria for distribution of resources based not only on a balance within the ministry of a given church (the original concern of the ECMY) but also on a balance in the global distribution of spiritual care, with the aim of greater justice in serving the total man and of a more responsible church ministry in today's world.

Source: *Proclamation and Human Development: Documentation from a Lutheran World Federation Consultation, Nairobi, Kenya, October 21–25, 1974* (Geneva: Lutheran World Federation, 1975), 11–17.

8

Pastoral Letter:
The Evangelical Church Mekane Yesus
in the Ethiopian Revolution

In cooperation with the Lutheran World Federation's Department of Studies, the ECMY conducted a seminar on Christianity and socialism at the Mekane Yesus Seminary from February 20 to 25, 1975. The very next weekend, Gudina Tumsa invited a number of people who had participated in the seminar to go with him to Woliso for further discussion, in which Gudina especially was an active contributor. At its conclusion, the assembly asked Rev. Paul E. Hoffman, formerly of the LWF's Department of Theology, then of the Department of Studies, and, from 1973 to 1978, a teacher at the Mekane Yesus Seminary, sent by the Hermannsburg Mission, to draft a potential statement to be adopted by the ECMY regarding the new political situation in the country. Hoffman, with the assistance of Dr. Gunnar Hasselblatt, a pastor and development worker, did so—till far into the night. The next morning, the draft was presented, discussed, and revised. As general secretary and the obvious choice for carrying the matter further within the ECMY, Gudina had the last word on the statement. He brought the document to the other ECMY leaders, who after discussion in the executive committee issued this "Pastoral Letter."

1. Ethiopia finds itself in transition. The old regime has gone. Ethiopian socialism has been proclaimed. New economic policies have been announced. Hopes and expectation have been awakened. However, as the structures of the old society have not been fully replaced, confusion, uncertainty, and hesitation are widespread.

2. The Evangelical Church Mekane Yesus is part of the body of Christ in the world. It is a church that proclaims the gospel of Christ in its full sense and is sustained by the sacraments. Deriving from the poor, the church rededicates itself to living for others, serving the whole human person, meeting his spiritual and physical needs. Through its health, educational, and other services, the ECMY has contributed meaningfully to the development of Ethiopia and has, at the same time, prepared people for change. It sees its continuing task to be the full liberation of the whole man. It welcomes the opportunities that the new situation provides for building a more just society. Having set the goal of self-reliance for itself, the ECMY supports the goal of self-reliance for Ethiopian society. As a church that petitioned the Parliament in 1973 to press forward on land reform, the ECMY fully supports a just implementation of land reform.

3. The church has been called into being as an instrument of proclamation of the gospel of Jesus Christ and for service. Because of this calling, the church differs from other institutions. It is a society for witness to the gospel of Christ and service to our fellow men, not a company set up for profit. Its employment policy is of necessity determined by this its particular character.

4. The institutions of the ECMY (hospitals, schools, development projects) are not aimed at the self-preservation and prestige of the church. They were brought into being to serve the whole man and for the human and social development of the country, in places where opportunity offered itself and the needs were not easily met by any other organization. The government has indicated its intention to take care of all the educational, medical, and development needs of the people. The church welcomes this move by the government and plans to hand over these institutions. This has been the expectation of the church from the start. The ECMY envisages that opportunities for development and service programs will be found in which it will be possible to cooperate with communities in the future, thus continuing to contribute to the development of the new Ethiopian society.

5. We welcome the prospect of participation by the people at all levels of decision-making, where the power of the people is channeled

from bottom to top. We aspire for justice, respect for human rights, and the rule of law. Ideologies cannot be considered as absolute. Complete allegiance is due to God and God alone. We recognize the urgent need of making the people aware of unjust practices. Structures for the exploitation of others must be discarded, and the crucial task of building a new society based on equality and a fair share for all undertaken with determination. In enthusiasm for this task, the means to accomplish the desired goals must, however, be in accord with the ends to be achieved.

6. In the revolutionary situation in which the country finds itself, internal tensions and animosities must be overcome if Ethiopia is to achieve justice for all. It is the duty of Christians, as individuals and in congregations, to pray and work for peace and reconciliation. As the body of Christ in the world, the church itself is made up of many people and various classes. In claiming the name of Christ, we must overcome differences of opinion by dialogue, suspicion by trust, and hatred by love. Such dialogue, trust, and love must be extended to those outside our particular fellowship, to Christians of different confession and to people of other faiths and ideologies. Our fellowmen are brothers created by God and redeemed by Christ. Special prayer should be made for our sister church in Eritrea and for peace in that province.

7. In its proclamation and prayer, the church interprets the situation in which it lives and finds in Scripture an understanding of God's dealing with men.

Through his Spirit, the Lord Jesus Christ calls for repentance and announces the coming of the kingdom of God. It is this kingdom that we must seek above all else. In order to liberate man from the power of sin, selfishness, death, and the evil one, Jesus Christ died upon the cross.

God is the God of all creation, the God of history. He has called into being a people to serve him in the world. He liberates this people from oppression, brings them into the judgment, defeat, and exile, and restores them time and again. God's final judgment and victory will only come after a time of distress and upheaval.

The people of God have been called to discipleship, pilgrimage, even suffering in this world because true life is found only through suffering and death. The church is challenged to find itself by giving itself for the true liberation of the whole man. In this, its witness to the gospel of Christ and its service to man, it teaches that salvation as wrought by

Christ must be experienced in this life, but that fullness of life is to be realized at the second coming of our Lord and Savior.

Addis Ababa, February 1975

Source: EECMY, Thirty-Fifth Executive Committee Meeting, EC Minutes EC-35-27.

9

Memorandum: Some Issues Requiring
Discussions and Decisions

It became increasingly clear in the course of the second quarter of 1975 that major changes were being contemplated by the new Marxist government of Ethiopia, which would in turn have a profound effect on the life and work of the ECMY. With the support of the LWF's Department of Studies, the ECMY undertook a "Self-Studies" program with several events: a seminar in April 1975 in Debre Zeit called "The Role of the Church in Socialist Ethiopia" involving the church's educational, medical, and development institutions; a seminar at the Mekane Yesus Seminary in the same month; and a workshop in Addis Ababa called "Church Economy in Socialist Ethiopia," which took place June 9–14, 1975.

At the same time, there was unrest among the employees of the church and its institutions concerning their right to organize and negotiate as a labor union, as well as the employment and salary policies of the ECMY and its synods. In June 1975, Gudina Tumsa asked to be temporarily relieved of his normal duties in order to go on retreat, reflect, and write on the issues facing the ECMY. The result was this "Memorandum" to Emmanuel Abraham, then-president of the ECMY, which was discussed in detail at the Special Executive Committee meeting on August 19–24, 1975.

Appended is Gudina's "Motivation for Policy Decisions by the Executive

Committee in 1975," which he wrote and presented along with the Memorandum to the General Assembly at Najo in April 1976.

To: Ato Emmanuel Abraham, President, ECMY
From: Gudina Tumsa, General Secretary, ECMY

A church may continue her activities as if nothing has happened in this country. However, this will be ignoring the complex social issues, a disservice to the cause of the gospel of Jesus Christ. A church may be aware of the revolutionary changes taking place in the social structure of the society as well as in the minds of the people and neglect making radical decisions demanded by the situation, to be an effective instrument for witnessing to the gospel of the risen Christ and giving useful service, salt, and light to the world. It is out of such a conviction that I presented a memorandum to the church officers of the ECMY on June 5, 1975, requesting that I should be partially released from the daily office routine to reflect on some issues relevant to the life of the ECMY in the light of the revolutionary changes taking place in our society. The points listed in the memorandum presented to the church officers are as follows:

1. a) Help church members to be aware of the emerging danger of unbelief
   b) Define the border between the Gospel and socialism
   c) Study ecumenical issues
   d) Through extensive travel in the synods, foster a closer relationship among the church leaders
2. a) Is integration a reality?
   b) The policy of the ECMY toward the missions

Prior to reflecting on the issues enumerated in the memorandum to the church officers and on some other aspects of the revolutionary changes affecting all dimensions of human existence in our society, I take the liberty of raising some issues in general that I consider to be worthy of deliberation at the forthcoming Thirty-Fifth Executive Committee Meeting, September 1975,[1] and copies of this memorandum are being sent to the members of the Executive Committee of the ECMY

---

1. Ed. Note: The meeting was rescheduled to take place in August 1975.

in order to give them time to ponder on the issues raised before they come to the meeting of the Executive Committee of the Church.

As indicated in the pastoral letter sent to our congregations in March 1975, fundamental changes have taken and are taking place in our country. What are taking place are not only changes affecting the social and economic life of our society as was customarily thought. Revolutionary changes affecting all aspects of the societal life, philosophies, economy, politics, religion, history, social life as a whole, are taking place at very high speed, unprecedented in the recorded history of this country, in a manner, to the best of my knowledge, not forecast by social scientists in our country. The high rate at which the Ethiopian revolutionary changes are marching forward is winning a mixture of surprise and admiration from national and international circles. The church being part and parcel of a given society, to say nothing of the type of revolutionary changes taking place in Ethiopia, any change in the general sense is bound to affect the Christian community either negatively or positively.

In the case of the ECMY, a statement in connection with the present revolutionary changes has not been issued, with the exception of the pastoral letter referred to above. This is to say that there is a lack of theological reflection regarding the changes that affect all aspects of the life of our society. Theology is a relative statement on the central message of the Christian gospel, in an attempt to translate that message to the people in the process of revolutionary changes in this country of ours. Lack of a sound theological reflection in the present Ethiopian situation has, in my opinion, affected our work in a negative way, which if allowed to continue uncorrected, will be very harmful to the life of this church to which we have committed ourselves for service.

Institutions

The ECMY is running quite a number of institutions established for the benefit of the poverty-stricken sector of our society. These institutions are schools on elementary and secondary levels, hospitals, clinics, vocational training schools such as carpentry, auto mechanics, masonry, and so on. In recent years, a number of hostels have been built to provide conducive facilities for students flocking to the areas where there are high schools. In our opinion, these institutions have rendered useful services to the Ethiopian people, and through these institutions, the church has been enabled to contribute her share to the present revolutionary movement taking place in our country.

Now, it appears that these institutions are becoming hindrances to our original intention of contributing to the improvement of the living conditions of our society, due to lack of understanding on the part of the public as to what the institutions stand for. The ECMY has not had any profit-making undertaking in this country. All our institutions are service organizations, non-profit-making undertakings to improve the lot of needy people in our society. The complaints against this church come out of ignorance of what the ECMY is working for.

Due to the significant number of institutions run under the auspices of the ECMY and the substantial amount of contributions being made to help Ethiopian society to reach a level of economic takeoff and self-sustained economy through these manifold activities, there are misunderstandings from within (for example, the Bako project and Wondo Gennet) and from outside (for example, the Ministry of Finance through its Inland Revenue Department has filed a case against the church for more than Eth. $57,000 as tax on the ECMY Hostel). These examples are cited to indicate the magnitude of the problems arising out of misunderstanding. Unless ways are found to solve these problems and the misunderstandings are corrected urgently, it will bring disaster to the ECMY before too long.

It would be wise for the ECMY to hand over these institutions to the government departments concerned on a time schedule to be agreed upon.

Functional Approach

This functional approach (noninstitutional) to development service (i.e., handing over the institutions run under the ECMY) does not hint at all at reducing our contribution toward helping the Ethiopian people to help themselves. It means, from the standpoint of the ECMY, that the approach used so far is to be changed due to the policy of the government (see Economic Policy Statement) and to correct the misunderstanding that has arisen between the church and her workers, as well as with some people who have no idea about the nature of the church. A few examples of what I call a functional approach to nation building are seconding agriculturalists, economists, cooperative experts, and engineers to the peasant associations being organized all over the country. Secondment of experts will depend on those interested in the assistance of the ECMY and on the resources available to our church.

This new approach, the noninstitutional, will show that the ECMY is

1. not running business in any form, and
2. it will reassure anyone interested in knowing that we are working not from motives of prestige but out of Christian love, to serve the Ethiopian people because the needs are very great.

There are people in our church who think that raising the question of handing over the institutions would be looked at from the side of the government as sabotage, and that therefore an unfavorable relationship might develop between the government and the ECMY. According to this view, the ECMY should continue to run the institutions out of fear, regardless of the demands of the situation. The biblical understanding of service is that it flows out of Christ's love poured into the hearts of his followers. The demand of the living Jesus Christ is that "you should love God above all else and your brother as yourself" (Matt 22:37–39).

This is the guiding principle for all forms of Christian ministry and service. It should be clear to all, therefore, that Christian integrity does not allow us to do Christian social service out of fear. What is not done out of faith is sin.

There is another point to be raised in connection with this issue or any issues to be discussed with the government: the ECMY should be reasonable and justify her decisions on Christian grounds. We should be aware that those leading the country understand reasonable arguments, and there is observable evidence for this contention.

The ECMY has won credibility for working not only for but with the people, and the evidence for this is that through the Yemissrach Dimts Literacy Campaign, recognition was given by an international organization to the fact that she has been working with communities at the grassroots level.

According to the government policy issued recently, peasant associations on twenty "*gashas*" of land—the smallest unit—are to run their own schools as part of developing their areas. This is a happy development in our country and should be supported as much as possible. For us, there is no need to run our literacy schools as done in the past under the feudal structure, when the Ethiopian people were denied right, ability, and knowledge in working for the betterment of their lot and their living conditions.

At present, the Ethiopian people are in active process of being organized, taking their destiny into their own hands, marching forward toward handling their own affairs and deciding for themselves. Our literacy schools should be handed over to the farmers' associations and the subsidies given now to the YDLC should be integrated into the work of the farmers' associations. Our grants should be given to the associations. As far as I know, this is in line with the original intention of our literacy program.

Integration

The Integration Policy Agreement has been implemented in a satisfactory manner since it was signed in 1969, and big steps have been taken in the synods of the ECMY. Integration between the ECMY and the Cooperating Lutheran Agencies was a natural process of the culmination of Lutheran mission activities as organizations on Ethiopian soil. The right implementation of the Integration Policy of the ECMY is that foreign organizations ceased to exist in our country as separate bodies and are integrated with the national church. What does this mean as regards expatriate personnel?

Expatriate Personnel

To the best of my knowledge all expatriate personnel are here because the ECMY has taken the responsibility of calling them out here to work under this church, due to a shortage of Ethiopian personnel to carry out the manifold ministries the ECMY has undertaken for the benefit of our people. The synods of the church normally request the services of expatriate personnel; the central office applies to the government department concerned for their entry into Ethiopia, taking the responsibility for their stay and work in Ethiopia. This is to say that the expatriate personnel are an integral part of the workers needed by the ECMY to carry out her responsibility to the Ethiopian people. The only difference between the national personnel and the international personnel is that the latter are supported from outside Ethiopia as far as their remunerations are concerned. As regards assignments to specific areas of work and obligations in carrying out their duties, there is no difference, and there should not be any difference, between nationals and expatriates. Our constitution is quite clear in defining the obligations and rights of missionary personnel under the ECMY. It appears that there are unnecessary misunderstandings as to the role of expatriate personnel in the ECMY. Incidents have arisen in a number of places creating unfavorable situations for the relationships required for the achievement of our objectives.

The reports of the president to the previous assemblies of the ECMY have been taken as basic policies for our relationships to foreign organizations so far. It is about two and a half years since the last assembly at Yirgalem where the president defined our policy as regards missionary personnel.

It should be understood that the ECMY has been able to maintain her integrity and credibility before those with whom we are working in this country, as well as before international organizations of all sorts. The ECMY should redefine her policy in a clear manner as regards expatriate personnel and ecumenical relationships. To make statements out of courtesy is a disservice to the cause of the gospel we are committed to serve. To find justifications for expatriate personnel to work in Ethiopia is against Christian integrity, if we are convinced that there is no actual need for their services in the ECMY. The ECMY as a mature church is able to make clear policy decisions guiding her activities and regulating her relationships with ecumenical organizations and cooperating agencies that send us expatriate personnel.

Moratorium

Moratorium has become a burning issue in ecumenical circles, attracting attention from all Christian denominations, calling for negative and positive reactions from churches and ecumenical bodies, depending in some cases on the specific economic situation out of which one speaks.

In my opinion, moratorium is in the first place a theological issue, and one's specific economic situation should not be allowed to overrule theological conviction. Understanding that the position of my church was quite clear as regards the relationship with missionary personnel as well as other personnel connected with evangelistic outreach, and based on my own theological reflections, I have spoken against moratorium whenever opportunity offered. In Adelaide, Australia, at the Commission Meeting of the LWF Church Cooperation, I made it clear that moratorium lacks theological basis in the biblical sense. Contending that moratorium lacks theological basis, I have so far neglected spending time on digging deep into the subject, since I consider it a luxury for the churches who have more personnel than they need for the essential work of their churches. In short, moratorium is defined as withdrawal of resources and expatriate personnel, for a certain period of time, from the former mission fields, in order to give the churches in the Third World time to find their identity as they make efforts to depend on their own personnel and finances, thereby attaining self-reliance.

Self-reliance is the final goal of any church; however, for the sake of self-reliance, moratorium should not be applied to the primary task of the church, which is the proclamation of the gospel of Jesus Christ. I contend that proclaiming Christ to his world is the responsibility of every Christian and every church, regardless of the varying situations in which we find ourselves.

The church of Jesus Christ is one, and we all belong to her. Our Lord is the head of the church; all who believe are members of the body. The resources available to any particular church are to be used by all other churches wherever there is a need—we are all stewards. In my opinion, we are responsible for the use of resources in whatever form they are available, whether personnel or finances. To argue that the availability of resources from overseas reduces the responsibility of the national churches in the Third World is misunderstanding the nature of the church and the responsibility that belonging to the church of Jesus Christ entails.

Planning an Alternative to Moratorium

The ECMY has been and is operating on a planned five-year basis. The first five-year plan started in 1971 and will end in 1975. In outlining the first period, 1971–75, the object was to get a clear picture of the situation within our congregations. Now this has been done. The second period, 1976–80, will be launched in January of next year. The intention was that during the course of the first period, a realistic plan should be set forth for the second period to enable the ECMY to increase her local resources so that grants from abroad should not be increased. The third period, 1981–85, should see a gradual decrease of grants from overseas. The fourth period, 1986–90, should be the last period for any financial grants from abroad. This planned way toward self-reliance is an alternative to moratorium, which is a withdrawal for a certain period of time.

Christian responsibility demands that we should march toward self-reliance in a planned manner, while at the same time maintaining Christian integrity and avoiding unnecessary contradictions. The spirit of hypocrisy should not be allowed to operate in the church of God; to talk about moratorium while applying for grants from abroad is dissimulation.

A paper will be presented on moratorium to the Executive Committee Meeting in September of this year.

Labor Union

The formation of a labor union under the ECMY has been discussed at the various meetings of the executive committee of the ECMY. At its thirty-fourth meeting, the executive committee decided not to recognize a labor union under the church. Being on official duty in Australia, I was not able to participate in the discussion. In the pastoral letter circulated to our congregations, it was hinted that the church was not a profit-making company. Because of the institutions the church is running for the benefit of the Ethiopian people, there is a misunderstanding that the church is a profit-making organization. Such a notion is maintained not only by outsiders but also by many who are working in the church. Some people think that the ECMY can bring bulks of money from abroad if she applies for it. All such views are partly due to ignorance of the nature of the church of Jesus Christ and partly due to lack of information. It is regrettable that, so far, the ECMY has not been able to run an information office.

Labor organizations stand for justice in general, and justice is the final goal of Christian social service (see Amos; Matt 23:33).

Since the aim of labor unions is in line with what the ECMY believes to be social justice, why doesn't the church wish to recognize a labor union in the various institutions of the ECMY?

To reply to this question, one should define the sources of income for the ECMY. There are two sources: (a) voluntary contributions by members of the church (since this is voluntary, the church can never have a guarantee as to the amount of money she can dispose for the next year. We do not have any business to help us secure ten thousand dollars for the year 1976), and (b) our sister churches and mission agencies from overseas (from these organizations, there is no guarantee that we can obtain funds for the year 1976. We may be informed in August or September of this year what they would be able to grant).

The grants the ECMY receives from abroad may be stopped for various reasons:

1. The ECMY may stop applying for grants from sister churches and missions on her own initiative.
2. The sister churches and mission agencies may stop granting on the assumption that enough has been done and that the ECMY is now able to carry on her task as a church.
3. The government, if it so wishes, can stop the ECMY from receiving grants from her sister churches and mission agencies. Either of these three possibilities or any other reason may happen.

This is to say that to enter into an agreement with any organization or union for the following two or three years is out of the question as far as the ECMY is concerned. How does the ECMY continue her work if there is no guarantee for the following two or three years? "We walk by faith, not by sight." We believe in the providence of the Lord of the church, speaking spiritual things to spiritual men.

We plead with those concerned not to judge the church on the basis of rules and laws issued to regulate profit-making organizations. This is to say that the inability of the church to recognize the formation of a labor union under her should not be taken as a reactionary attitude and defiance of social justice.

This apologetic approach is to solicit reasoning and understanding of the position the ECMY is maintaining. As the church by nature is not interested in making profit, those who do not desire to serve in such an uncertain situation should decide for themselves. An organization having no assurance of a fixed guaranteed income can never guarantee its employees for years to come. To look for security where there is no guaranteed income is unreasonable (Luke 9:58).

Contributions to Nation Building

In the light of the present situation, I have contended in the preceding paragraphs that the functional approach is preferable to the institutional, as far as the church is concerned, as regards our contributions to nation building for various reasons.

One reason is that the present government has declared that it would look after the welfare of its citizens, and the ECMY should not give any hint that she is competing. As stated in the pastoral letter, the ECMY welcomes the present changes that promote the cause of the masses and serve their interest. As a matter of fact, the ECMY has contributed her share for the changes that are taking place all over our country. In the event anyone doubts the validity of this statement and the integrity of this church, one should be referred to the resolution of the Eighth General Assembly of the ECMY held at Yirgalem. In January 1973, the General Assembly of the ECMY extensively discussed matters concerning land reform and passed a resolution requesting for a land reform law. The resolution of the Assembly was communicated to the two Houses of Parliament and to the Ministries of Land Reform and the Interior (see Eighth General Assembly).

The ECMY has been a pioneer in settling landless peasants under the oppressive feudal system, and if anyone is interested in ascertaining this one should visit the settlements of nomadic Shanqellas in the Didessa valley. Anno-Gambella is another model community. The contribution the ECMY makes to eliminate poverty, ignorance, and disease is not to win favor from anyone. The ECMY does it because the need is there and Christian love compels us to make as much contribution as possible, so that our country may be a beautiful and comfortable place to live in.

The ECMY will continue to contribute her share to the economic development of Ethiopia, to improve the living conditions of the people, and to the political orientation of the people in being useful to society, in knowing their rights and obligations as citizens.

Training literacy school teachers selected by the bodies concerned at the expense of the church is a possibility to contribute to the mental development of society. The provision of radio receiving sets at reduced prices, in consultation with the government, is something to be explored.

The contribution of the ECMY to the famine and rehabilitation program should be reinforced from within our congregations as well as from abroad, knowing that our sister churches are showing great interest in continuing to help the drought-stricken areas of our country.

Training cooperative workers for the farmers' associations at our own expense is another way to be explored to accelerate the development of socialist Ethiopia.

At Yirgalem, a paper was submitted to the Eighth General Assembly exploring different ways of providing work opportunities to some of the prostitutes in Addis Ababa. However, due to lack of a concrete plan, we have not been able to make a contribution toward the elimination of this social evil.

Now, because of the government's intention to change this condition, we should be able to cooperate with the government department concerned to do our best.

Undertaking small-scale industries to provide employment for urban and rural communities is something within the possibility of the ECMY, on the basis of the experience acquired in past years. In past years, the ECMY invested millions of Ethiopian dollars annually in development projects. For the sake of discussion, I have just mentioned a few examples to show the manifold ways in which we can contribute to the development of Ethiopia.

Identity of the Church

The identity question is occupying the minds of many theologians and church leaders presently, and rightly so. As the Zulu theologian, Dr. Manas Buthelezi, has once remarked, in order to produce indigenous theology, there must be an indigenous man. The sources of Christian theology are found in the Scriptures as well as in the classical confessions inherited from the fathers and have come to us through the church of Jesus Christ.

The Reformation tradition, as well as the traditions of the revival movements that took place during the nineteenth century (especially in Scandinavia: Rosenius and Hauge), out of which the Lutheran missions have grown and started work about the second quarter of this century in Ethiopia, are part of our Christian heritage.

An indigenous theology in the Ethiopian context may be defined as a translation of the biblical sources, the various confessions, and the traditions transmitted to us throughout the history of the Christian church to the patterns of the thought of our people, that they may feel at home with the gospel of love as revealed in the life, death, and resurrection of Jesus Christ. Contextual theology is making the message of the gospel of the risen Lord meaningful and relevant to our life situation, economic life, political life, and social life as a whole. In our case, theology must grow out of concrete daily experiences, from our dealing with the ordinary affairs of life as we experience them in our situation, in our cultural setting, in our economic life, in our political experience, and in our social practice.

Has the ECMY any theological experience to share with her sister churches, a contribution to the church universal? The ECMY is in the process of developing an indigenous theology grown out of her experience in dealing with the Ethiopian situation, taking the spiritual and physical together in an inseparable manner. This theological position of the ECMY was communicated to the Lutheran World Federation and has attracted interest beyond expectation from ecumenical bodies around the world.

A Holistic Theology

Western theology has lost the this-worldly dimension of human existence, and holistic theology is an effort to rediscover total human life. Apolitical life is not worthy of existence, uninvolvement is a denial of the goodness of creation and of the reality of incarnation. We are interested not in creating medieval monasteries, in setting up ghettoes (modern monasteries), but in being involved in the complex social life of our people as we find it daily, with full knowledge of our Christian responsibility.

The history of the people of God in the Old Testament starts with the liberation of a group of slaves from oppression. Nothing is more political than this biblical narrative. In our continent, what is prevalent is the basis to define economic policy, agricultural development, foreign relations—"Politics decides who should die and who should live." African theology should develop a political theology relevant to the African political life. During my recent visit to the South Ethiopia Synod, it was encouraging and inspiring to observe how the elders of our congregations who were elected as leaders of peasant associations were making efforts to practice their Christian faith in the leading positions they occupy. Political theology should grow out of such experiences on the local congregational level.

Nurture and Evangelism

There are two inseparable responsibilities, nurture and evangelism, confronting us at present as at any time, although sharpened because of the present changes taking place in the country. We may be tempted to maintain the one at the expense of the other, rather than maintain the two in a dialectical relationship—a healthy tension to be appreciated. Looking at the situation of our church and at her history up to the present, one may conclude that evangelistic outreach was at the heart of the ECMY, while nurture was at its minimum. There seems now to be a shift of emphasis from evangelistic outreach to nurture. These two aspects of the Christian ministry should be maintained in a balanced manner. The responsibility for evangelistic outreach is laid on the shoulders of the ECMY, for this country as well as elsewhere, and there is no one else to carry out this responsibility for her. The only reason for retaining expatriates is for evangelistic outreach, which can never be neglected without entailing serious consequences for the life of the church. The ECMY has many ethnic groups in her fold, speaking various languages. One of the handicaps to nurture was the policy of the feudal system, which had hindered the use of the vernaculars spoken in the country by the different ethnic groups.

The present policy of the government encourages the development of the various languages, and the use of these languages should be taken as a good opportunity for the production of Christian literature in the languages the people understand. A substantial amount of funds and sufficient personnel should be assigned to produce Christian literature in the mother tongues of our membership. Those who preach should be requested to keep their sermons and devotions in writing.

The Cost of Discipleship

To believe in Christ is to take the form of a servant, to be a servant for others. The full implications of the suffering servant in the Old Testament (see Isa 42:1–4; 52:13; 53:1–12) as fulfilled in the New Testament (John 13:12–17; Phil 2:5–11) should be practiced by the ECMY today. There is a turning point in the history of any nation, any church, or any individual person. September 12, 1974, was a turning point in the history of this country. Ethiopia can never be what she was before September 1974. Fundamental changes, especially in the economic field, have taken place. One should expect that changes in the economic aspect of the country would generally affect the salary scales introduced under the feudal system.

Ethiopia, with one of the lowest per capita incomes in the world, will not be able to maintain the salary scales in practice at present. My contention is not whether the government will be able to pay people on the basis of the salary scales in practice or not; the point is that a socialist government will not be able to operate on scales introduced by a feudal system.

As a church, the ECMY has a prophetic role to play in this society. It is our duty to remind the government of some issues that we consider to be of vital importance to the life of our country.

The aim of this memorandum is not to discuss our relationship with the government but to raise some vital issues as they relate to the life of the ECMY, so that they may be discussed with a view to making drastic policy decisions to meet the needs of the time we are confronted with, due to the process of historical development as Ethiopia marches forward into the future.

The ECMY has to interpret the signs of the time, as we believe in the God of history who determines the destiny of nations. History is the field of activity of the Creator of the universe, and it is our duty to detect and interpret the guiding hands of God in the present historical development in our country, and to cooperate with the God of history in order to shape her future history.

One of the demands of the time for the ECMY is to take drastic steps in matters pertaining to the present practices of payment for the employees under her. There are arguments in favor of a drastic review of payment practices now in operation. One may bring up a number of points in support of this view. But as it is impossible to dwell on all the points in this outline, let me mention two or three reasons for the sake of argument. A drastic review of payment practices must be made for the sake of the church: "Though he was rich, yet he became poor for our sake" (2 Cor 8:9). We should be prepared to give up luxury for the sake of the gospel of salvation. Another point is that the ECMY should be an example to others. This church has been able to set an example in showing interest to the outcast in our society. The third point is that a realistic view of the economic situation of our country requires a drastic review of the salary scales now in operation in the country as well as in the church.

In this matter, which is so personal to every one of us, we have to make decisions affecting our personal interests, our living standard, the luxury that we enjoy, thereby setting an example for the government as for others concerned, not by words but by actions of sacrificial nature. This is what it means to be the church for others. Jesus Christ lived and sacrificed himself for others.

In my opinion, the minimum payment for anyone working under the ECMY should be seventy Ethiopian dollars, while the maximum payment should be four hundred fifty Ethiopian dollars per month. My suggestion is that, as of January 1976, payments should be adjusted in such a way that, for those receiving less than seventy dollars a month, increments should be made to bring them up, and cuts should be made from those getting more than four hundred fifty dollars a month, so that will be maximum. Those in categories between ninety and four hundred fifty dollars will have to face a cut of a certain percentage of their salaries, but those with less than ninety dollars should not be affected by this reduction.

Personnel working in project undertakings for a limited period of time should be employed on contract not exceeding a two-year period at a time. Thus, their salaries will not be affected by this decision.

In my opinion, this is the cost of discipleship we have to pay for the sake of the gospel and for the sake of our country. This is what the love of Christ demands of us in the present historical development. This is what it means to love God above all and our neighbor as ourselves in the present, concrete Ethiopian situation.

Let not anyone deceive himself in taking Christianity as one of the social systems or ideologies. To be a Christian is to be a follower of the risen Christ, confessing him as the Lord of history. The confession that "Christ died for our sins" implies that we, the confessors, are ready to sacrifice whatever the Lord of history demands of us in a concrete situation. To pay the cost of discipleship is not to buy our salvation; it is to demonstrate the quality of love that led Jesus of Nazareth to the cross. To pay the cost of discipleship in the present situation means for us to take a concrete decision to go from Jerusalem to Golgotha (Matt 20:17–19; Acts 20:22–24).

The demands for the cost of discipleship will be met by various responses from each one of us. To some it will mean a reduction of pay in a drastic way. To others it will mean giving everything away to be members in farmers' associations. Still to some who earn their means of living either through the employment of wife or husband, it will mean serving in a different manner. Whichever may be the way we respond, the inevitable demand of the cost of discipleship is that the saving power of the gospel should be preached regardless of the sacrifices it may entail (Rom 1:17–18).

Higher Theological Education

The best theological scholarships should be afforded to those who have proved to be committed to the ministry of the church. However, the purpose for higher theological scholarship must be redefined in the light of the biblical understanding of the ministry of the church. This is to say that the purpose for theological scholarship should be to give better service to the church of Jesus Christ, rather than to earn a better salary. From those to whom much is given, much is required, says the Bible. There should be no difference of salary on the basis of certificates, diplomas, or degrees. Any payment to be made to those serving in the ECMY must be the minimum to enable the person concerned to live. An opportunity to attract someone to work under the ECMY should never be given in the form of salary or scholarship. Serving in the church must come out of a calling from the Holy Spirit. The purpose, therefore, for a higher theological scholarship should be explained to the prospective students in such a way that they should be clear in their minds that they are being given higher education not to earn higher salaries but to render better service to the people of God. The expectations of the ECMY from the seminaries should be clearly defined in such a way that these expectations should, in turn, influence preparation for theological education.

The Central Administration of the ECMY

The central administration as well as the synod administrations must be simplified and reduced to the minimum. At present, there are about forty people working in the central administration. In the light of the changes taking place in Ethiopia, these must be reduced by 50 percent beginning January of 1976 as concrete steps toward self-reliance. There are positions to be discontinued and other positions to be created, which, in my opinion, will call for amendments to the Constitution and Bylaws of the ECMY.

In restructuring the ECMY, the heavy expenses incurred in the Yemissrach Dimts, as well as the wisdom of running two seminaries under a church of the size of the ECMY, should be studied in terms of good stewardship.

Information Service

Our congregations need information on what is taking place in the various parts of our country and within our church. So far this has been neglected, and in a way, we are suffering from the consequences of this negligence. It is not necessary to discuss the need for an information service in the ECMY. The point is that ways and means of making information available to our congregations, in the languages they understand, should be discussed and steps taken at the forthcoming executive committee meeting.

Conclusion

The gospel of Jesus Christ is God's power to save everyone who believes it. It is the power that saves from eternal damnation, from economic exploitation, from political oppression, and so on. Because of its eternal dimension, the gospel could never be replaced by any of the ideologies invented by men throughout the centuries. It is the only voice telling about a loving Father who gave his Son as a ransom for many. It tells about the forgiveness of sins and the resurrection of the body. It is the good news to sinful man, the only power to save mankind from its sinfulness. It is too powerful to be compromised by any social system. It is too dear a treasure to be given up (Matt 13:44). Nationalism has its own place, but it can never replace the gospel of Jesus Christ.

I hope and pray that the ECMY will be able to make the right decision at this critical moment in her history.

Addis Ababa, July 21, 1975

Source: EECMY, Thirty-Fifth Executive Committee (Special Meeting), August 1975, Minutes EC-35-5.

* * *

Motivation for Policy Decisions by the
Executive Committee in 1975

1. It is the prerogative of a higher authority to review the decisions of a lower body in a given hierarchy. The decision of the executive committee at its thirty-eighth meeting was based on this principle when it directed that an explanatory note be submitted to the ninth General Assembly in connection with the policy decisions made in August and October 1975. This is to say that this General Assembly as the supreme organ of the ECMY can confirm, modify, or reverse the major policy decisions passed by the executive committee of the church. Without going into an analysis of the situation that came about as a result of the changes taking place in our country, I would like to

point out a few of the main factors that led the Executive Committee of the ECMY toward the adoption of a new policy. What should be clear to all concerned for the life of this church is that there is no hidden motive whatsoever behind the actions taken by the Executive Committee in adopting the new policy.

Raising the minimum salary to seventy-five dollars a month had to lead to the reduction of a certain percentage from the salaries of those receiving over two hundred Ethiopian dollars a month, setting the maximum of six hundred dollars. The point of the argument is not that those who received over two hundred dollars are getting too much but that those earning less than the minimum are in a worse economic condition and should get seventy-five dollars a month. In a society where there is a class struggle among the rich and the poor, among the bureaucrats and the laborers, it is logical to make an effort to narrow the wide gap between them as much as possible. It is assumed that the animosity, or rather the tension, existing between the workers of the church will be reduced to the minimum as the result of minimizing the existing gap between the classes. The decision on salary reduction should be understood as an act taken out of Christian love for our coworkers rather than as a law directed to any group or groups. Christian love compels us to share the burdens of our brothers, thereby enabling us to practice in our daily life the love enjoined by the Lord of the church.

So far as the downtrodden and the unfortunate are concerned, Christian love and Marxist humanism complement each other.

2. Another factor to be seen in connection with the reduction of salaries is the policy that one should be allowed to be engaged in only one type of activity. It is a well-known fact that quite a number of our coworkers have had plots of land owned or rented to do some farming to help support their families. In the present situation, it is not clear whether one would be able to obtain any kind of income besides the salary or wage one earns. It is because of such an uncertain situation that the executive committee had to act in favor of reducing the higher and increasing the lower salaries.

3. It is a confirmed fact that local income from our congregations had been decreased for the year 1974. It has not been reported as yet for 1975 as to how much of the expected income had been collected, but the prospect seems to be that the financial situation of our church does not appear to be better than that of 1974. Adjustments are therefore needed.

4. If we take a look at the international scene, there are economic crises caused by the oil-producing countries. As a result, communications have been received from some of our cooperating agencies overseas informing the ECMY that their financial situations would make it difficult for them to meet the requests of the church. As a matter of fact, the budget worked out by the church for this fiscal year and presented to the cooperating agencies was not met in full. Seven hundred thousand dollars less was granted than requested. In short, this indicates the complex problems facing the ECMY due to the present social and economic changes taking place in the country as well as the impact the international situation is making on our church.

5. The political and economic situation, such as the one in which the ECMY finds itself, calls for a decision on new policies, exploring possibilities for existence and making every effort to find her role in a socialistic environment.

Historically, churches were too late in reacting to emerging new situations, which were regrettable and damaging to the lives of those churches. This is not to pass judgment on the positions taken by churches in the past. However, in times of revolutionary change affecting all dimensions of life, a church must define, on a theological basis, its relationship to the new situation.

6. Time has gone once and for all when theology was defined as the queen of the sciences. At present in our society, the theological task is to make all possible efforts to interpret the signs of the times and to clarify issues as they relate to the life of the church and to that of society. It should be noted that this is not an easy task, as it demands rededication to the God of the Bible (Isaiah 50:4–5).

7. Another point is the test of our faith in practicing being honest and frank in our dealings with one another as a Christian community and with the society in which we live as citizens. This is to say that baseless rumors circulating around should not be allowed to misguide us. Issues of whatever nature should be discussed openly at any time in any meeting. One may ask why anonymous letters are being circulated. The answer to this question must be that those who spread such letters do not have facts to be presented for discussion and clarification. People engaged in such baneful activities are not only dishonest but, for the sake of their interests, will do all in their power to destroy the church of Jesus Christ. Their theology is that the church lives for them as opposed to the teaching of the gospel. Christian commitment requires the maintenance of integrity. This is foreign to the mind of

those who have the form of religion but deny its power (2 Timothy 3:1–9).

8. The ECMY has been practicing democracy since the establishment of its present form. Our congregations have been and are the source of authority. No one commands power at *any* level of this church unless they are elected. The democratic system being introduced into our country has been in practice in the ECMY for years. This must be appreciated and acted on.

9. That theory and practice are essentially inseparable cannot be overemphasized in a socialistic environment. Christians are good at talking about the theory of love rather than practicing this biblical truth, by which the Christian is shown as separate from others. Socialism as explained by Karl Marx is to change the world, not to indulge in abstract theories only. The desire of our God is that "you shall love the Lord your God with all your heart, with all your soul, and with all your mind" and that "you shall love your neighbor as yourself" (Matt 22:37, 39). This should be lived in the present situation, sharing with our brothers and coworkers whatever is made available to our church in the interests of the kingdom of our God and Savior.

10. This is just a brief explanatory note on the motivation for the policy decisions made by the executive committee of the ECMY at its two meetings in August and October of 1975. This is not a position paper; there is a big difference between a note and a position paper. As background material to the decisions, the Memorandum of July 1975 should be studied in relation to the present situation. The policy decisions were made about nine months ago. The trends in the country since August 1975 support the actions taken. To get the feel of the magnitude of the problems involved, the issue must be studied from different aspects, theological, political, and economic.

For a national church to be always dependent on overseas grants is a sure way of saying that it can never stand on its own feet. This would be tragic for this church in a fast moving and changing world. As the General Assembly well knows, the question of stewardship and eventual self-support and self-reliance has been a matter for study during the past several years. The ECMY has set this goal for herself. Can anyone in his senses say that what the executive committee undertook to put into effect in the name of this church is not in line with our goal or the present situation in our country? As followers of Christ, we cannot do less than those who profess that Christ is irrelevant to the problems of this age and so strive to bring social and economic justice to the underprivileged through ideologies thought out by men.

Source: EECMY, Ninth General Assembly, April 1976, Najo.

10

The Moratorium Debate and the ECMY

It was Rev. John Gato of the Presbyterian Church in Kenya who first launched the idea of a moratorium on all foreign funds and personnel in the recently founded churches of the Global South. His hope was that during a period without input or interference from the older churches, the newer ones could find their own identity, address their own contextual challenges, and finally divest themselves of mere "mission" status to become full churches in their own right. His idea was endorsed at an international conference of the World Council of Churches' Commission on World Mission and Evangelism held in Bangkok, Thailand, in 1973, and by the All-Africa Conference of Churches meeting in Lusaka, Zambia, in 1974.

As a part of the LWF's "Self-Studies" program coordinated in Ethiopia by Terfassa Yadessa in cooperation with Olof Joelsson from Geneva, an advisory committee was set up to examine the issues at stake in the proposal for moratorium, including Paul E. Hoffman at Gudina Tumsa's request. The two men had distinct perspectives on the subject: Gudina focused on the interdependence and worldwide character of the church; Hoffman strove to reflect the input from the advisory committee. In the end, it was agreed that a joint paper should be presented to the Special Executive Committee Meeting in Addis Ababa that met from August 19 to 23, 1975. The nuanced, ecclesiologically thoughtful result is evident in the following document.

Background

"Moratorium" became a worldwide slogan at the Bangkok meeting of the Commission on World Mission and Evangelism of the World Council of Churches in 1973. It became a matter for debate all over Africa because of the call issued by the Lusaka Assembly of the All-Africa Conference of Churches in 1974. Since then, despite older, clear statements by representatives of the ECMY concerning the continuing need both for personnel from abroad and for support from overseas for the development and the evangelistic tasks of the ECMY, other voices have been raised by various persons who might be seen as speaking for the ECMY. There has been talk of a partial or a full moratorium, a moratorium on both funds and personnel from abroad, or merely on personnel from abroad. The [ECMY/LWF] Study on Identity and Resources of the Church has fostered debate of the moratorium issue in order to focus on the ECMY's "identity problem."

The debate, though certainly not being carried on at all levels or in all areas of the ECMY, has been sufficiently widespread to cause foreign coworkers within the ECMY to ask themselves: Are we still welcome within the church? Is our service still needed? In fact, at an orientation course for new missionaries just finishing language school, the finance director of the church indicated that missionaries—at least new missionaries—were not needed in the ECMY, though foreign subsidy was still necessary. The legitimate question raised in the minds of those being oriented concerning the work of the ECMY was: If we are not wanted or needed, why were we called by the ECMY in the first place?

The debate within the ECMY has also been carried overseas. It would be foolish for us to imagine that a debate here in Ethiopia would not have repercussions among our donor agencies. Mission societies and other overseas partners must be asking themselves: What is the stand of the ECMY? Or, who actually speaks for the church? Personnel of the ECMY, speaking overseas, have spoken favorably of moratorium or positively responded to questions concerning it, while others have rejected it. That the diverse opinions expressed have the effect of confusing donor agencies and persons who support our work should be obvious. For the sake of clearing up the confusion within the ECMY as well as overseas, it is essential that the ECMY express its own mind clearly. Above all, the ECMY should not give the impression of being double-tongued or not knowing what it is doing by talking moratorium, while at the same time requesting new personnel and even increased funds.

To reestablish the credibility of the ECMY, it is essential that the executive committee debate fully the issues at this time and—even if only provisionally, since the next [Ninth] General Assembly [at Najo in April 1976] should finally decide matters—define the position of the ECMY amid current issues. It is to help in the debate on these issues within the executive committee that the two of us have been asked by the church officers to present the issues to the executive committee. We are not fully agreed, as will be seen from the following. But we have agreed to present the matter in a common paper, in such a way that Gudina Tumsa presents the arguments against moratorium and Paul Hoffman presents a number of reasons that have led to proposals for moratorium. We agreed, in the final part, to make concrete proposals.

Fundamental Objections to Moratorium

What "moratorium" is, is the temporary stopping of funds and personnel from abroad. It is proposed so that mission churches may find their own identity and ways of working without interference from foreign personnel within the church and from overseas mission agencies. The usual period for moratorium is mentioned as five years. The assumption behind the proposal is that a church can only find its true identity and only decide its own projects and programs if there is a radical break with the overseas personnel and funds. Only the complete break can lay the foundation for a truly independent, indigenous church.

1. The first thing that must be said against the moratorium proposal is to point out that it is based on a false assumption: whatever may be the situation in other churches around the world, this church surely cannot be said to be hiding its identity for the sake of getting personnel and subsidies from abroad. To assume that a moratorium is necessary is to assume that a church is not free enough to determine its own policies. The ECMY can assert its freedom from any and every kind of foreign dominance, even with the continued presence of foreign personnel and funds. This is a firm conviction.

2. But issues as important as the proposal to stop all personnel and financial assistance should never be decided on grounds of self-pride or national feeling. We must think and argue theologically. And moratorium must be rejected in principle on theological grounds. The church of Jesus Christ on earth is universal. A national church is part of the

universal church. This is not to deny that the church in each nation does take on and should take on national characteristics. The church is always subject to the influences of national cultures, laws, ideologies. But this aspect of the church belongs to the law, not the gospel. The gospel and the sacraments are locally proclaimed and administered but, at the same time, are signs and evidences of the universal church. A national church's constitution is not the final law. A national president or bishop is not the head of the church—Jesus Christ is. Let me explain this by citing two concrete experiences which I have had: (a) In the United States in 1965, in a place called Jamestown, North Dakota, I was asked to distribute Holy Communion, as the pastor of the congregation was on a consultation. (b) In the Federal Republic of Germany, in October 1972, I participated in baptizing children of the congregation where I was visiting. These experiences are unforgettable. I was acting not as an Ethiopian but as a minister of Jesus Christ. Because of the gospel of Christ, the church is one, whether it is found in Russia, Sweden, Germany, China, or Ethiopia. The various parts of the universal church are and should be interdependent. Independence is a legitimate national political aim; it can never be an acceptable theological aim for a church.

3. In rejecting moratorium in principle, the ECMY would not be alone. Even the way in which some within the AACC after Lusaka are talking about moratorium shows that a complete break is not the only option, as the first impression was. In any case, by rejecting moratorium in principle the ECMY would find itself in company with sister Lutheran churches in Africa: Liberia, Madagascar, and Tanzania, which, according to reports through the Lutheran World Federation, have all come out in opposition to moratorium.

4. The most convincing argument, however, is that the ECMY needs the continuing assistance of sister churches around the world, both in funds and personnel, because of the development and evangelistic tasks that the church must continue to tackle and that it cannot suspend for any period, much less for a period of five years. The opportunities and needs for outreach and service are so great that the ECMY cannot possibly tackle them alone. As long as the government permits receipt of personnel and funds from abroad, the ECMY should not make a break simply to assert its own identity. Its identity consists of service of others—not self-assertion. In fact, the ECMY should, in the new Ethiopia, seek to find as many ways as possible to foster the well-being and development of the people. And an important way for doing this is

to secure the assistance of foreign personnel to aid in the development tasks of the country.

There is really no other answer for the ECMY than a "No" in principle to the call for moratorium.

Reasons—Nevertheless—for Consideration of Moratorium

Despite the objections to moratorium, reasons can be advanced for consideration of moratorium in the particular situation of the ECMY:

1. Identity questions are all interrelated. What is the economic identity of the ECMY? Its political identity? Its cultural identity? What is its theological identity? Is the ECMY in its worship life, for example, Ethiopian, indigenous? To the extent that the ECMY is not truly indigenous, does not have an identity of its own, and has difficulty defining its identity apart from its heritage from the respective missions, the cause can be traced—at least in part—to the continuing presence of the missionaries and their influence within the ECMY and the ongoing subsidy of the ECMY in all aspects of its work. How shall the ECMY attain an identity of its own? If moratorium, which was proposed to achieve the true identity of mission churches, is to be rejected on grounds of principle, then more concrete answers must be given to such pertinent questions, and concrete steps taken to work toward an ECMY identity that takes the various facets of the identity question seriously.

2. The extent of the missionary presence within the ECMY and the availability of seemingly unlimited funding from abroad leads to projects or programs that are either conceived in overseas patterns, can be financed solely from abroad, and/or can be staffed initially only by foreigners. How can the ECMY ever develop truly indigenous programs so long as the missionary influence is as strong as it is, or so long as the first question in any financing scheme is how to raise the funds from overseas donor agents? That moratorium is not just raised in the interest of academic debate can be understood when one takes note of the problems into which the ECMY hostels were put when the availability for funds from abroad changed the very purpose for which the hostels were built, or when missionaries promise funding for this or that scheme if it only finds at least the reluctant approval of the decision-making bodies of the ECMY. Has not much of the difficulty in which the ECMY has come over the past year developed precisely because the ECMY has been pressured, in one form or another, into adopting

a scheme or program that in its focus or extent was not really indigenous?

3. It might be argued that all the recent problems relate not to evangelistic work but to development projects, and that at least for evangelistic work—especially new evangelistic work—it is essential that the ECMY continue to request new missionaries from overseas. But it should be pointed out that—in part, because of foreign staffing and financing—the training of evangelistic workers (pastors and evangelists) has never found financial support from the ECMY congregations, and would therefore collapse immediately if foreign funds and personnel were withdrawn. Equally, foreign missions have often been willing to engage in work in new areas; the ECMY congregations and indigenous staff have never been challenged to take on responsibility for new mission work within Ethiopia.

4. Missionaries and missionary financing are real, not imaginary problems. When missions cannot promise the funding of an Ethiopian replacement if a missionary is withdrawn, when continued financial support from overseas seems to be dependent upon the ECMY's continued willingness to host foreign missionaries, when missionaries set patterns of housing and payment that cannot be met by the ECMY for the personnel it hires, when missionaries are elected to posts in part as insurance that overseas donor agents will look favorably upon projects or requests, then the ECMY is deeply enmeshed in problems that "unity of the body of Christ" and "interdependence" cannot solve and only hide.

Concrete Proposals for Action

Despite our differences, we are agreed in proposing concrete steps that should be taken. Whatever the merits of a moratorium might be, the ECMY's answer on the moratorium issue could consist of a "No" in principle—plus concrete steps to become less dependent on foreign sources for (1) theological identity and worship patterns, (2) the planning of its work, (3) its cultural identity, (4) its economic identity, (5) personnel, (6) structure, (7) local Bible schools, (8) finances, (9) missionary outreach, and (10) theological education and training.

1. The identity of the ECMY as a church in Ethiopia—in particular its theological identity—should be fostered at all levels and in all facets of the life of the ECMY. Concretely, the liturgy and hymnody of the ECMY, in Amharic and in the other Ethiopian languages, should be fostered

by a renewed Theological Commission of the Church, as well as by the synods, which should also be asked to look into the issue of the "theological identity" of the ECMY.

2. All planning for new projects or programs should from now on be done within the framework of socialist Ethiopia and be consistent with the goal of self-reliance. That means that in all the work of the church that can never be given up, programs should be ultimately financed by congregational giving, not overseas subsidy.

3. Cultural and linguistic studies of the peoples of Ethiopia should be fostered (for example, by Mekane Yesus Seminary). Proposals for such cultural and linguistic studies should be brought to the next meeting of the executive committee.

4. In a socialist Ethiopia, the patterns of housing and living set by foreigners should not be the patterns adopted by the ECMY. The adoption of a reduced salary scale will be a major step in decreasing financial dependence upon overseas donors and place the ECMY in the forefront of adapting positively to the new Ethiopian society, thus identifying with the social and economic direction in which Ethiopia is moving.

5. At all levels, there should be a review of just what missionary personnel are needed in the new situation of Ethiopia. No missionary should be retained in a post simply because the finances for finding an Ethiopian replacement are lacking. In such instances, funds should be available once the salary scale has been scaled down. It is no service to a missionary to retain him when he is no longer needed or does not fit the present Ethiopian situation. In instances where missions cannot promise funds to finance replacements for their personnel that are withdrawn, funds should be sought from other sources. Furthermore, personnel from such missions should not be concentrated in limited geographical areas, but be scattered throughout the ECMY, so that the ECMY in those geographical areas should not be bound to continued receipt of missionaries solely for the sake of the "cheap labor" they seem to represent. Furthermore, before a new missionary is requested, or an older missionary is recalled, every effort should be made to find an Ethiopian to take on his particular task or responsibility. And where new tasks or new work is to be undertaken by a missionary, the church, the synod, or the institution concerned should indicate how someone is to be recruited and trained to take over for the missionary concerned.

6. It should become an essential principle not only in theology but for the structure and organization of the ECMY, for its administration

and strategy, that the congregation is the fundamental unit and the main center of the church. Pastors and evangelists should be employed not by the synods but by congregations.

7. Congregations should normally be understood to be self-supporting and not eligible for subsidy from overseas. Local Bible schools should become part of the congregational structure, not any longer to be considered institutions of the synods. Teachers in such local Bible schools should be the neighboring pastors, salaried by the congregations, who are so convinced of the value of their Bible school to the mission of their congregations that they are willing to see their pastors engaged part-time as teachers in the Bible school.

8. To foster less dependence on foreign subsidy, the giving from congregations should, in the financial reports of the synods and the ECMY, clearly be distinguished from the subsidies received from overseas.

9. The executive committee should charge the Evangelism Department of the ECMY to lay plans for an ECMY Home Mission, to be staffed by Ethiopians and financed by special appeals to all congregations of the ECMY. The ECMY, in other words, must begin a strategy of self-propagation and mission.

10. The synods should agree with Mekane Yesus Seminary and the Synodical Bible Schools on a method of informing the congregations of their work and on appealing to them for annual support. Every effort must thus be made to engage the congregations in increasing support for essential functions of the synods and the ECMY.

The "No" in principle and these steps would be the ECMY's answer—at this time—to the call for moratorium.

Source: EECMY, Thirty-Fifth Executive Committee, August 1975, Minutes EC-35-11, Minutes C0-75-133.

11

———

Unbelief from Historical Perspective, or Kairos

Gudina Tumsa presented this paper to the Ninth General Assembly of the ECMY, which met in Najo from April 21 to 28, 1976. On one mimeographed copy of this paper, an additional or alternate title appears in Gudina's own handwriting: "Kairos," a biblical Greek word meaning a decisive time, a pregnant time, a time for decision. In the presentation, Gudina points out how ancient unbelief is and challenges both materialism and atheism. It is interesting to note that the intellectual history recounted by Gudina follows the standard narrative of Western civilization, which, for good or for ill, had traveled to Ethiopia as well in the form of—among others—Protestant missions and communist politics. This paper should be read together with his brother Baro Tumsa's paper "The Church and Ideologies" (see the appendix), which demonstrates Baro's Marxist sympathies.

Unbelief—the lack of faith in God or the denial of his existence—is spreading in Ethiopia today: among the youth, among the educated, among those in political power, but also among the common people. Where does such unbelief come from? How should we Christians respond to the spread of unbelief?

The Nature and History of Unbelief

1. The first thing that we should note is that unbelief is not something new. It is as old as humankind. Two of the psalms of our Old Testament begin with the statement: "The fool says in his heart, 'There is no God'" (Pss 14:1 and 53:1). The psalmist, though he calls such persons "fools," admits that such men and women existed then, and they exist today. Sometimes unbelief takes the form of denial of God's existence. At other times it takes the form of questioning the truth or wisdom of God's word, as when Eve accepted the serpent's question concerning the truth or wisdom of what God had forbidden (Gen 3:1–6). Sometimes it takes the form of trying to cover up one's misdeeds and denying one's responsibility for them, as when Cain tried to escape responsibility before God for murdering his brother Abel (Gen 4:8–9), or when people hide their deeds and say, "Who sees us? Who knows us?" (Isa 29:15). Sometimes it simply takes the form of denying in one's heart or in one's actions what one confesses with one's lips (Isa 29:13; Mark 7:6; Matt 15:8). Unbelief thus takes many forms. At different times and in different circumstances the characteristics of unbelief change. It was when the "fortunes of Israel" seemed lost and would never be restored that unbelief was spreading in Israel in the psalmist's days (see Ps 14:7; 53:6), much as, when misfortune strikes today, an individual begins to question the existence, power, or goodness of God. Unbelief thus has always been known throughout our human history. Its source is the human heart.

2. However, intellectual argument, intellectual considerations, are put forward that strengthen the unbelief that arises in the heart. Historically, the source for these intellectual arguments and considerations is to be found in Ancient Greece. The religion of the ancient Greeks contained a multitude of gods. None of these gods created the world; they were part of the world, they had lusts and feelings, they were arbitrary in their actions, and in this they were very much like ordinary men and women. Except that they had immortality; men and women did not. About 600 BC, there arose in Greece a remarkable intellectual movement that began to inquire into the nature of the world, the nature of things. In this intellectual movement was born what we today call philosophy (a Greek word meaning "knowledge"). At first, philosophy turned its attention to the world, in order to find explanations for things in the world, and a surprising amount of accurate observations and solid information was gathered about the world and

its nature, which resulted in the growth of science. Soon, however, the philosophers began to turn their attention to the Greek gods, and philosophers became increasingly skeptical about what the Greek myths told about the gods and their behavior. Yet, as a whole, philosophers, though they might discount the gods, believed that behind the world and men and women were principles or elements that were "divine" or "godlike."

3. But there was a strand in Greek philosophy that abandoned such thinking altogether in favor of what we call "materialism": belief that "matter" is the only and final reality. It is usually Democritus (born 460 BC) who is thought to have put forth the first theory to explain the world and human beings solely in terms of "matter." He was the first to propose that everything in the world and in human beings has its explanations in "atoms," tiny units of "matter" in motion that cannot be cut down further (from Greek *a-tome* = "unable to be split further"). These "atoms" are in helter-skelter motion in a void. Gods may exist in some other world, but not in this. Two followers of Democritus, Epicurus (born 342 BC) and Lucretius (died about 58 BC), draw the consequences for the goal of life. Virtue consists in avoiding pain and in seeking pleasure. Lucretius, in a masterpiece of Latin poetry, "On the Nature of Things," is openly antireligious, feeling that belief in this world undermines the pursuit of happiness. The Bible knows of a popular Epicureanism that, as in the parable of the rich fool, describes the aim of life as "eat, drink, be merry" (Luke 12:19).

4. The main body of Greek philosophical thought decided, on the other hand, that whatever one thought about the gods, one could identify some principle or element in the world or in humankind, be it "soul" or spirit, as divine. Plato (died 347 BC), in particular, is responsible for this side of Greek thinking, which saw in "matter" and "soul" or "spirit" opposing principles, without attempting to explain how "matter" came to exist. It was Plato's pupil Aristotle (died 322 BC), himself a student of natural science as well as of philosophy, who tried to do justice to both strands of the tradition, maintaining that the divine (God in the singular, not the gods in the plural) was the Prime Mover or First Cause to put everything into motion. The world as it existed was capable of being studied and explained without reference to action or activity of the gods.

5. The Greek philosophical tradition posed a problem for Christian theology as the Christian church evangelized the Greco-Roman world. The materialist tradition was easily rejected. But Plato and Aristotle

could not be rejected out of hand. Plato had taught the immortality of the soul. And Aristotle was understood to have come close to the doctrine of creation with his teaching about the Prime Mover and First Cause. Was not Aristotle, in particular, proof that human beings had a natural knowledge of God, and that one could prove by human reason that the God revealed in the Jewish and Christian Scriptures actually existed? It was with such reasoning that the Greek philosophical tradition and the Greek impetus to study the natural sciences were maintained in Christian Europe.

6. But the problem of relative authority persisted between revelation and natural revelation and natural knowledge, faith, and reason. While with the help of Aristotle, the chief theology of the Catholic Church maintained that faith and reason were complementary, revelation and faith simply supplying what natural knowledge and reason could not achieve, there grew up in the late Middle Ages the philosophical teaching of the nominalists that "universals" like "man," "nature," and so forth do not "exist," they are simply human names for particular, individual things. The nominalists gave up any attempt to "prove" the existence of God. They taught that reason cannot prove the main teachings of Christianity, including the existence of God and creation of the world by him, but that these must be believed on the authority of the Bible and the church. Reason and natural knowledge, which largely up to then were seen as supporting the Christian teachings, were now understood as ending up in skepticism or agnosticism.

7. It was in the time of nominalism that the Renaissance brought a new interest in Ancient Greece—and a new skepticism and agnosticism into European culture. The Renaissance also brought with it a new impetus to study natural science: the world, the planets, the universe. In seventeenth-century Europe, noting the regularity with which the earth and the planets moved around the sun, and being convinced that the whole universe moved by inherent natural laws, a group of thinkers who are called "Deists" borrowed from Aristotle's teaching about the Prime Mover and First Cause to claim that while God created the world and set it in motion, the world was like a watch and God like a watchmaker. God could not interfere in the orderly running of the world without bringing the whole thing to a stop. With this view, the world was understood as a sphere in which God is not, in fact cannot be, active. The universe is a closed system in which nothing new can or does happen. It is this understanding of the world and of natural

science that lies behind much of the unbelief at present spreading in Ethiopia.

8. Contributing to present understandings about man and God and the world among educated Ethiopian youth today are the teachings of the German idealist philosophers of the early nineteenth century. The concern of Immanuel Kant (1724–1804) was to maintain the truth of both the natural sciences and the truth of such ideas as God, freedom, and immortality. Kant basically accepted the Deist understanding of the world as a closed system and came to the conclusion that God, freedom, and immortality cannot be proved by observation or experiment, the methods of the natural sciences. He tried to show, however, that these concepts were in the structure of the human mind. The human mind cannot prove that it is free, for instance, but it knows itself to be free. Furthermore, God, freedom, and immortality are essential assumptions for "practical reason," reason as it deals with ethics and religion.

9. Out of this teaching arose the teaching of Ludwig Feuerbach (1804–1872). A former student of theology, Feuerbach came to the conclusion, on the basis of reading Kant, that the idea of God is a creation of man. "God is not the Creator of man; man is the creator of God." He believed that man makes God in his own image, not the other way around!

10. The thought of Feuerbach profoundly influenced the thinking of Karl Marx (1818–1883) and Friedrich Engels (1820–1895), the founders of what is called "scientific socialism." These men were followers of Friedrich Hegel (1770–1831), who had taught that Spirit was the origin and end of all things. Marx simply reversed the philosophy of this German idealist. He and Engels adopted as the basis for their philosophy or ideology the materialist worldview of Democritus and Lucretius, that all things are to be explained in terms of matter. They built upon Feuerbach's views; not only is God the creation of the human mind, the human mind or consciousness is itself a product of matter. This had led to a philosophical and practical denial of human nature or human dignity. Man and his history are purely to be explained on the basis of economic causes, economic forces. Marxist ideology, arising as it did in the nineteenth century, also accepted the basically Deist [opinion that the world is a closed system].[1] Engels eagerly accepted the teachings of Charles Darwin (1809–1882), who put forth the theory of evolution.

---

1. Ed. note: Reconstituted text from the Amharic translation.

Neither in the philosophy of Marxism, nor in the popular worldview called Darwinism, is there any place for God as an active creative agent in human affairs or in the world.

11. Mention of Marx and Darwin, a German and an Englishman, show that unbelief is not restricted to one nation or culture. Atheism—the philosophical denial of the existence of God—is not just a constitutive element of Marxism, or of socialism as understood in the Eastern countries, it is constitutive of much modern philosophy in the West and of much popular thinking also in capitalist societies. Unbelief does not confine itself to one social or political system.

Our Christian Response

1. Our Christian response to expressions of unbelief and attempts to spread unbelief cannot be one of repression. If we Christians wish that our right to believe and to see belief spread should be respected, we should equally wish that the rights of those who do not or cannot believe should be respected. To repress those who hold other views is no way of convincing them. We must vigorously exercise, however, our own right to believe and to propagate our faith. To such as have no hope and are without God in the world (Eph 2:12), we are bound to give witness, but not in a proud or overbearing manner: "Always be prepared to make a defense to anyone who calls you to account for the hope that is in you, yet do it with gentleness and reverence" (1 Pet 3:15).

2. Our response to unbelief should be based on a clear and full testimony to the nature of God, the world, and man from the biblical perspective. It is God who created the world, the heavens, and the earth and all that is in them, not like Aristotle's "Prime Mover" or "First Cause," who simply puts all things in motion, or like the Deists' "Watchmaker," who after starting the watch cannot interfere in the working. Jesus said, "My Father is working still, and I am working" (John 5:17). The creative power of God is still at work in this world. God is busy and active in this world, creating ever new. And Jesus, the Son of God, came with this same creative power. The one who is Alpha and Omega, the beginning and the ending, is the one who still promises, "Behold, I make all things new" (Rev 21:5–6). This creative power of God extends also into the affairs of men. God is not far off (Acts 17:27), but in his providence he is constantly bringing good out of evil. The God to whom both Jews and Christians witness is the God who, in the

midst of the nations, has called into being a people peculiar to him (Deut 14:2; Titus 2:14; 1 Pet 2:9; Ps 135:4), who leads his people out of bondage, who uses even the rulers of the world who do not know him to do his bidding (Nebuchadnezzar of Babylon, Jer 25:8; and Cyrus the Persian, Isaiah 45). This God is "our refuge and strength, a very present help in trouble." "He makes wars cease to the end of the earth; He breaks the bow, and shatters the spear, He burns the chariots with fire!" (Ps 46:1, 9). He is the God whose

> mercy is on those who fear Him
>> from generation to generation.
> He has shown strength with His arm,
>> He has scattered the proud in the imagination of their hearts,
> He has put down the mighty from their thrones,
>> and exalted those of low degree;
> He has filled the hungry with good things,
>> and the rich He has sent empty away.
> He has helped His servant Israel,
>> in remembrance of His mercy,
> as He spoke to our fathers,
>> to Abraham and to his posterity forever.
> —Luke 1:50–55

3. The biblical view of God demands an open understanding of the world and of man. The world is neither an arbitrary collection of atoms in a void nor a closed system. Man is not just matter. He does not just have consciousness, awareness. He has been created in the image of God (Gen 1:26–27). And human beings have freedom, creativity, honor, and dignity deriving from that image of God. To have a closed understanding of the world and a materialist understanding of man is to deny essential elements of science and human nature. No truly scientific worldview can be closed or dogmatically rule out the possibility of essential new occurrences taking place.

4. The truly effective testimony against unbelief is a life lived by faith. Unbelief does not accept the possibility of the sick being healed; faith does (Mark 9:22–24). Unbelief scoffs at resurrection (Matt 22:23–32; Acts 17:32); faith sets its whole hope on resurrection (1 Corinthians 15). Unbelief scoffs at the providence or presence of God to save (Matt 27:43); faith, even in death, places one's spirit in God's hands (Luke 23:46; Acts 7:59). Faith is not holding the form of religion but denying its power (2 Tim 3:5). Faith puts one's trust in the presence and power of God—Father, Son, and Holy Spirit—in all the activities and cir-

cumstances of life: in preaching and teaching, farming and business, conferences and administration, in joys and sorrows, honor and dishonor, praise and persecution. Faith puts its trust in him who fed the five thousand (Matt 14:13–21; Mark 6:31–44; Luke 9:10–17; John 6:1–13). That is the faith that trusts in him who "supplies seed to the sower and bread for food" and who therefore blesses also what we share with others, in full confidence that he will also multiply resources and increase the harvest of righteousness and justice (1 Cor 9:6–11, especially v. 10). The important thing is to turn to him with all one's cares, concerns, and problems. It is then that we experience the reality of God, and in turn can speak and witness to him in defiance of all expressions of unbelief. Then can we say with Isaiah, the prophet:

> The Lord God had given me the tongue of those who are taught,
>> that I may know how to sustain with a word him that is weary.
>> Morning by morning He wakens,
>> He wakens my ears to hear as those who are taught. . . .
> For the Lord helps me:
>> therefore I have not been confounded:
>> therefore I have set my face like a flint,
>> and I know that I shall not be put to shame;
> He who vindicates me is near.
> —Isaiah 50:4–8

It is such faith that receives miracles and that removes mountains, yes even mountains of unbelief (Mark 9:14–29; cf. Matt 17:14–21).

Addis Ababa, April 14, 1976

Source: ECMY Ninth General Assembly, 1976, Minutes GA-9-44-76, Doc. L.

12

The Responsibility of the ECMY toward Ecumenical Harmony

At the second "Christianity and Socialism Seminar" on April 25-29, 1975, hosted by the ECMY and the LWF's Department of Studies with participation from other churches, the idea of creating a Council for Cooperation of Churches in Ethiopia surfaced. It was to include Orthodox and Catholics as well as other Protestants. The matter did not come up for discussion at the Ninth General Assembly in Najo in April 1976, but at the Tenth General Assembly, which took place at the Mekane Yesus Seminary in Addis Ababa from January 24 to 31, 1978, Gudina presented this paper, putting forth reasons for the ECMY to foster ecumenical harmony and exhorting cooperation in the founding of the prospective council. He also anticipates the positive decision by the General Assembly to join the World Council of Churches, but the focus of the paper is on ecumenical harmony in Ethiopia. It was Gudina's efforts to connect the Christians of Ethiopia to speak with a common voice that ultimately led the Derg government to consider him a threat to their security. It is fair to say that Gudina's ecumenical activism sealed his death sentence.

Slight emendations have been made to the paragraph numbering.

1.

1.1 When we speak about ecumenical relationships, I believe that we need a definition of the term so that what we are talking about will be clearly understood by all concerned. The term "ecumenical" is not what our Lord prayed for in the Gospel of John, chapter 17. The prayer of our Lord was and still is for the oneness of his church.

1.2. The word "ecumenical" describes the common strategy of the churches in working together for the furtherance of causes of common interest. The word describes two or more churches engaged in common responsibilities. Practically, this may mean churches of the same confessional family or various denominations with different confessional backgrounds.

1.3. The Amharic word *andnet* is misleading when we discuss ecumenical affairs. This became quite clear to me in the course of the discussions we have had with our sister churches during the last two years. The Amharic word *andnet* describes the "oneness" of the church spoken of in John, chapter 17, particularly verses 11, 21, and 23. To avoid confusion, another word, *hibret*, which may be translated "association," is preferable in describing ecumenical relationships.

1.4. For the sake of clarity one may distinguish different stages as we march forward in working together for the unity of the people of God, the church of Jesus Christ.

a) The first stage is the ecumenical stage where the churches have a readiness to come together for discussions, prayers, and reading of the Scriptures, thereby doing away with their historical hatred and paving the way for joint activities.

b) The second stage is "that they may be one" (John 17:11, 21). This we may call the complete stage. The priestly prayer of our Lord is not only for the ecumenical affairs of the churches but primarily for the oneness of his church.

1.5. The ECMY has an inescapable responsibility to make all efforts that the prayer of our Redeemer for the oneness of his church may be fulfilled. Specific areas for actions to be taken will be mentioned later in this paper.

2.

2.1. In discussions on the unity of the church of Jesus Christ, we come across opposing views or theological positions.

a) One school of thought spiritualizes everything to the extent that tangible, visible things are denied proper consideration. This group condemns all forms of structure and fails to see the place of structure or organization in carrying out the mandate of Christ's church.

b) The second group is what we may call the secularizers. This view contends that the church is an organization like any other worldly organization and refuses to recognize the church of Christ as an assembly called by God for a purpose, redeemed by Jesus Christ, and enlightened by the Third Person of the Holy Trinity.

2.2. The spiritualizers and the secularizers are diametrically opposed to each other. Whereas the spiritualizers try to transfer everything to the other world and refuse to accept responsibility for the pressing social problems of our planet, the secularizers are blind to see other than the material, and see their responsibility only as contributing to the improvement of the living conditions of human society.

2.3. In my opinion, neither the spiritualizers nor the secularizers are true to the biblical understanding of reality. Whereas secularizing is a denial of the Creator of the universe, the God who has revealed himself through Jesus Christ, spiritualizing is interpreting the Scriptures in such a way that all social problems find their solutions in the hereafter, thereby denying the reality of the incarnation and leaving the world to atheism.

2.4. The third school of thought is what I would call the holistic position. In holistic theology, both the spiritual and the physical are taken seriously in an inseparable manner. This theological position contends that the right biblical understanding takes seriously both dimensions of human existence, the spiritual and the physical life. The God of the Bible is the source of life both in its spiritual and physical dimensions. He has the proper claim on human life both on this planet and in the world to come. There is no portion of human existence that can be free from God.

2.5. Since the purpose of this short paper is not to present the basic theological positions of churches represented in the ecumenical movement in our country but to define specific responsibilities of the ECMY toward ecumenical harmony, it would be out of place to deal with the various presuppositions of the different views toward ecumenical matters.

2.6. Prior to proceeding to the third part of this paper, let me recite the classical Lutheran definition of the church as "the communion of saints where the word of God is proclaimed rightly and the sacraments are administered rightly." This is to say that the church is located where grace is offered, the bitterness of sin is taken away, the blessings of God appropriated, and the joy of the Lord's forgiveness is experienced. This is meant to remind ourselves that when we are clear about the primary purpose of the church and our ecumenical responsibilities for the unity of the church of the Savior, then whatever structure is chosen is of lesser significance.

3.

3.1. Comments are heard that the ECMY does not interest herself in ecumenical affairs, thereby placing herself in isolation. Such comments are due to lack of information on the active participation of the ECMY in ecumenical endeavors, even before she was organized into her present structure in 1958. Lutheran groups were playing active roles in the annual meetings of evangelical believers, who came together to discuss the common problems they faced as new groups left behind by the missions who left the country during the Italian occupation during the Second World War. That our congregations received delegations from various Christian denominations, and in turn sent representatives to annual evangelical meetings, is evidence of the longstanding interest of the ECMY in ecumenical affairs.

3.2. Documents from the meetings of those days were kept by the late Pastor Bodima Yalew of the Addis Ababa Mekane Yesus Church and are available for reference. It is very interesting to note how the evangelical believers were trying to find solutions to the problems confronting them in an ecumenical manner when they were neophytes with minimal experience.

3.3. One may wonder why the ecumenical movement begun during the difficult days of the Second World War ceased to exist about the end of the 1950s. The main factor for the dissolution of the evangelical ecumenical movements was the ready answers that the believers received from their respective missions to the burning issues facing them in their daily work, such as polygamy, relationship to the state, and so forth. Thus, they didn't need to consult and work with each other.

3.4. By way of criticism let me say, the evangelicals formed an ecumenical movement out of practical needs, without defining the biblical or theological basis for the unity of the church. Lack of precise definition of objectives beyond the practical needs led to the dissolution of the ecumenical movement when their immediate needs were met.

3.5. To bring about desirable results, an ecumenical movement should set a clear goal for itself. In my opinion, this clear goal is a united witness to the saving power of Christ as we unequivocally work for the unity of the church of God.

3.6. Those who contend that there is no possibility for the unity of the church of Jesus Christ, except in the hereafter, should be refuted on theological grounds. The point I want to make is that we do not need to define the limits of what God can do, including in our prayer only that which we think is possible for him and leaving out of the agenda the impossible, or what we imagine he cannot do.

3.7. In case there is a god for whom man has to think and put limits to what he can do, such is not the God we have known in the Scriptures, or rather by whom we are known. Such a finite god is not the God of the Bible, the Father of Jesus of Nazareth, but the god of human creation, the projection of human imagination (the god of Feuerbach).

3.8. Ours is the God who orders light out of darkness, brings order out of chaos, life out of death, peace out of anarchy. This mighty process is beyond the human mind and refuses to be manipulated by men. What he can do in his church and with his church should be seen in eschatological perspective, not only in terms of the long future but also in the context of today. He is the God who performs miracles today as he did in the past, saving his people from slavery, liberating them from oppression, providing them with the necessities of life on their journey to the promised land, judging them when they are disobedient, and forgiving them when they have confessed their sins.

3.9. A question may arise: Is it necessary to refer to the omnipotence of God when we discuss the unity of the church of God? It seems to be necessary to remind ourselves of the mighty power of the Bible's God, because there are Christians who argue that there cannot be a unity among the churches. Biblical faith is based on the impossible, on miracles. In the Old Testament, the deliverance of the people of Israel from Egypt and the dividing of the Sea; in the New Testament, our Lord's birth from the Virgin Mary and his resurrection from the dead are central to what the church of Christ confesses as a faith by which she lives. These are impossible miracles, and miracles are contrary to the laws of nature. Ours is still the God of miracles, and one of the miracles he may perform today is to bring about unity among his churches. Let us then talk about his church rather than our churches.

4.

4.1. Presently the ECMY is contributing to the strengthening of ecumenical endeavor in our country. These contributions are in various ways. As indicated in preceding paragraphs, the history of the ECMY is partly the history of the evangelical ecumenical movement. During the 1960s, the involvement of the ECMY was limited almost entirely to negotiations with the Evangelical Church Bethel, with occasional invitations to other churches to attend our General Assemblies. The negotiations with the Bethel Church resulted in the merger of the two sister churches in 1974. This in itself is a big step forward in setting an example for Christian denominations in our country, and it can be said to be one of the results of the ecumenical movement started during the Second World War.

4.2. Ecumenical relations among the evangelical churches are looked at very naturally, at least on an informal level, even to the extent that pulpit fellowship has been in practice since the founding of the evangelical churches. What does irritate many evangelical leaders is when we begin talking about the possibility of initiating discussions on ecumenical affairs with the Ethiopian Orthodox Church. Although evangelicals are irritated when the question of relationship with the Orthodox Church is taken up, foreigners are confused as to the actual position of the evangelical churches, especially the attitude of the ECMY, since among the evangelical churches in this country, the ECMY is more widely known in broader ecumenical circles.

4.3. In the circumstances of today, it is not necessary to discuss problems of a historical nature, which are seen as hindrances to real ecumenical dialogue with the Orthodox Church. When the discussions were under way for the formation of a council of cooperation of the churches in Ethiopia, naturally the possible membership of the Orthodox Church was discussed. At that point, one of the evangelicals related the bitter experience of his church at the hands of the Orthodox Church. However, all were willing to participate in a Council for Cooperation of Churches with the Orthodox Church.

4.4. Some of us in the ECMY leadership are maintaining personal contacts with some in the leadership of the Orthodox Church in order to pave a way for ecumenical leadership to be established between the two churches. It gives me pleasure to say that some of the personal contacts I have had with some of the leaders of the Orthodox Church have been refreshing experiences. I feel that these informal contacts should be broadened to include as many as possible of the leaders of the Orthodox Church and the ECMY. (For additional information see the paper I presented to the [Lutheran World Federation's] Commission of Church Cooperation in Tokyo, Japan, 1971 ["Report on Church Growth in Ethiopia"].)

4.5. In case this Tenth General Assembly of the ECMY decides in favor of membership in the World Council of Churches, this may accelerate the time when the two churches, the ECMY and the Ethiopian Orthodox Church, may start discussions on how to discharge their responsibilities for the Ethiopian people. From one point of view, it appears to be easier, in case real efforts are made, to work for a meeting among the three churches, Orthodox, Catholic, and ECMY. There are theological and historical reasons for maintaining this view. As a matter of fact, in some areas of concern there have been real contacts and discussion with the Orthodox Church in a semiofficial manner. One instance is the seminar on Urban Industrial Mission conducted last year, which was more or less sponsored by the Orthodox Church but jointly planned with the ECMY and the Catholic Church. We should remind our congregations that they may make as an object of their prayer the good relationship among the churches of Ethiopia, especially between the Orthodox Church and the ECMY.

4.6. A Council for Cooperation of Churches in Ethiopia was formed in 1976. The occasion was brought about by a series of seminars on Christianity and socialism in Makanisa, sponsored by the ECMY. The majority of the evangelical churches, the Catholic Church, and a small section of the Orthodox Church (one Orthodox mission headquartered in the Trinity Cathedral) are represented in the Council for Cooperation of Churches in Ethiopia.

4.7. It is essential to increase the participation of the ECMY for the strengthening of the council, whatever form such participation may take. The council has not found it possible to rent a room for an office, a place to keep its documents and where the secretary could coordinate the activities of the council. This is a specific responsibility for the ECMY. Ato Tesfatsion Delelew, reactor to this paper, has contributed in many ways to the formation of the Council for Cooperation of Churches in Ethiopia and is still making strong efforts, inviting others to be members of the council. I hope he will enlighten us on the specific needs of the Council for Cooperation of Churches at this initial stage in its history and for the long future.

4.8. As stated in the preceding paragraphs, involvement in ecumenical affairs with the evangelical churches of Ethiopia is part of the history of the ECMY from her beginning. Earlier, I mentioned that during the 1960s the main involvement of the ECMY was with the Bethel Church. The evangelical churches have shown a strong interest in ecumenical involvement for about the last three years. This interest is being promoted through a very active committee set up to make the necessary preparations for evangelical church leadership conferences held two times in Nazareth, September 1976 and September 1977, with a wide representation from all evangelical churches. Speakers are invited from abroad as well as from within the country for revival preaching. Revival meetings and movements should be encouraged and guided in such a way that the various gifts within the different churches can be shared for the enrichment and edification of the church of our Lord Jesus Christ (1 Corinthians 12 and 14).

4.9. The importance of work among the youth cannot be overemphasized in the present situation within our country. It is quite clear that the young people in this country, perhaps as elsewhere, are not interested in denominational doctrines but rather attracted by Bible studies, prayers, and discussions with any Christian from any Christian denomination. The ECMY contributed in the formation of associations for high school and university students. A young man, Ato Tekste Teklu, who was employed for this responsibility did a tremendous job in achieving the objectives set for him. For me, it was inspiring to listen to five of the representatives of the students tell of their activities among the youth. There is much more awaiting the ECMY in this area of ecumenical endeavor.

4.10. A study on ecumenical movements to do away with prejudice and misunderstandings may be one way of discharging the ecumenical responsibility of our church. Lack of information and personal prejudices are contributing causes in hindering participation in ecumenical movements.

4.11. In obedience of the Lord of the church and in order that the prayer of our Savior may be fulfilled, the ECMY should continue its efforts and strengthen its work in areas of ecumenical cooperation.

Source: ECMY Tenth General Assembly, 1978, Minutes GA-10-62-70, Doc. 33.

13

The Role of a Christian in a Given Society

Gudina Tumsa was arrested for the first time on October 11, 1978, and released on November 7. He was detained a second time from June 1 to 23, 1979. Upon release, aware that a third arrest would likely end in a death sentence, Gudina set down in his own hand an essay that he entitled "The Role of a Christian in a Given Society." It can justly be called his last will and testament, his final confession of faith, for on July 28, 1979, he was abducted after leading a Bible study at Urael Mekane Yesus Church in Addis Ababa and murdered, though his body was not found and identified until after the fall of Derg regime.

According to Dr. Yonas Deressa, who was then working in the Information Office of the EECMY, Gudina's original manuscript included a preamble setting forth his personal political convictions. Those preparing for the Eleventh General Assembly of the EECMY on January 23 to 31, 1980, half a year later, felt it would be imprudent to disseminate the opening section. The rest of the essay was distributed and read as a complete lecture to the Assembly in Makanisa. The original handwritten manuscript with the political preamble has not been found, as all of Gudina's papers from his period as general secretary were confiscated and presumably destroyed by the Derg regime not long after his disappearance.

Strikingly, in the first paragraph of the essay's conclusion, Gudina alludes to Dietrich Bonhoeffer's famous line from R. H. Fuller's translation of The Cost of Discipleship: *"When Christ calls a man, he bids him come and die."*

Introduction

A Christian lives in a society, among whom God created, saved from sin, and placed him to bear witness to the gospel of the risen Lord Jesus Christ. A given society cannot be free from the different competing forces like other religions, atheism, and pluralism. A Christian is placed by God to live and proclaim the gospel of Christ to the people that are in need and difficulty so that they can turn to God to get their needs met and their problems solved.

A Christian in a Society

1. A Christian lives in a given society where he carries out the mandate given to him by the Lord of the church. We have not been given a choice as to where we should be born. We believe that God has placed us where we are to do his will as Ethiopian Christians and to fulfill his purpose. It seems to be proper to speak about what a Christian is prior to speaking about their given responsibility. A Christian is a person who is transformed by what the God of the universe has done in the person of his Son, Jesus Christ.

2. The Lord Jesus Christ is the basis for our Christian faith. What God has done for the salvation of mankind can never be undone, simply because it is the God whom we know in Jesus Christ who has done it.

3. In response to faith, in what has been accomplished by the sacrifice of the Son of God for the salvation of mankind, the Christian has tasted heavenly gifts in earthly life. A life of relationship with the Lord of the church is possible only through faith.

4. When we as Christians state that nothing in the universe can separate us from the love of God made ours in Christ, it is not a bringing of human strength but an acknowledgement of the fact that the relationship our heavenly Father has established with us through his Son can never be broken (Rom 8:35–39). It is even beyond the ability of death, the greatest enemy of mankind, to destroy the relationship we have with God through our Savior.

5. When Christ died for our sins on the cross and became our cure, the power of death was broken. The battle was won for us by our Lord Jesus Christ. What is going on in the world between good and evil is not a real war but the final operation after the war has been won, because death has been destroyed and victory is complete (1 Cor 15:54). It is

only the Christian who can ask the question, "Death, where is your victory? Death, where is your power to hurt?" (1 Cor 15:55).

Thanks be to God, we have complete victory through him who loved us and sacrificed himself for us. The most death can do now is to be a stepping-stone for the Christian to be transferred to fullness of life in and with the Lord Jesus Christ.

6. As the theme for this Eleventh General Assembly indicates, we confess that "God is with us." In the Lord's Supper, he who assures us of his presence that renews his covenant with us, thereby forgiving us and ever leading us to fulfillment of his purpose for his world.

7. A Christian has not chosen God, but God has chosen them, and in the act of being chosen they are set apart for service in the kingdom of God. Because of what has happened to them, the Christian is encouraged to let God transform them, inwardly, by a complete change of mind. Romans 12:1–2:

> So then my brothers, because of God's great mercy to us, I make this appeal to you: Offer yourselves as a living sacrifice to God, dedicated to his service and pleasing to him. This is the true worship that you should offer. Do not conform outwardly to the standards of this world, but let God transform you by a complete change of your mind. Then you will be able to know the will of God—what is good, and is pleasing to him, and is perfect.

8. The Christian knows that he/she has been made by an act of God through Jesus Christ. If he/she is holy, God by his grace has made him/her so. The Christian knows that he belongs to "the chosen race," he/she belongs to "the holy nation," he/she belongs to "the king's priests," he/she is part of "God's own people." All those named belong to the chosen race, ordination as the king's priest, being a member of the holy nation, God's own people, all done by God in order that the Christian may be equipped to "proclaim the wonderful acts of God, who called him out of darkness into his own marvelous light" (1 Pet 2:9).

9. Sin is not human weakness, it is rather a rebellion against God the Creator. It is a refusal to accept God's gracious gift through his Son Jesus Christ. Sin is a departure from the Father's house in rebellion. It is a denial of one's own source. Sin is an attempt to dethrone the one who rules above. It is a futile effort of mortal man to replace God. The Christian is aware that he lives among people whose lives are ruled by the power of sin.

10. The Lord's Supper is a foretaste of the heavenly banquet that the

Christian is entitled to enjoy here on earth. By the coming of our Lord, the new age has dawned on us. He has inaugurated the messianic age, the sole rule of God has started: the demons are cast out, the gospel is preached to the poor, the blind are given sight, the lepers are cleansed.

In participation in the Lord's Supper, three things come to mind:

a. What has been written about the Messiah by the prophets has been fulfilled.

b. The power of God is at work, all because the Son of Man has shed his blood as ransom for many, thereby making the forgiveness of sin a reality for those who respond in faith.

c. The third aspect of the Lord's Supper is expectation of the Lord's return to subject all things to himself. Recollection of God's mighty deeds in the past, experiencing forgiveness of sins today, and expecting the second coming of the one who has shed his blood for us are ways of being equipped for a life of witness in society.

A Christian Is Responsible to God and Man

1. In the preceding paragraphs and the prior part of this paper, attempts are made to show what a Christian is. A Christian is a transformed person by believing the gospel of Christ (justification) and is in the constant process of being transformed (sanctification) by the power of the Third Person of the Holy Trinity, the Holy Spirit, who dwells in the Christian. God has counted the believer as righteous without any contribution on their part, with the exception of accepting the gracious gift of God through the Lord Jesus Christ.

2. The Christian is made a citizen of the kingly rule of God. By belonging to the realm of that rule, the Christian is charged with the responsibility to proclaim: "The right time has come, the kingdom of God is near. Turn away from your sins and believe the Good News" (Mark 1:15). In carrying out this assignment from heaven to be fulfilled on earth, the Christian is aware of two things. The first is that the risen Lord is ever present within, and second, that the Christian is never alone. He has joined, as a companion of Jesus Christ, millions of Christians who have responded in obedience to the command of the Head of the church and are engaged in working for the acceleration of the day of the Lord Jesus Christ.

3. The Creator and Redeemer of the Christian has total claim on the life of the one who confesses him as Lord and Savior. When the Christian confesses that Christ is Lord, he proclaims that Jesus Christ is the

King of kings, the President of presidents, the Chairman of chairmen, the Ruler of rulers, the Secretary of secretaries, the Leader of leaders, and the Head of the heads of State. Christ is the Lord of the universe and the one who guides historical developments to their right fulfillment according to the purpose of the Creator. At the same time, he guides us both collectively and individually in such a way that the hairs of our heads are well known to him, so that we can relax in carrying out the commission he has given to his church. This assignment has the first and top priority in the life of the believer.

4. To promise second place to the Lord (anyway, the Lord would never accept second place in human life) is openly to worship idols and is a breach of the first commandment: "Thou shalt have no other gods before me" (Exodus 20:3).

5. It has already been stated in this part of this paper and in the preceding paragraphs that a Christian is citizen of the kingly rule of God in this messianic age. A Christian is also a citizen of a given country and, as such, is under the laws and policies of the country of which they are a citizen. Should the Christian obey the laws and policies of their country? There can be no doubt about obeying government. Two classic examples should be sufficient (Rom 13:1–7 and 1 Pet 2:13–14). All authority is given from above, from God. Whether those in authority believe it or not is not the issue. The Christian knows that anyone in a position of authority is placed there by the God who is the source of all authority and power. According to Romans 13:2: "Whoever opposes the existing authority opposes what God has ordered; and anyone who does so will bring judgment on himself."

6. The Christian does not only obey the authority of the State; they do more than that, they show honor and respect to the person in authority. A Christian does not stop with paying what is due to the State, such as various taxes; they do more than that by being honest and by fulfilling the demands of the State for the sake of conscience.

7. Considering the present special situation of our country, the Christian should not think only in terms of paying tax, as if it were sufficient. The Christian should invest their money, time, knowledge, and life, as well as anything else they may treasure, in the interest of their country. A Christian knows that their country is God's gift to them and their posterity. The Christian is part of society, and as such, they should cooperate with governmental as well as other organizations, such as Rural and Urban Associations, in working for the well-being of the Ethiopian people. Everything possible should be done by

the Christian in contributing to the current Green Revolution, so that hunger, one of the three enemies of developing countries, should be done away with.

8. When speaking about obedience to the authority of the State and making contributions of whatever we may have to change the living conditions of the Ethiopian masses for the better, it seems to me to be unfair to pass without expressing my opinion on what I call a very sensitive issue in our situation. The sensitive issue is that there are Christians who debate on the recitation of "slogans." In the program of the National Democratic Revolution of Ethiopia, three archenemies are listed, namely imperialism, feudalism, and bureaucratic capitalism. These are systems to which the Ethiopian masses are firmly opposed. Today, "down with feudalism," "down with capitalism," "down with imperialism" mean simply that as Ethiopians we do not want to live under these systems any longer.

As a matter of fact, feudalism, capitalism, and imperialism are things of the past as far as the Ethiopian masses are concerned. There are other numerous slogans that have cropped up during the various stages of the revolution to inspire people in the progress of the revolution and to urge them to do their part with enthusiasm.

The writer has talked with Christians who believe that reciting slogans is a betrayal of their Christian faith. With all due respect to those who consider repeating slogans as a denial of their commitment to the faith, I think that they are of nonreligious significance, and if slogans are of a nonreligious nature, joining with others in reciting them will have no effect on one's Christian commitment.

9. A Christian should know the essentials of his faith. Ignorance of the central theme of the Scriptures should not be identified with Christian commitment. Our Lord Jesus Christ is the center of our faith. The Old and the New Testaments bear witness to him. We do not believe in a person who died almost two thousand years ago and remained in the grave, but we believe in a person who gave his life as ransom for many and who was raised from death for our justification. In my opinion, a Christian has to make a choice only when he is faced with the demand not to confess Christ as Lord, and when they are denied the right to teach in his name (Acts 4:16–20). Many things were considered "adiaphora" (nonessential for salvation) by the early church, but when it concerned the denial of the person of Christ as Lord, the believers preferred physical death to earthly life and went for martyrdom. The term

martyrdom is derived from a Greek word that means witness. Martyrdom means a believer witnesses for Christ by dying.

10. A responsible Christian does not aggravate any situation and thereby court martyrdom. It is the duty of the Christian to pray for the peace of the country where they are placed by the Creator and work for the well-being of the society of which they are a part (1 Tim 2:1–2). Something that we could not sufficiently remind ourselves of is that to be a Christian is not to be a hero to make a history for oneself. A Christian goes as a lamb to be slaughtered only when they know that this is in complete accord with the will of God who has called them to his service.

11. It should be clearly understood that the good news of Jesus Christ can never be seen as a part of the systems that came about at the various stages in the process of historical development in world history. The gospel is the power of God working in the human heart with a view to transforming man and thereby putting him in a right relationship with God, who is the source and goal of his life, regardless of the stage in the process of historical development at which man finds himself. The Christian gospel refuses to be identified or to be considered as part of feudalism or capitalism, and as such it cannot fade away with these systems, since by its nature the gospel of Christ is totally different from them. Christ himself is the gospel. There is no gospel apart from his presence with us in our daily labor. Christ is the living Lord who was raised from death by God the Father. A living person cannot be identified with any impersonal system. A person can work in any system, and the living Lord Christ commands us to go out and proclaim his presence, the good news. He forgives us our sins and saves us from the bitter experience of sin. Only a living person can perform such things.

12. Recognizing that our day and age is quite different from that of the first century of the Christian era when the apostles of Jesus Christ traveled around the Middle East and Europe preaching the good news of Christ, my assumption is that there are some principles in the New Testament that we should make use of in order to get our cue to be able to chart our way with the guidance of the Holy Spirit. Right at the beginning of his ministry, Jesus of Nazareth was faced with opposition. At times his opponents, the Pharisees, the Sadducees, and searchers of the law, wanted either to arrest him or to kill him. To enable them to achieve their purpose, the opponents of Jesus addressed to him various questions. From some of his replies, we learn that Jesus knew the wish of the evil one but avoided confrontation to show he was someone

great (Matthew 4; Matthew 6). Whenever they wanted to arrest him, Jesus left them and went to another district to carry out his ministry (John 7:44 and 8:59). The supreme purpose of Jesus was to know his Father's will at the right time. Jesus was always in touch with his Father and received guidance for the actions he had to take in the interest of man. When the hour came for him to be sacrificed for the sin of the world, he knew it was the will of God and said, "Father! Your will be done" (Matt 26:39). A Christian should stay in prayer for guidance, so that they know the will of God for any action they may take. If this is not the case, one may be considered as giving oneself for what is less than the will of God, which is human adventure, heroism.

13. A glance at the book of Acts provides us with the basic information that Paul of Tarsus, the apostle of Christ to the gentiles, followed in the footsteps of the Lord Jesus in a life dedicated to constant prayer, searching to know the will of God as he carried out his missionary task. As we know it, Paul did not hesitate to proclaim the whole truth of the gospel of the one who called him to be a missionary, the preacher of the good news of Christ. The world in which Paul understood his ministry was sophisticated in the Greek philosophy of that age and in the Judaism of the time. At this period in world history, the Roman emperors were worshipped as gods. It was in such a tense situation that Paul had to proclaim Christ as Lord, but always avoiding, as much as possible, confrontation or aggravation of the situation. To be sure, Paul was ready to reason with the Jews and the Greeks, but this was a challenge, not an aggravation. Whenever he saw the situation aggravated, Paul had to change his tactics (Acts 23:6–9). This is to say that Paul did not preach the gospel of Christ to create an opportunity for himself to pose as a hero. The supreme purpose in the life of Paul was to know the will of God and follow it regardless of the cost it might entail for his life (see Acts 21:1–13, when he went to Jerusalem). Paul was the seeker of the will of God, and once he was assured of that will, he was ready to submit to it wholly as his Master did. The will of God is the goal of the Christian's life.

Conclusion

It must be crystal clear to the Christian that they have a double purpose to live for:

1. As someone has said, when a person is called to follow Christ, that person is called to die. It means a redirection of the purpose of life

that is death to one's own wishes and personal desires and finding the greatest satisfaction in living for and serving the one who died for us and was raised from death (2 Cor 5:13–14). In other words, the Christian has been crucified with Christ and has no life that they claim to be their own. The life the believer leads is a life of faith, and the risen Lord lives in them (Gal 2:19). It is a life set free from the power of sin, and it is beyond the capacity of death to destroy it. Because it has its source in the resurrection of the Lord Jesus Christ, that resurrection life is at work in the life of the believer. Being in Christ, the Christian is already the possessor of eternal life by being placed in a new order of existence, where the law of life is the love of Christ (2 Cor 5:13). And where the power of the resurrection of the Lord is at work, the life of the Christian is a life of witness to the risen Lord.

2. It has been stated that a Christian is a citizen of a given country and, as such, under the laws and policies of that country. Because they are under the laws of the country of which they are a citizen, it is their duty to pray for the peace of that country and cooperate with their fellow citizens for its well-being. The only limitation to their cooperation or obedience to the laws of their country is if they are commanded to act contrary to the law of God (Acts 5:29).

Source: EECMY Eleventh General Assembly, 1980, Minutes GA-11-55-72, Doc. 3.

PART II

Tsehay Tolessa's Story

Preface to *In the Fiery Furnace*

Lensa Gudina

For you, O God, have tested us;
　　you have tried us as silver is tried.
You brought us into the net;
　　you laid a crushing burden on our backs;
you let men ride over our heads;
　　we went through fire and through water;
yet you have brought us out to a place of abundance.
　　—Psalm 66:10–12

It took me two decades to find the courage I needed to be able to read this book that Aud Sæverås wrote about my parents, *In the Fiery Furnace*. This phrase from the book of Daniel was used repeatedly by my mother during the interviews she had with the author—in a hiding place, for fear of military reprisal—to describe the sufferings she had to endure while in prison.

The book tells of atrocities committed against prisoners by the Ethiopian Military Regime, physical and mental torture committed on men and women, young and old indiscriminately. Ethiopia had become a testing ground for torture equipment, chemical weaponry, and strategies of war from the Soviet Union, Cuba, and the Eastern European countries.

The torturers were ruthless, merciless, brutal wild beasts, as my mother described them. It is impossible to make any sense out of their inhuman acts or why they did them. They considered torture sessions joyous occasions, a time to get drunk and mock victims as they hung them upside down on wooden bars and took turns beating them. They got pleasure from listening to the victims' agonizing screams and seeing the blood dripping down from the beaten bodies. The guard who witnessed my father's brutal assassination told how Mengistu Haile Mariam, the head of the Military Regime, and his officials came to the torture chambers to watch victims being slaughtered.

This is why it took me twenty years to bring myself to read this book. Each time I picked it up and tried to read a section of it, I cried uncontrollably and had to put it down. The book had been translated from its original Norwegian into other Scandinavian languages, German, Swahili, and even Mandarin. We heard that Aud had arranged for an English translation, but before it was finalized she passed away. This is how the English-speaking world has failed to hear the story of a courageous woman who unconditionally loved the Lord despite imprisonment, torture, the loss of a husband she loved dearly, and separation from her children for decades.

The brutal acts, inhumanity, and injustices described in the book may trigger anger, remorse, and outrage in the reader. At the same time, reading of how both my parents responded to the brutality inflicted upon them will demonstrate vividly the power of love, the cost of discipleship, determination, faithfulness, and victory in the way of Christ. My mother was once asked in an interview what she would like to see happen to her tormenters. Her response was: "That they may come to know Christ and through forgiveness inherit the kingdom of God." This kind of response is beyond human understanding. Only through the grace of God can it be achieved.

While reading some sections of the book, I began to wonder whether Aud may have considered naming it "Born to Suffer." My mother's childhood, coinciding with the Italian occupation of Ethiopia, portrays fascism at its worst. Italian soldiers set fire to fields ready for harvest, annihilated innocent villagers, burned whole villages, and scattered families mercilessly, reducing them to poverty and homelessness. Mother managed to escape the wrath of the Italians, who killed her merchant father and made her mother a refugee, only to be kidnapped and abused by slave traders. A traumatic childhood! She was ill-treated, beaten, sick, and starved at the hands of vicious men. A similar kind of brutality recurred many decades later when she found herself in the hands of ferocious military men who took pleasure in shredding her flesh to pieces and breaking her bones as they tortured her.

As I was totally immersed in the thoughts of the indescribable atrocity committed against both of my parents, I was led to reflect on the words spoken to the church of Pergamum in Revelation: "I know where you dwell, where Satan's throne is." This, I thought to myself, could also have been a suitable title for this book: "Where Satan's Throne Is." Such an act of cruelty, savagery, mercilessness, and injustice against the innocent can only be expected in Satan's kingdom. Throughout the different eras and regimes, Ethiopia suffered in this way. Underneath the superficial image that Ethiopia likes to show the rest of the world—as hospitable, never-colonized, biblical—lies inhumanity, injustice, and brutality indescribable in human words. The true stories told in this book expose the ancient Ethiopian camouflage, loaded with fairy tales and myths, while unveiling the true face of Ethiopia.

Heaven and earth will pass away, but my words will not pass away.
—Matthew 24:35

In that dungeon, where my mother was kept for the first thirteen months of her imprisonment, life had become unbearably bitter. She told me that open wounds all over her body were left untreated, her whole body was rotten, full of worms and stench, not to mention the creepy-crawly bugs and the throng of rats that invaded the prison cell every night. She had to lie on a bare cement floor night and day, unable to drink or eat, with nothing to cover her body. The worst of it all, she said, was that no sleep came to her eyes for the first twenty-one days after her first beating. On the twenty-first night, she couldn't stop crying and murmured to herself that she was going to die there and no one would ever find out what had happened. As she uttered those words, she fell asleep and saw Jesus coming toward her, saying, "Do not be afraid. You shall not die here!" He took her by the hand to show her how he was going to bring her out of prison in due time. He said, "You shall pass through four gates to get out of prison, and afterward I will give you a spacious compound where you will reside." After that encounter, she had no more sleepless nights. Her hopes were renewed.

Ten years passed before the promise came true. On the day of her release from prison, she thought of that dark and gloomy dungeon where she saw the extraordinary figure of Christ. As she walked out to freedom and new life, she began to count the gates. When she stepped out of the fourth, she said to herself, "Now I know I am finally free!"

Yet you have brought us out to a place of abundance.
—Psalm 66:12

The fulfillment of the second half of Christ's words, spoken to Mother in that prison cell, took another fourteen years. When she entered the "promised compound," she vowed to set up a church right there to serve and honor him who answered her in the day of her distress and who had been with her wherever she was taken, who never forsook her as she walked through the valley of the shadow of death.

Biftu Bole Mekane Yesus Congregation came as a reward for the long suffering and grief, wounds and bruises, widowhood and loneliness, loss and humiliation. Gudina Tumsa was in his eternal home; on October 12, 2014, Tsehay Tolessa joined him. The passion and selflessness with which God endowed them—passion to take the gospel to all peoples suffering under the bondage of the evil one, passion to reach out to the poor and downtrodden, passion to bring the message of hope to the despairing millions—continues to thrive through the Gudina Tumsa Foundation (GTF) and the Biftu Bole Congregation.

Holistic ministry, which has become synonymous in church circles with the name of Gudina Tumsa, has found a fertile ground among the underprivileged and marginalized persons that the GTF has been serving for the past two decades, addressing their physical and spiritual needs. Biftu Bole is actively engaged in spreading the good news and planting churches in remote areas. There in that "promised compound," a new generation is rising to take the vision forward, a generation that, in the words of the prophet Joel, "march each on his way; they do not swerve from their paths. They do not jostle one another; each marches in his path. . . . The Lord utters his voice before his army, for his camp is exceedingly great; he who executes his word is powerful" (2:7–11).

The year is 2014. Three and a half decades have elapsed since Gudina Tumsa's assassination and Tsehay Tolessa's imprisonment. In the "promised compound" stands the Biftu Bole Congregation. It's Sunday morning and people flock into the church by the hundreds. Tsehay, now in her mid-eighties, takes her seat in the back of the congregation, surrounded by her children and grandchildren. The worship leaders spread out in front of the altar, dressed in traditional Oromo costumes, adorned with colorful beads. They lift up their voices to worship and praise the Lord and the whole congregation joins in singing and dancing. Tsehay, who was once forlorn, battered, and locked up in a dark dungeon, lifts up her arms to worship and praise, remembering God's mercy and faithfulness along that treacherous and dark path of life.

> Truly, truly, I say to you, unless a grain of wheat falls into the earth and dies, it remains alone; but if it dies, it bears much fruit. Whoever loves his life loses it, and whoever hates his life in this world will keep it for eternal life. If anyone serves me, he must follow me; and where I am, there will my servant be also. If anyone serves me, the Father will honor him.
> —John 12:24–26

In the Fiery Furnace

The Story of Tsehay Tolessa and Gudina Tumsa, the Assassinated General Secretary of the Mekane Yesus Church in Ethiopia

Aud Sæverås with Tsehay Tolessa

Originally published in Norwegian as *I Ildovnen* (Oslo: Lunde Forlag, 1992). Translated into German by Antje Meier and Ralph Meier, *Der Lange Schatten der Macht: Augenzeugenbericht: Die Geschichte von Tsehay Tolessa und Gudina Tumsa, dem Ermordeten Generalsekretär der Mekane-Yesus-Kirche in Äthiopien* (Giessen: Brunnen, 1993). Translated into English by Sarah Hinlicky Wilson.

Revised and updated by Lensa Gudina.

All Bible quotations from the English Standard Version.

> Whoever does not bear his own cross and come after me cannot be my disciple.
> —Luke 14:27

Kidnapped and Disappeared

Gudina Tumsa, a church leader and the general secretary of the Mekane Yesus Church in Ethiopia, could not deny his Christian faith. He had to stand by the truth, even if it would cost him his life. On July 28, 1979, he was arrested by the henchmen of a terrorist regime that had officially declared that God did not exist. No one ever saw him again.

His family tried to find him, and many international groups and organizations, in concert with Western governments, tried to exert political pressure on the Ethiopian powers-that-be. They wanted to find out what had happened to Gudina. But there was no answer. Gudina was not to be found—and no one would admit to knowing anything about his disappearance. He appeared simply to have vanished into thin air—but that was hard for those who knew him to believe. A man of such conspicuous size and, furthermore, of such personal charisma doesn't just disappear.

For thirteen long years, the world went without any news of Gudina Tumsa while his wife, Tsehay Tolessa, endured a more-than-decade-long nightmare as a prisoner in an Ethiopian jail. For years, Amnesty International featured her prominently on its list of unjustly imprisoned persons.

Finally, toward the end of the Derg regime under Mengistu Haile Mariam, the dictator of Ethiopia, she was set free. Mengistu's efforts to transform all of Ethiopia into a totalitarian communist state had failed.

Then, on April 28, 1992, the terrible news was shared with the world: the body of Gudina Tumsa had been found near the residence of Ras Asrate Kassa in Addis Ababa, buried in the garden. This palace was already known to be a prison and torture chamber for especially important prisoners of the Ethiopian regime.

The opening of the grave was broadcast live on Ethiopian television. This time there would be no rumors; this time the truth would be brought to light.

The discovery confirmed long-held fears. Gudina Tumsa had become a martyr for the church of Christ in Ethiopia.

But what really happened? What did Gudina Tumsa and his family, his wife and his children, have to endure? That's what I wanted to find out when I visited Ethiopia not long after Tsehay had been set free.

My husband had been one of Gudina Tumsa's closest coworkers in the Mekane Yesus Church, and we had grown very fond of his family. Thus, during my work as a missionary I often visited Tsehay in jail. Anyone who suffers for faith and pays for it with both life and family should not be forgotten by other Christians.

When we visited Tsehay in jail, we had to hand over the food and the other things we'd brought for her for inspection. We were able to speak together but only under the strictest surveillance and at a wide distance from one another. She always greeted us with her hands folded, then stretched them up high over her head. It was a Christian witness that was not allowed to be expressed in words.

Now I wanted to interview her in order to bring to the world in words the witness of God's people in Africa during our times. What follows is the report that she gave me. It was a report that she had never been able to share with anyone else. She was never permitted to express the thoughts that were such a burden upon her, that she had been almost unable to carry. A single word spoken to the public would have put her directly under the shadow of power. During that period, the walls had ears. For this reason, her story remained untold for a long time.

Ethiopia

We know of Ethiopia through the reports of the mass media, and we immediately connect it with famines and endless civil war. But Ethiopia is much more than that.

Immediately north of the equator lies this beautiful land at high altitude, "Africa's roof," in the horn of Africa. It is an old kingdom that was mentioned in several places in the Bible, although the borders of today's Ethiopia have changed a bit.

If a Northerner wants to travel to Ethiopia today, the obvious way is to go by air. In the early morning hours, you float slowly over the land while the fire-red sun rises up higher and higher in the sky. Far below, you see first the dry desert areas before the earth starts getting greener and greener. The landscape is quite varied. If the day is clear, you can plainly make out how the inhabited area is partitioned off into groups of huts with cultivated lands all around. Everywhere the eucalyptus trees grow luxuriantly.

So near to the equator you would expect it to be extremely hot, but the high altitude makes for a pleasant climate. If you experienced this beautiful and varied natural setting, you would easily assume that it was the source of all peace in the world.

But peace is something that the people there have hardly dared to dream of for centuries. The history of Ethiopia is marked by violence and upheaval. Kingdoms rise and fall. One kingdom devours the next, and the suffering of the people is great.

The old cultural territory of Ethiopia consists of many kingdoms. In spite of this, you have the impression that Ethiopia has always been balancing on the edge of a volcano. And sometimes it has simply lost its balance altogether.

But what moves you the most is the people of the land, who take in foreigners with openness and heartfelt warmth. And now we are going to meet these people.

A Daughter of the Land

Tsehay Tolessa, Mrs. "Sun," daughter of Tolessa Boru, wife of Gudina Tumsa.

To meet Tsehay was to encounter a formidable woman: tall, upright, an attractive woman—even after the cruel experiences of her more-than-ten-year detainment in prison. When asked about it, she gladly told that God is a living God who keeps his promises and who was present during the whole time of her need.

She was born in 1931 near the city of Nekemte in the Welega province, northwest of Addis Ababa.

Her world was the huts on the marketplace, which were dominated by a constant coming and going. Her well-to-do family employed many servants. Everyone lived together in a great grass hut that protected them from the heat of the sun by day and the cold by night. You felt just right when everyone was gathered around the warm fire within the hut at sundown while supper cooked in the pot. Then the big and small events of the day were told and you felt the mutual togetherness. Servants and masters were one big family who lived and worked together.

Tsehay's home was a beautiful place with fertile land in the vicinity. The yield of the coffee trees brought in good money. Tolessa Boru, Tsehay's father, counted among the well-to-do farmers. He not only ran cattle-ranching and farming operations but also bought goods that he transported by mule to other vendors. Up to forty fully packed mules on each trip assured not only good earnings but also that everyone had enough to do. Life was good.

In Nekemte, many people felt oppressed and discriminated against since their land was ruled by the Amhara, who in fact lived farther to the east and north. The Oromo and all other ethnic groups in Ethiopia were not allowed to use their own language in written form but had to write in Amharic, which had been declared the national language of the country. Also painful was the annexation of other areas of land by the Amhara. But the little girl understood nothing of such matters yet.

For Tsehay and her siblings, the future looked full of promise. There were five of them altogether, three boys and two girls. Tsehay was the fourth, after the other sister and two boys. Technically she was the fifth child, but the oldest sibling, a boy, had already died at a year old.

That happened in most families; everyone knew of such things. For that reason, people were happy with every single child they got. After Tsehay came another boy into that gaggle of children—three boys who lived! Everything was as it should be.

Dark Clouds

Then the first dark cloud appeared on Tsehay's horizon. The war with Italy had begun in 1935. In 1936, the Italians managed to conquer Nekemte. Italy had counted on it being a trifling matter to take this militarily weak African country in order to get access to the mineral wealth that was there. But it wasn't that easy. The Ethiopians put up fierce resistance, although they had had to suffer terribly under the barbarity of the Italians during the war years.

In the middle of Addis Ababa, there stands a columnar statue depicting human beings piled up on top of each other. It does not symbolize life. Instead, it stands there as a memorial of the great mass of adults and children who were burned alive by the Italians on that very spot as a deterrent and a warning. The column speaks plainly about the barbarity of the Italians. White skin is not an automatic qualification for being civilized.

The Italians afflicted the Ethiopian people with brutal violence. It was felt not only in the cities but also out in the country. The Italians came and seized everything that wasn't nailed down. They didn't ask—they just took. And thus all the belongings of the Ethiopian population disappeared.

The Italians needed vehicles in particular, as there were no cars in the Welega province at that time. The supplies that were always pouring in had to be transported onward to the next location. So again, the Italians simply took whatever vehicles were there. The merchant with mules, Tsehay's father, was forced along with many others to work with the occupying powers.

But it wasn't just ordinary wares that they needed to transport. Tsehay reports:

One day, a coworker of my father came screaming and running into our house. One of the mules had veered off course from the caravan and was heading directly for the house. The animal wanted something to eat. It could have tipped over along the path at any time—and the mule was carrying grenades on its back.

"Out! Quickly! Out of the hut! Get the children out of the way!" bellowed the man as loudly as he could. He was scared to death, imagining what might happen. A great panic reigned—everybody tumbled out of the huts and ran into the thickets. At the last moment, the man managed to grab the animal and tie it up. The dangerous goods could now be unloaded carefully and were stored just as carefully in the hut for the time being.

After this experience, my father didn't want to transport such burdens anymore.

"You have to," said the Italians.

"No," replied Father. "These sorts of goods I will not transport. I refuse to work for you Italians anymore."

Not long afterwards, they forced him to transport goods to Gimbi anyway. Then we got news that he was sick. Since he had refused to obey the Italians, they poisoned his food.

In absolute despair, Mother borrowed a mule from her father and made her way to her husband. The distance was great and she ran for her life to get there as quickly as possible. But by the time she arrived, Father had not only already died but was even buried.

There stood Mother. Alone. Desperate. Powerless. And all the mules! In any event, she had to find the mules. They were her whole fortune; they were her source of income. Mother searched and searched, but she never found the mules.

"They are dead," said the people. No one would help her, and no one looked after her. Someone must have gotten rich off those mules. All of them had disappeared. She came back home with empty hands.

On top of everything else, Mother was pregnant. In the midst of all these problems, of all these difficulties that she had to manage all by herself, she brought a little boy into the world, my youngest brother.

It was a very hard time: Mother had to be both mother and father to us. Today I admire how she managed to pull it off! We had lost so much, which made it harder to deal with. One servant after another had to be let go. It was impossible for the household to continue as before—Mother had to take care of more and more of the work alone. She tilled the land, cared for us children, cooked the food, and drew water. And we, the children, had to help with ever more difficult tasks. Our family that used to have it so good was now fighting for mere survival.

One day, my mother gave my oldest sister away in marriage. The times were so dangerous for young women, as many were molested by the Italians. And after a rape the outlook for marriage was no longer good.

Therefore, it was important to marry a girl off as soon as possible. My sister was just fourteen years old, but it was not uncommon then to marry so young. Besides that, it was one less mouth to feed, and in this hard time you had to arrange things as well as you could.

Everyone dreamed of the day when the Italians would shove off and leave the country. The Ethiopians fought for freedom and dreamed about it.

The Italians Strike Hard

It happened: by 1941 the Italians could no longer hold on, militarily speaking, and had to pull out of Ethiopia. But again sheer horror descended: the Italians used the "scorched earth" tactic in their withdrawal. They may have had to cede the land back to the Ethiopians, but the Ethiopians weren't going to get anything out of it. The Italians just set huge areas on fire.

It was morning in Tsehay's hut, but this morning was different from normal.

The family woke up as usual. Mother was always up first to make breakfast. Before everything was ready, she wanted as usual to go for a minute over to the neighboring hut of Grandmother and Grandfather. Carefully Mother pushed away the mat hanging in the entryway to go out.

I took the opportunity to tag along, for it was always nice to go to Grandfather and Grandmother's.

Suddenly the air was filled with screams of terror. What on earth was going on? Tsehay peered out—the whole horizon was up in flames! At the same time, the cries of neighbors could be heard: "The Italians are coming. They're going to kill us all. They're burning our huts down! Run for your lives! They're already nearby. Take the children and run!"

Mother stood there helplessly for a moment. That's what you do when in a split second your life shatters into a thousand pieces. Then she came to her senses and disappeared into the hut. She packed up us children just as we were. There was no time to think of provisions. There was no time to take anything along.

It was a matter of life and death. She took the smallest of us on her hip and pushed the rest of us forward. "Children, run! Come on!"

All the neighbors screamed as they ran away. People tumbled out of their huts to save their skins. Everything else had to be left behind—the only goal was to reach the thickets in the hope of not being discovered there.

Together the horrified people ran under cover through the thorn bushes, between coffee trees, toward the thickets on the riverbank. We ran barefoot without even noticing how the thorns were tearing up our feet and legs. Blind fear drove us on. "Psst! Psst! They must not see us. Keep crouching down! Lie down flat so they won't see us!"

And then the Italians came into view. Wildly shooting all around them, they came on the attack with their bayonets pointed outward. Children and adults who hadn't found a hiding place in time were wantonly slaughtered. Blood flowed and people groaned and wailed while the Italians mercilessly threw burning torches on the dry straw roofs of the huts. In a flash, everything went up in flames.

Sometimes I dream of that day. It comes into my mind again and again. I see the terrible flames and the poor people who were still in their huts, who didn't have the chance to get out. They were burned beyond recognition. And all that occurred out of a naked lust for murder. The Italians pursued the fleeing people and stabbed them with their bayonets until they were dead.

The whole village stood in flames. What did Tsehay's mother think and feel in that moment? Who can say? Her despair can only be guessed at. But all eight members of her family were still alive—that at least was something—even Grandmother and Grandfather had been able to get to safety. At the same time, her fear for her oldest daughter was great. Did she survive as well? And where would they all go now?

For the rest of the day, they lay low so as not to be found. At least their clothes were the same color as the sand, so it wasn't easy to spot them. Food? No one even thought of it on that day.

Slavehunters

Finally that terrible day came to an end and darkness set in. Hyenas! Jackals! The thought of wild animals got the adults and children moving with terror again. Normally hyenas wouldn't attack people, but anyone who went to sleep out in the open was in danger, a tempting prey for the predators.

Desperation gave Mother courage. She darted over to us and said we should lie down to sleep near our neighbors. She herself crept over to the huts during the night in order to pick some coffee beans that were still hanging on the trees. Naturally, that was dangerous.

We had to hide in the wilderness for many days without getting anything to eat. Finally, we reached a village that was more than a day's march away from our house. There Mother sought a fresh start in a small, miserable hut that belonged to an acquaintance of ours.

A mother with small children would try as well as she could to prevent them from falling into the hands of abductors—still necessary at that time. We always lived in fear of being captured by slavehunters and being taken away. There was no longer much respect for human life, and the sale of slaves was a good source of income.

The thought of how terrible the life of an enslaved family was didn't cause the slavehunters any concern.

In the midst of this time of horrors, it happened again. The mother and father of a family that used to live near us didn't arrive at a prearranged meeting point. One of their daughters was also nowhere to be found. Their two other children, a boy and a girl, had joined us during our flight. Suddenly they couldn't find their family anymore—they had disappeared without a trace.

The thought of slavehunters gave you a shiver all down your spine. Poor children! But Mother looked after them. They stayed with us the whole time, and Mother took them in as her own children. But how was Mother supposed to take care of herself and her own children and these children too and look after their food and everything else they might need? Often we had absolutely nothing left. Yes, it could happen that we went for five days at a time without anything to eat.

Together with my grandparents, we lived in this way for three years in a simple hut. Then something else happened. I was about seven and a half years old and still remember that evening.

Mother had already made a fire on the floor in the middle of the hut. There she crouched by the fire and made coffee. The girl that Mother had taken in along with her brother had borrowed Mother's dress and sat with us other children by Mother while she was getting everything ready.

Suddenly a man jumped in at us through the hut entrance. We drew together and, terrified, screamed in chorus.

In a moment, the man had grabbed the girl and also us other children. Mother threw herself on top of us to hang on. We cried and screamed. The man and his companion beat Mother fearsomely in order to get her away from us. They beat her so brutally in the face that her teeth fell out and blood flowed.

Mother couldn't hang on to us against the superior force of the abductors, and they disappeared with us. Against such great force, she had no chance.

Everywhere in the huts people were crying. The abductors had struck every one of them. They stole everything they could find. They combed through our hut, too. Mother lost everything, even her children!

It's hard to put oneself into her state of despair. I only remember what fear I felt when the men beat us and made off with us double time. But they really had to hurry to get out of there. So after a short time, they left behind all those who couldn't keep up with their tempo. That was our salvation: my brother and I were free again.

Battered and miserable, we came crying back home. They had taken nine children away with them—and they never came back again. Oh, we thought of how awful it must be to be slaves. I remember how Mother cried.

Many years later, I found out more about what had happened. I was already Gudina's wife and had two children myself. While Gudina was away on a trip, a woman came up and spoke to him. She was the disappeared sister of the two children that were stolen from us. Gudina brought her home to us, and she told us how she and her parents had been captured by the slavehunters. These slavehunters were not just any old criminals. They were soldiers of Commander Kebede Tessema, leader of the provincial administrative authority.

The soldiers had taken the captives with them and sold them to rich people in Gojjam in the Ethiopian highlands—people who spoke other languages. The same fate befell the other children who had been taken from us. She herself managed to flee sometime later. Now she lived in a far-off place.

One day she had heard of Gudina and his wife Tsehay Tolessa. She recognized the name of my father and inquired whether Gudina had gotten married to the daughter of Tolessa Boru. Yes, that was the case—and in this way we learned how it all turned out.

After the robbers had stolen our things, everything was hard again. All of our miserable possessions had been taken from us. The same happened to Grandfather and Grandmother and also to the people around us. Terrible. Who could help us? Who could free the children that had been stolen from us? And Mother had not one single dress to wear. Her only dress was the one she'd lent to the girl when the slavehunters pounced on us. With them, her only dress was gone too. Luckily a relative had pity on her and bought Mother a dress.

Soon after, we moved again. We didn't dare to stay in that place any longer. My two oldest brothers were sent to relatives because Mother was no longer in a position to take care of them. In Ethiopia, it was customary for relatives to help one another. Those of us who were left built ourselves a simple little hut to live in.

Now Tsehay, at the age of eight, was the oldest child at home and the most important helper for her mother in the care and upbringing of her two little brothers.

The Typhus Epidemic

My mother was so depleted after everything that had happened to her that it seemed as though all her strength had been used up.

We were small and it was an enormously difficult time, with much hard, unfamiliar labor. We children had to learn early on how to help her. For that I am actually thankful, for amidst all the hardships we got a good education, and Mother didn't need to feel so worn down.

In spite of that, it seemed that Mother's will to live had finally been broken. She was already quite drained when then the next blow came. A typhus epidemic struck. The lamentation was great—in one hut after another the people got sick, and the families could only look on helplessly. There was nothing they could do; their laments reached up to heaven. In retrospect, it is not hard to understand that the people were exhausted after the many cruel experiences they'd had. Their power of resistance was no longer very great.

Weak as she now was, Mother quickly became sick. The situation was a desperate one, and for the neighbors all around it was just as hard. Everyone was impoverished after the war and its horrible results, and when they got sick many died, very many of them. In every house there was death. The whole village was in despair. We children also got sick.

Mother, who had no strength left at all, died very quickly.

Although I was then just eight years old, I grasped that something terrible had happened. I had a high fever myself—and we had nothing to eat. The situation was desperate.

What were we to do? My sister came and took us home with her. She cared for us as well as she could, but after a short time she also got sick. Everything was getting worse and worse.

Things couldn't go on that way, and in the end someone brought us to the mission hospital in Nekemte. There we met Sister Ruth Perman, a Swedish missionary nurse. I will never forget how she cared for us. She knew the Oromo language, too, so we could understand her.

One of my brothers was too weak to be able to fight against the sickness. He died in the hospital. My sister got well again so she could travel back home, but my other brother and I needed time to recuperate. Bit by bit we got better again. But how was I, an eight-year-old, supposed to survive on my own? And what was to become of my little brother?

We were lucky. Sister Ruth took care of us and helped us get a place in the school dormitory. We were allowed to attend the mission school and live in the dorm.

When I look back on it now, how God has led me through life, I recognize how much good he has done me. When Mother died, I didn't want to go to live with her relatives. I wanted so much to start school. My sister had enough to do with her own family. I wanted so much to learn something—and God was good to me. In school, I got knowledge not only for my mind but also for my soul.

In the years to come, the workers at the mission station cared for me with exceptional affection. Sister Ruth was like a mother to me. Later, Elsa and Torsten Persson came to Nekemte, and Elsa was also like a mother to me. They sang Christian songs with me and told me about Jesus. In their house I got to know God.

Torsten Persson was a pastor, and he got me acquainted with the Bible. In all things they both helped me. We wrote letters to each other all the time, and while I sat in prison, they used up many ballpoint pens for my sake!

Their daughter Signe married a Norwegian missionary, Rydland. They were missionaries in Ethiopia for many years, and Signe was like a sister to me.

Signe visited me later in prison, and it was always a great joy to see her there. I remember her last visit. She cried. And later when I was in the hospital, Signe asked after me. "Is Tsehay seriously ill? Does she suffer much?"

I can see her before me still, and how much she cried over me—the way you cry over a good friend who lies at death's door. I cannot give back her tears. I give back prayers instead. If someone will cry so much for my sake, I will pass the tears onward to God.

We haven't been able to see each other again.

Nekemte

Nekemte is a beautiful green place with high rustling eucalyptus trees. All around lie fruitful fields in which wheat and corn are cultivated. The climate is pleasant, not too warm and not too cold, the way it can be in Addis Ababa. Sufficient rainfall is the reason for the fruitfulness of the countryside.

The mission station with its school dormitory and many residences stands high and free on the hillside. It offers instruction from first to sixth grade. Below in the valley, the river snakes through the most fertile area of Nekemte. The mission station was founded by Swedish missionaries of the Swedish Evangelical Mission (*Evangeliska Foster-lands-Stiftelsen*).[1] The names of Swedes who supported the missions during the nineteenth century, such as Lina Sandell and Carl Olof Rosenius, are still well known today.

The hospital attached to the mission station not only creates work for many people but also provides adequate housing for them. The very visible church on the heights is closely connected with the parsonage.

I remember that Sister Ruth kept some animals. She even had pigs, which is rare in Ethiopia. The Ethiopians—like Jews and Muslims—view the pig as an unclean animal. They don't even want to touch it.

In Nekemte it was as if I were at home. It was not that far from the old house of my father. From nine to twelve in the mornings we went to school. Then was the midday break, and school resumed from three to five in the afternoon. After school there was always a lot to do still. We cleaned the house and washed our clothes. Until late in the evening we did our homework. But we managed well—we were still young then. There was water on the premises so we didn't have to run to the river to draw water. The house where we lived was made of stone—quite different from the huts that I had lived in before.

In the dorm we also got our food. Naturally we had to help with its preparation, but it was good for us. I was already used to working from the hut where I used to live.

Tsehay went to school for six years. She learned easily and loved school. After finishing her schooling, she got work in the children's home, which had been established for orphaned children from the hospital. Signe and Allan Stefansson took over responsibility for the children's home.

Pastor Allan and Signe were like a good father and a good mother to me. Later on they even gave me away at my wedding.

Seventy-three children lived in the children's home, and of those, twenty had come from Addis Ababa—healthy children of leprous parents.

In Addis Ababa, there was in fact a house for lepers, and sick people from all parts of Ethiopia came there. It is terrible to be afflicted by this awful disease. Since the children can no longer live with their parents for fear of infection, it was necessary to bring them to a location far away until there was no longer any risk of infection.

Tsehay was like a mother to these children. She wanted to take care

---

1. Trans. note: "Evangelical" in European usage generally means "Protestant" and often means "Lutheran." It does not have the same connotation as "evangelical" in North America.

of them and give them the love they needed. Tsehay gave to the children all of her care, a protective care that she had experienced from her own mother in her early childhood and later from the missionaries in Nekemte. Once again Tsehay had a large family.

Life was tragic for these children. And I thought a lot about their mothers. For this reason, I gave them so much love and care. For four years I was their mother, and I loved them. God had entrusted them to me.

Love at First Sight

God gave even more to Tsehay. For there in Nekemte, the tall, beautiful young woman met an even taller and slender young man: Gudina Tumsa. He was exactly two meters tall—nearly 6′7″. Gudina Tumsa had just completed his training as a surgeon's assistant in the hospital. It was love at first sight.

I had had a number of suitors before, seventeen or eighteen of them. But Gudina was the only one that I wanted. I was so in love with him. And I saw how devout he was. That made an impression on me.

Gudina fell in love with me, too, and asked for my hand in marriage two years later.

The wife of the doctor reported at home: "You know what I saw today? Gudina and Tsehay, hand in hand!"

In Ethiopia that was very unusual. People only went hand in hand with friends. But these two were so in love with each other.

I wanted him or nobody! For that reason, all the hard things that happened later were so difficult. It hurts because we loved each other so much. This weight presses on my chest like a stone. But I must keep it to myself; I cannot burden another with it. They would not endure it.

Gudina from Boji

Gudina was born in 1929 in Boji, to the west of Addis Ababa. His family was Ethiopian Orthodox, not Lutheran.

Gudina's uncle was a *qaaluu*, which is the Oromo word for an animist who makes contact with the spirit world and demonic spirits and offers sacrifices to the demons so that they will be pacified and to prevent bad luck. The *qaaluu* had great authority and power in the society since the belief in spirits, even in Orthodox circles, was great.

In Boji, there was a primary school run by two Ethiopians. These two teachers were Lutheran Christians, and they took every opportunity to tell their pupils about Jesus.

Gudina had a great desire to go to school, but his parents wanted him to help his father on the farm. The yearning he had to learn was so strong that he defied his parents' command and attended school anyway.

There in school Gudina heard the gospel. He heard about Jesus, the redeemer, the Son of God, who loved people so much that he died for them all in order to give them eternal life. And Jesus was stronger than Satan and all the other evil spirits. Whoever accepted Jesus no longer needed to make offerings to spirits, because Jesus had triumphed over all powers.

Gudina accepted this message and immediately drew the consequences of his faith. He went home and felled the great tree where the locals always offered their sacrifices, as they believed that the spirits lived in the tree. And the spirits always had to be humored with constant sacrifices that the people left nearby or blood smeared on the tree. That was the way to keep illness and need at bay—so thought the people.

So Gudina cut that tree down. He believed in God and, therefore, had no fear. He never had any fear. If ever he thought he had to do something, he never hesitated.

In chopping down the worship tree, Gudina brought the wrath of the people upon himself. "You are ruining everything," they said. Gudina had to get out of town as fast as possible. From then on, because he wasn't willing to renounce his faith in the gospel, he had to depend on himself to get by.

There was no other option for Gudina—he had to leave the area. He went to the village of Najo to a mission station that, just like the mission station in Nekemte, was run by the Swedish Evangelical Mission.

Gudina was a ten-year-old child, but now he had to look out for himself, all alone in the world. Luckily, he was able to live in the school dormitory. He was able to work for the missionaries in the garden there. That way he earned enough to live on, and he stayed in that school for about two years. That it was a strenuous time made no difference—the decisive matter for Gudina was that he was doing the right thing.

The Prayer Meeting

Gudina's only fear was that he might do something contrary to God's will, opposing the Holy Spirit. And one experience from that time, which he told about much later, is characteristic of him. In his words:

It was while we were going to the mission school in Najo. We had Bible instruction and were to be trained as surgeon's assistants. All the pupils lived in the mission compound together—in small groups in little wooden houses with corrugated iron roofs.

Each evening before we went to bed, we boys read the Bible together. We prayed together and spoke about what we'd read. One evening, I heard a boy near me praying, "Dear God, take your Holy Spirit away from me! I don't want to preach anymore. I don't want to be in your service anymore!"

I jumped up and cried, "What's wrong with you? That is the sin against the Holy Spirit!"

But my friend continued his terrible prayer: "Please let me be a pharmacist's apprentice, and show me how I can earn money so I can take good care of my family. Oh, my God, take your Holy Spirit from me, so that he stops driving me to preach! I don't want to proclaim your word anymore! I want to be a good surgeon's assistant and a good pharmacist and nothing more!"

I tried again to stop him, and again I was angrily refused by my indignant friend. He said, "I don't want to preach anymore! I just want to learn a trade. The Holy Spirit should look for someone else."

I will never forget that evening. It was terrible. Who can oppose the power of the Holy Spirit? I never would have risked it! I also—just like my friend—received the education to be a surgeon's assistant. I worked in many provinces as a surgeon's assistant—but at the same time I always preached the gospel and prayed with people, and in this way, I was always pointing to Christ. But my friend opened his own practice and earned good money.

God's call and God's will were the decisive thing for Gudina. Nothing would be able to lure him away from them.

Bad News

After about two years in Najo, Gudina traveled to Nekemte to continue school and further his training. His family still refused to have anything to do with him—to say nothing of helping him. They didn't want to know anything about his faith. Without parental support, he languished from lack of food and clothing.

While Gudina was in Nekemte, his father, Tumsa Silga, died. He was originally a farmer and supported himself with farming. But on the side, he also ran a thriving cotton business.

One day, he was on a trip deep in the Blue Nile Valley to buy cotton. After the transaction was finished and he had started on his homeward journey, he suddenly felt unwell. He quickly got worse, and on the steep uphill path he could hardly breathe. Tumsa realized quickly what was wrong with him. His business partner had mixed poison into his final meal. The way home was terrible agony. Despite fierce pains, he fought his way back home, but in the end the effort was too much for him. The pains overpowered him and he died. Gudina was sixteen years old at the time.

While in Nekemte, Gudina got engaged to Tsehay. Soon afterwards, he got the news from home that his mother had also died. It was clear to Gudina that he'd have to look after his younger siblings who were still at home. Tsehay explains:

"Oh," he said to me, "Mother is dead! I must hurry home to the little ones."

It must have been a hard trip back to Boji. He hadn't seen his mother or father for many years. Now they were both dead. But there had been no way to go home as long as he remained in Christ. And at home there was nothing left for him to inherit. The family of his father had taken everything—after all, Gudina was gone.

Gudina found his little siblings, a sister named Dinadge and two brothers, Negasa and Baro. He quickly decided to take them with him. They had no belongings or even the smallest bag. Gudina arrived on foot with all three of them. I still remember their arrival perfectly. Dr. Gunnar plucked a pretty rose and gave it to Gudina. "Your mother is now dead," he said, "and this is to remind you that you have a new one now, a new rose for yourself—you have received Tsehay in her place."

I will never forget that.

The problem now was what to do with these three children, since we didn't have enough space. The room we got after our wedding was just barely big enough for the two of us. But the missionaries were good to us and gave the sister and brothers a place in the school dormitory and permission to go to school.

Fortunately, Gudina had begun to work during this time. He worked as a surgeon's assistant in the hospital while at the same time keeping busy with preaching the gospel in the area. Everyone had to have a chance to hear the gospel; that was important to him. His siblings also accepted the gospel and became Christians. That was a great joy.

The Wedding

We got married on a Saturday, a wonderfully beautiful day. Our friends butchered a whole ox and several sheep and prepared a lovely feast in the big hall of the hospital. We got so many nice presents!

I had already been a mother for the little children in the children's home for several years by then. On this day, they all got dressed up festively and arranged themselves in a receiving line with flowers and candles, all seventy of them! It was such a wonderful thing to see.

So we got married, and for a while I could work in Pastor Allan Stefansson's house. We needed the money, and anyway I was very pleased to be there. We moved into a little house, a room with a little kitchen, that was in the neighborhood of the hospital where Gudina worked.

A year went by. Then we were given our little Emmanuel. He was big and strong. I don't know how much he weighed exactly. But our last child was also big, and he weighed almost ten and a half pounds. And that's no small amount, is it?

Emmanuel arrived on schedule, but it was a difficult birth. I was very skinny and had immense difficulties bringing that big child into the world. I fought for three days. Fortunately, I was brought to the hospital where the doctors did everything in their power to help, so it all turned out well in the end.

And God rescued me—early in the morning, the baby finally arrived. All our friends came storming in and congratulated me. When I came home four days later, the ladies brought me the "labor porridge," as was our custom.

But my husband was not at home. He was on the road, evangelizing, as he did at every free moment. Not even this could keep him at home, so he wasn't there when his first child came into the world. But I managed just fine while he was away.

Emmanuel was a lovely little boy, and we enjoyed the time with him. He learned to walk early—after only nine months he was walking! He was a magnificent child. In addition, I worked during the day at the Stefanssons'. That went well, since I had a girl at home who looked after Emmanuel while I worked.

The Tragedy

Then it happened. I remember it as well as if it were yesterday. Emmanuel was already a year old. My little sunshine toddled jauntily on his crooked little legs through the neighborhood. On that day, I needed to go to work, as always, and leave the boy in the care of the young woman, as usual.

But I felt that something bad was going to happen. It is rare, but I have known each time beforehand when something really terrible was about to happen. It was the same on that day. I didn't know why nor who would be struck, but something told me that I shouldn't leave Emmanuel in the girl's care that day. For that reason, I put him in another woman's care that day. But what could happen? It was a morning just like any other.

Then I went to work. A short time later I got a call.

"What's wrong?" I shouted. "Is my child dead?"

"No," they answered, "but he has inhaled a dried corn kernel and it is stuck in his throat."

The weather was at that time already very dry, and Emmanuel loved picking little things up off the ground and shoving them in his mouth.

I ran to my child and saw that he was hardly able to breathe at all. I drove with him to the hospital, but they weren't able to help him in Nekemte. He had to be brought to Addis Ababa immediately and be operated on there.

I nearly lost hope. Addis Ababa was far away and the road was not good. But this time Gudina was at home, so we could drive together. We wrapped the boy in a blanket and Gudina took him in his arms. The hospital doctor drove us with his car to the city.

The journey lasted the whole day. We drove in a cloud of dust, and we shook and bumped along. Our hearts bled for our little treasure, whose need for air was getting ever more dire. Would we arrive in time?

The road was longer than ever to us that day. But Emmanuel was still alive when we arrived at the hospital in Addis Ababa. Immediately the doctors began with the operation, and after a while he was doing passably well. But on the fifth day he suffocated and died. How poor and miserable we felt in the big city with his little body in our arms.

We bought a little coffin in which we laid him. Then for two hundred Birr we rented a car—more than three months' wages. In Ethiopia, it is expensive to transport corpses. The rental agencies know perfectly well that mourners are totally dependent on cars since the burial has to happen quickly, if possible even on the day of death. We drove back to Nekemte to bury our little Emmanuel there.

The book of Daniel tells of three young men thrown into a fiery furnace. But there, in the midst of the flames, God was with them. So it was with us also. For that reason, I can still praise his name, even though I lost my little boy and later another of my sons as well.

I know that those who have never experienced such calamities know little about what kind of God we have, what a great God we have, who himself is with us in all our tests and trials. Therefore, I thank him that I was able to know him, and how great and glorious he is in all things. I am not the same person today that I was twenty-eight years ago. Everything that I endured changed me and drove me much closer to God.

When things are going well and we don't have any pressing need to seek for God's presence, we think about him only now and then. But in this situation, Gudina and I experienced God near to us and accompanying us.

The way home lasted a day and a night. When we drew close to our goal, our friends and neighbors came to meet us. They came to mourn with us. For ten days, we had a house of mourning. The neighbors brought us food and stayed with us, standing by us in our grief. It was hard to lose sweet little Emmanuel. The path from the greatest happiness to the deepest grief was so short.

Pastoral Training

There was something else that helped me cope: for three years already I had wanted one of our sons to become a pastor. When little Emmanuel came along, I was not surprised that he was a boy—surely he was the one to become a pastor. Just like Hannah in the Old Testament, I had promised him to God.

But now little Emmanuel was dead. He would never become a pastor—so, therefore, Gudina had to become a pastor in his place, even if people in Ethiopia said that a pastor was as worthless as a woman. "You have to!" I said. "You must become a pastor! I made the promise three years ago already!"

We began to pray to find out whether there was a call from God for Gudina.

Ten months later, I had another child, a little girl we named Kulani. She also was born in Nekemte, and this time Papa was around and helped. He had already been trained as a surgeon's assistant and could see to the delivery. After the birth I stopped working. I could not imagine ever letting another person look after my child again.

And then Gudina received the call. The church asked him to become a pastor. That may sound strange—Gudina already had work as a surgeon's assistant and plenty to do. But it was the answer to our prayers, the confirmation of a calling that God had first laid upon me. Yes—it was, after all, God's will.

A difficult time lay before us. The educational center for pastors was in Najo, so we had to move there. Kulani was just one month old. I remember well the day we moved out.

"This will definitely not be easy," I thought. We had not a drop of water for the trip, and the sun burned hot upon the dusty road. Only someone who has experienced such a journey knows how the dust penetrates through every fiber of your clothes and practically into your body.

I prayed to God that we would arrive all right with our little child. The majority of our belongings we'd sold off before the trip because we had no way of transporting them. We could only take along what we ourselves could carry, and that wasn't much.

There was no housing option at the theological seminary in Najo for married students. Gudina had already scoured the town and found a little place for us. It was located in the city, just a short walk from the school.

It was not exactly a home that awaited us—there was not so much as a mattress to lie on. When we arrived, we had to begin with the setup and didn't dare to allow ourselves to think how exhausted we were.

Heavy Burdens

Our house was dilapidated, dark, and uncomfortable. And it was even a two-family house. We lived wall to wall with Pastor Gammachu and his family, who quickly became close friends of ours. Pastor Gammachu was much older than my husband. He had married late, and later still began his theological studies. But he was in good health and managed all right. The Gammachus had two children at the time, and we ended up having a really good relationship with our neighbors.

We had to take care of all the basic necessities for the house ourselves. We had nothing beyond the basics anyway. Everything was as simple as could be—everyone had their own key, which hung on the wall. There were only the most essential kitchen utensils.

At that time, nobody thought of teaching women as well as men. And in fact, we had to work so hard that it would have been impossible to find the time to do so anyway. We not only had to take care of our children, but just to fetch water we had to run some distance to a well. We went to the well with empty pitchers and then had to carry the water home on our backs.

That really was drudgery. The pitcher contained about five gallons—and it was very heavy to carry back. It took fifteen minutes to get to the well. The well was deep, and we had to scoop the water out laboriously by ourselves. And then there was the trip home that took even longer because of the full pitcher on our backs.

I was not used to that, which is what made it so taxing. Sometimes I had to fetch water four times in a single day—which meant back and forth each time. But you have to have plenty of water in the house when you have a little child. Happily, an old lady in the neighborhood looked after Kulani while I went to get the water.

In the area, there was no mill, so I had to grind the grain myself by hand between two big rocks. But I was young then and could take it. Today I would never manage. And above all I wanted to do everything I could for the people I loved.

I often worked until late in the evening. Many guests came to the house. That meant making coffee and roasting grain to serve to them. And then there was the floor to clean, the laundry to wash with as little water as possible, and tidying up. Those were hectic days.

Sometimes we picked corn, and then I would have to strip the kernels off the cobs with my fingers. The kernels were cooked or roasted over the fire.

I got the firewood for the cooking myself. I just went into the thicket and collected both light and heavy wood and carried the heavy burden back home. I chopped branches off the bushes and trees, and when I came home I chopped them up into convenient sizes. Long logs were needed that could be pushed bit by bit into the fire until they were all burned up.

Gudina went every day on foot to the theological seminary outside of the city. When he finished his pastoral training and started to work, he still went everywhere on foot, often far distances. He even went as far as forty miles away to preach.

We had sixty Birr each month to live on. That had to cover everything—and it was hard. But God's goodness is great—and we had it good together. Gudina always showed love and concern, and whenever he did get angry it never lasted more than five minutes before he came and apologized.

In Ethiopian families, it is quite common for a husband to hit his wife and even drive her out of the house whenever he is dissatisfied with her. It was never like that between us—our house was always a house of peace. We made it cozy for ourselves, told nice stories, and laughed a lot together. We read a lot in God's word and often prayed together. Yes, we had a really happy marriage.

In all those years, Gudina never liked to be at home if I wasn't there; he would wait outside for me before going in.

When the children came, they also showed a great deal of mutual love and took care of each other. They say that when they have the chance to start their own families, they hope to have the same kind of loving relationships that we did.

Bringing the Gospel to the World

The tiny salary in Najo made it difficult for us to manage. We often went without necessary things. Finding food to eat was often difficult, to say nothing of clothing. Gudina never complained. I was a mother and had to take care of my children; I wanted him to take the time to locate the things we needed.

"No!" Gudina said. "Instead let us use our time and strength to build God's kingdom."

And with that he was off and running to found a new congregation or church. God wants us to seek his kingdom first. Then he will provide the other things we need, too. Even if that didn't exactly mean abundance, we experienced it to be true. God keeps his promises. But God's kingdom must come first. That was Gudina's life motto, and it became mine, too. By and by, I learned that this was the right path to take.

But I also felt that the afflictions of Satan were always coming at us. Take, for example, prayer. At the very moment of prayer, Satan sticks all other possible thoughts in our heads. It is a battle to remain steadfast in prayer when everything else wants to interpose between us and God. These afflictions come because it is so important for us to put God first in our lives—and that is what God's adversary wants to prevent.

Already during his studies, Gudina was on fire to preach the gospel. He constantly gathered people around him with whom he prayed. He gathered evangelists around him and gave them instruction. He walked, taking the gospel with him—and walked and walked. Often he walked far; he could go for a good six or eight hours on foot in order to host gatherings. Then he would spend the night before coming home again. People gladly took him in. And everywhere they accepted the gospel in droves and became Christians.

"Help us build a little church," they asked. Such requests got to Gudina, and again and again he returned to these places to teach them.

Once he met with a female qaaluu, a necromancer. This woman had been practicing her sorcery for thirty-five years. There and then she accepted the gospel and destroyed all her conjuring paraphernalia. From then on, she used all her time to bring the Bible close to people. She lived for the Bible.

And she wasn't the only one: many qaaluus came to faith and began new lives. They were freed from their dependence on the occult. They had been delivered from it.

"Come to God, and you will be redeemed!" Gudina invited them. And they came. One time a qaaluu tried to stop him, but that happened less and less often. Most of those Gudina came in contact with turned to God and became Christians. More resistance came from the Ethiopian Orthodox Christians. They

didn't like his preaching about the gospel. "That is foreign doctrine," they said, "an absolutely foreign doctrine."

Only a year after we moved to Najo, our third child came along—a little girl. Later, still in Najo, I brought another boy into the world, and then we had two more children, a boy and a girl. They were born after we'd moved back to Nekemte. All my children were born in a hospital, though the two in Najo were born in the big clinic there.

Aster, our girl born in Najo, was very frail, as we once again endured a terrible epidemic. The city was struck with diphtheria. It is terrible when such epidemics come. Many, many people got sick and died. My little Aster was also terribly sick, and we feared that she would die. But she survived. I don't know how I would have been able to endure it if I had lost her then. The death of our little Emmanuel was always still so close.

Back to Nekemte

We lived in Najo for two and a half years. Life there pushed me to my limits. Then I got a chance to return to Nekemte with the children. We lived there in the school dormitory while Gudina pursued his last year of pastoral training in Najo.

I didn't see Gudina that whole time. It was hard—but traveling during that time was no trifling matter. So I had to deal with all the difficulties alone. Again, I became totally emaciated and had no strength left. But the missionaries looked after me—some of them looked after my children so I'd be able to work a bit in the missionaries' houses and have enough money to live on. In that way, we struggled along during the second year.

When Gudina was done with his course in Najo, he joined us in Nekemte, where he was to continue with one more year of education. All in all, it took three difficult years for him to finish his training to be a pastor.

When Gudina came back, we moved into our old house again, which had been rented out during our stay in Najo. Again, we had to manage everything for ourselves, for once again we could hardly take along any of our stuff from Najo. But I had already acquired some things during the year that I had lived in the dormitory. Moreover, we got a lot from "my family," the Stefanssons, which helped us greatly.

But still, it was no bed of roses. Gudina traveled a lot in the surrounding district, and most of the time he went on foot. That meant that he was often away for long periods at a time. So I was alone with the children a lot and had to manage by myself. During the week, he was occupied with his studies at school, and over every weekend he disappeared into the surrounding area. Everywhere he proclaimed the gospel, people came to faith. Gudina rejoiced over that.

People streamed together to hear the word, and even at home we gathered people around God's word. The sick came to us often to get help, because Gudina was also a trained surgeon's assistant. All the guests that came to us and filled up our house—how many can it have been? We had up to thirty overnight guests at a time, and our salary amounted to only sixty Birr a month.

We looked for a bigger house then. When someone gave us one hundred Birr, it was just enough to build a house. We repurposed the old house as a clinic. There were so many sick people who needed help, and at the same time they got to hear God's word. Later our salary grew to two hundred Birr a month, and then everything got easier.

Once Gudina finished his pastoral training, he was hired as a pastor in Nekemte. I'm no longer sure, but I think that he was there just barely three years. There was a lot of trouble and infighting in the congregation, because he wanted to work as close to the way it is in the Bible as possible. He didn't want to deviate from it in the slightest way, whereas others didn't want to follow it so exactly, in order to get through life more easily.

Gudina remained adamant. When God's word said something, there was to be no wavering. He wanted to go by the straight path only; he called sins by name and said clearly that it wasn't right to live in such a way. That caused trouble.

"It is not right to have two wives," said Gudina. "God's word teaches us that we should have only one wife."

Moreover, he said astounding things like: "The church is not composed only of older people; it is also composed of youth. They also belong to the congregation and serve it."

Previously, it had always been the case among our people that only the oldest could be elected as representatives. It was unthinkable that a young person would be elected to such a position. But Gudina wanted a young member of the congregation to take up the task when an older member died. That caused trouble. Gudina shook up the whole system.

Moreover, his practical proclamation of the gospel was oriented to everyday life, and many found it uncomfortable. There were always many people in the congregation who held a position on the council and at the same time would drink to the point of drunkenness. Everywhere people brewed their own beer at home. When Gudina preached that it wasn't right, there was conflict. It didn't please many people to be reminded of such concrete things.

Gudina wanted to follow the straight path. He could not take part in crooked business dealings. With that the conflict became official. The oldest pastor in Addis Ababa was sent to Nekemte to mediate.

"You shouldn't look at it that way," said Pastor Badima. But Gudina persisted on the same path.

"We must follow God's word," he explained, "exactly as it stands. We are not allowed to change it."

So the church undertook a brief process and arranged that Gudina should leave the congregation at Nekemte and go to work as an evangelist with a completely different people group in Kambata. But the problems in Nekemte were not solved this way. They continued. Someone else was appointed as pastor in Nekemte, and Gudina said, "Good; if they can get peace this way, it will be all right with me."

Transferred

Gudina traveled in the Kambata area, which lay much farther to the south. That was not easy for him. Gudina did not know the Kambata language. He preached and taught in Amharic, and a Kambata man accompanied him as translator. Gudina traveled for a year throughout Kambata as an evangelist. He spent the night in the huts of the people he visited, and the whole time he had no place to call his own. But he never complained, and the call to be a preacher drove him on.

When he had already been away a long time, I couldn't take it anymore. I wanted to be together with my husband. I had a boy who helped me with the children and the household tasks. He was smart and responsible, and so I entrusted him with the children and joined Gudina. I myself had a strong call to preaching, so I wanted to help with the evangelizing.

For six months, I accompanied my husband, and in that whole time I never saw my children. It was simply too expensive to travel back and forth.

But it was good for us to be together. We had a wonderful partnership, even at times when it was not all that easy to get by. Often it was difficult to find potable water, and food was also a problem. The food in Kambata was completely different from the food we were used to.

In Kambata they eat a lot of kocho. The dish is made from the roots of the enset or "false banana" tree—a tree that looks like a real banana plant but doesn't bear its fruit. The trees have large and powerful roots that are peeled, wrapped up in false banana leaves, and buried in the earth, where a fermentation process begins. The food reservoir is then ready. Now if someone wants to eat, he simply digs up the wrapped root, squeezes out the moisture, and warms up the root in a pan.

Many mix the fermented root with cooked cabbage or season it with herbs. Most of the time, however, it's eaten plain. You get full quickly eating it, but its nutritional value is quite poor.

We were used to baking bidenaa ("injera" in Amharic), a firm pancake that is made out of fermented ground teff. This bidenaa we would dunk in strongly seasoned sauce, a hot pepper sauce with vegetables and sometimes also meat, or we baked bread. So the food in Kambata was very unusual for us.

Gudina was very worried about me and I about him. We ate a lot of corn—only once in the whole time was there also meat to eat.

We went around on foot and sometimes also rode on mules. The landscape was very hilly; it went up and down through the fertile fields. When evening came, we stopped in a hut, where the neighbors immediately began to gather to receive their guests. We held our assemblies there and preached the gospel of Jesus, the Son of God, who is mightier than any powers and has come to redeem everybody. All who believe in him will be saved.

We experienced once again how people accepted this message. The joy that we had there was so great that it made all our troubles worthwhile.

In that area, there are two big ethnic groups, the Hadiya and the Kambata. They were always in conflict with each other. Gudina took a lot of time to mediate between the two groups. In this way also he was able to preach the gospel and reconcile them.

To America

When that year was over, an American by the name of Dr. Schaefer, recognizing Gudina's exceptional leadership qualities, requested the Mekane Yesus Church to allow Gudina to travel to America for further studies. He received a scholarship from the Lutheran World Federation, and in 1963 he went to Saint Paul, Minnesota, to study at Luther Seminary. He was supposed to be there only one year on a diploma program.

I went home to my children. Luckily, at that time the missionary Backlund arrived in Nekemte and helped me with lots of things. The mission was able to build a school on a small piece of land I'd inherited from my grandfather. I helped out with the evangelizing work of the church and attended many of the gospel meetings in the surrounding area. Many people came to Christ; those were very beautiful experiences.

I also helped with the building of a church for young Christians to meet in. The cooperation with Backlund was very pleasant.

And that was good, because after Gudina had been in America for a while, one of his student supervisors said, "We shouldn't have this man do just a diploma. He is so talented that he should absolutely do an advanced degree. He can manage it in three years."

Gudina wrote all this to me.

It wasn't easy for him, either, to be separated from his family for so long. At that time, there was no prospect of the family coming to America with him. But I told my husband that he should rest easy—we would get by just fine. This was his chance, and in 1966, he received his bachelor of divinity degree.[2]

When the three years had finally passed, Gudina came back and we rejoiced to be able to live together in our house again and to preach the gospel in our homeland together. But things turned out differently.

The General Secretary

Gudina was asked by the Mekane Yesus Church to become its general secretary. Mekane Yesus is the Lutheran church of Ethiopia that was established in 1958 as the fruit of Lutheran mission societies from Germany, Norway, Switzerland, and the United States. Later on, Lutheran missionaries from Denmark and Finland also worked with the church.

It was no easy decision to say yes to that offer, because we wanted so much to stay at home in Nekemte. Besides, Gudina felt that such a position was too high for him and humbly declined the offer. But the church leaders didn't give up, and they renewed the request again and again. Then it became clear to Gudina that this was a call from God, and he must reply with a yes.

It was also a sign of their great confidence in him, but it was clear to us that this post would bring a lot of work and responsibility with it. Gudina went about it as he always did, following the call of God. That was all that mattered. He could not disobey the Holy Spirit, and on September 13, 1966, he began his service.

There was plenty to do. In a short time, he was working day and night—not even stopping to catch his breath. The workload was unbelievable. From early in the morning till late in the evening there was work that had to be done. His lunch was usually cold by the time he got home. Home for a coffee? Home for tea? Out of the question. Someone was always there waiting for him, wanting to speak with him.

Often, he was terribly tired, but he allowed himself no rest if there was still

---

2. Trans. note: At that time, pastors received a bachelor of divinity rather than a master's of divinity degree after three years of seminary education.

something to be done. Everywhere they wanted his help and advice. There were evenings when he didn't get home from work till three in the morning. How I worried about him! At that time, it was not nearly as dangerous to be outside at night as it was later, but still.

We lived in a rented house in the neighborhood of the church office. It was not easy to find a house then. Houses farther away would have been a problem because we didn't have a car, and naturally the church office couldn't order a car service just for Gudina. We lived in that house for eight years, and often he remained late at the office night after night since the path back to the house was so short. When we moved farther away, he no longer stayed at work so late—then he at least came home before midnight most of the time.

I had no peace before he got home. "Maybe people are lying in wait to ambush him," I often thought, worrying about him. But God looked after him up to the day they took him.

Our house was always full of people. Gudina's siblings lived with us as well as other relatives. At times, there were sixteen of us in the house—and everyone needed a place to sleep and food to eat. Moreover, we always had guests, many guests. People came to see Gudina not only at the office. Often, they came to our home to be able to speak with Gudina. There was not much peace during the day, and often very little at night.

On top of all of this, he was away and traveling often. The Mekane Yesus Church has congregations in many provinces, in the north, south, east, and west. He had to visit them all, and often there were problems that he needed to solve. He was also wanted at many meetings as a speaker, and then there were all the forums and committees of the church that demanded his presence. So many important decisions that had to be made! He traveled to southern Ethiopia, he traveled to Welega, to Tigray, and to the many other provinces of Ethiopia.

Many times, he also traveled abroad. He went to Europe and America and many other African countries. Once he was at a meeting of church leaders in Johannesburg, South Africa. That was a shocking and humiliating experience: this great church leader was suddenly an undesirable sort of person. The conference participants from Europe and America discovered that Gudina was not allowed to use the same bathroom! He was told that he couldn't even travel on the same bus with the rest of the delegation! To Gudina that was unacceptable. Without the slightest fear, he resisted and would not submit. He opposed and spoke against apartheid everywhere he went. When you think of how long that system lasted . . .

The Church Leader

Gudina was not only a big man but an imposing shepherd for the church. His external appearance was striking and impressive. He couldn't buy clothes in Ethiopia that fit him. There were no shoes big enough for his feet. Everything had to be made to order.

First and foremost, he was a great spiritual leader. He was uncompromising and far-seeing. Under Gudina's direction, an article entitled "On the Interrelation between Proclamation of the Gospel and Human Development"[3] was written and sent out into the world—an article that formulated for the first time that the task of the church is to serve the whole person.

The gospel carries within itself a mandate toward development. Development without gospel proclamation, though, is only half the work. In that article, the one-dimensional material approach of the Western partner churches was heavily criticized.

It should not be this way. The soul is a part of the whole person, and the church has the greatest responsibility to look after that part. At the same time, evangelization and development belong together inseparably.

The article from the Mekane Yesus Church, sent out to all partner churches overseas, was posing a challenge to reconsider their views of partnership and the danger that one-sided development involves. Gudina strongly opposed how the Western churches made unilateral decisions, placing more value on development projects than on congregational work and training leaders in the church. Gudina underlined this idea in his talk in Tokyo before the Lutheran World Federation in 1971.[4]

Gudina felt assistance should be provided in all areas of need—that was a Christian duty. But first, and ultimately, the gospel had to be preached.

Gudina was compelled to advocate for all people, wherever he was. He could not compromise. He was not politically engaged, but when an injustice had been committed, he did not keep silent. Already during the regime of Emperor Haile Selassie, he condemned what was happening. Whoever had gold could acquire land and justice for himself while the poor remained helpless. As a Christian, Gudina was furious about

---

3. Trans. note: See section 5 in part 1 of this volume.
4. Trans. note: See section 4 in part 1 of this volume, "Report on Church Growth in Ethiopia."

that. He was not afraid to write a letter to the imperial government, requesting land reform.

When he conducted worship in the big Mekane Yesus Church in Addis Ababa, he left out the part in the prayers of the church asking for a long life and ever-enduring rule for the emperor and the royal family. He always left it out, and that was not without its dangers. He was often warned that he was putting his life at risk.

"No!" Gudina said. "Before the face of God everything must be done rightly. I cannot pray the prayer the way it is formulated. I could only pray that the emperor would repent so that all of his sins might be forgiven."

He thought about how the farmers were burdened with unjust taxes and how they were required to perform compulsory labor at the disposal of the landowners, with no rights over against their rich overlords. He saw already then how many people were blinded into thinking of the emperor as a good father of the nation.

During that first difficult time, there was an unbelievable influx into the church. The Mekane Yesus Church was the fastest-growing Lutheran church in the world. Animists accepted the message of Jesus, the Son of God, who is stronger than all powers. People who had been oppressed and humiliated accepted the message of how precious they were in God's eyes, so precious that he gave his only Son up to death so that they could be saved.

The gospel proved its liberating power. People recognized that they needed God. The administration of the church was faced with great challenges.

Much wisdom was necessary for the administration and leadership of the Mekane Yesus Church. The church was the fruit of Swedish, German, American, Norwegian, and Danish mission work. And the various mission organizations had brought along their own individual ecclesial traditions and their own understandings of the nature of the church. That naturally made a mark on the Ethiopian congregations that came into being.

The Norwegian Lutheran Mission (*Norsk Luthersk Misjonssamband*), for example, was a lay-run organization that didn't use an official liturgy in its assemblies. The congregations in the synods of the south that came into being as a result of its preaching developed accordingly. The other missions had, in varying degrees, stronger ecclesial ties, and so for them the form of the Lord's Supper in the worship service was more important. In contrast to the congregations of the southern synods, these pastors wore albs.

You can, of course, say that these differences are not decisive as long as God's word is proclaimed rightly and well. But these differing realities required a lot of thought and wisdom to sort out if all these different congregations were going to live together as one church. Gudina did not stand alone in this work; he had an able and dynamic church leadership behind him. Nevertheless, the circumstances placed great demands on the general secretary of the church.

The church was also responsible for a big program of instruction, from the schools for all age groups to the school of continuing education in Debre Zeit. The social work taken over by the church was absolutely enormous; there was a bunch of clinics and even a hospital. Besides this, the leaders—evangelists and pastors—had to be educated. Young Christians needed biblical instruction, although many of them couldn't even read. And the gospel always needed to be proclaimed to people who hadn't heard it yet.

Individual missionaries, the local churches, and the central church leadership worked closely together so that all the activities took place as the cooperation of one church, one national Ethiopian church. That alone spoke volumes about the leadership of the church and the missions, without forgetting that behind all of it stood the action of the Holy Spirit.

The System Breaks Down

When the great famine catastrophe broke out, the challenges were no longer minor ones. The government had hidden them for a long time, because they wanted to prevent the world from seeing the situation in Ethiopia clearly. It was too humiliating.

But the Mekane Yesus Church had congregations in the central area of the catastrophe, in Wollo, and knew early on what was in store. The Christian approach of the church being responsible for the human body *and* the human soul led it to take up numerous aid projects. Mekane Yesus offered itself as a solid and reliable contact for emergency assistance organizations from around the world. First there was the relief agency Bread for the World (*Brot für die Welt*) from Germany, Luther Aid (*Lutherhjelpen*) from Sweden, and Church Emergency Aid (*Kirkens Nödhjelp*) from Norway. Additional help came from America, Finland, Denmark, Holland, and other countries.

Dependable personnel who will pass on the aid through direct contact with the persons affected are irreplaceable. They make sure that the donations of the organizations actually arrive and don't disappear into somebody's pocket on the way there. That, in fact, happened many times to the aid organized by the Ethiopian state.

This tremendous catastrophe broke the neck of the imperial political system. The wish for change became a demand by the whole population and the tide could no longer be stemmed. Patience with landowners and the prosperity of the rich were over. The need was so great that it became stronger than fear of the mighty. The expected military putsch ended with the arrest of the emperor. The old feudal system had to get out of the way of the good of the people. The people rejoiced—now good times were coming.

Many people in the church had this attitude, too. The enthusiasm was great. You wanted to support it, be a part of it. During this fit of enthusiasm, a lot of people went overboard. That is understandable, in light of all the trouble that had come before. The majority of church members were poor farmers from oppressed ethnic groups.

Now there was supposed to be equality for all, freedom for all, and education for all. As Christians, they knew the value of individuals within the whole. The gospel had laid the basis for democratic thinking, based upon the responsibility of the individual and the notion of social equality. Now came the revolution, which said that all persons should participate in local political work. For the first time in the history of the country, the people were granted self-determination.

For a long time, Gudina was of the opinion that a revolution was necessary. But almost immediately, he realized that this particular revolution was not going to develop into something good. The new system came with the message: "There is no God."

That was not the guiding principle in Gudina's heart. He predicted very early on that difficulties were coming for the church and for Christians. He proved to be right. What had already been bad enough was going to get even worse. And he said so—loudly!

I asked him so often to be careful.

"No!" said Gudina. "I work for God and not for anyone else. They will forbid the preaching of the word of God. They will close down the church," he prophesied.

And everything happened just as he said it would.

Christianity and Communism

The new powers sought contact with the leading communist states: the Soviet Union, Cuba, China, East Germany, and the other nations of eastern Europe. They, in return, offered armed assistance and military and economic support. You can easily understand what a temptation this was for such a poverty-stricken country. The bad thing was that they bought into communism right along with the aid.

It was important, then, to prepare the church for this new future. Gudina saw that clearly.

At its educational site for pastors in Makanisa, the administration of the Mekane Yesus Church hosted seminars and workshops for church leaders from various congregations. Four such seminars were on the theme of Christianity and socialism. Other churches were invited to them as well: the Roman Catholic and Orthodox churches, the Pentecostals, the Sudan Interior Mission. Representatives of the Lutheran World Federation participated in them too.

The themes were: What is socialism? How can it be reconciled with Christianity? What approach should the church take? How should the church relate to it? To what extent should the church get involved in the class struggle?

With the thought that the church should be light and salt in the world—and not only in times of peace but also under revolutionary conditions—Gudina Tumsa wrote a memorandum in 1975 on how the church should relate to a socialist system.[5]

He argued that the many institutions of the church are good and useful for their work, but if they become obstructive in the new situation, the church should not cling to them. One problem was that the church's social institutions were often perceived as good sources of income for the church. That was not actually the case, but as long as the people thought so, the church had to draw the obvious conclusion and hand the institutions over to the state.

On a basic level, the church, of course, should not give up its social engagement. It must, as long as it is able, offer assistance, support, and help for the new organizations of farmers that were being established all over the country. In this way, it would become clear that the church is not out for money but wants to serve the people. Such is the attitude suggested by Jesus's words in Matthew 22:37–39, "You shall love

---

5. Trans. note: See section 8 in part 1 of this volume, "Pastoral Letter: The Evangelical Church Mekane Yesus in the Ethiopian Revolution."

the Lord your God with all your heart and with all your soul and with all your mind" and "You shall love your neighbor as yourself."

The church ran a few primary schools that had to be turned over to the new farmers' organizations. In this way, the church would be able to support the people—"the masses," as they were called. The church had to take every opportunity to help the broad masses of people.

Already in 1973, the church had passed a resolution in support of land reform to allow the people to get access to the land. In many cases, the Mekane Yesus Church had already helped farmers to access land under the feudal system. The church saw it as a service in the love of Jesus.

Gudina emphasized, however, the church must pledge its support independent of all political circumstances, and that Christians had the right to meet for the sake of spiritual edification and the growth of Christian life. Moreover, the church had always to obey the Great Commission and spread the gospel among the people. Otherwise the church could not survive.

In this very same period, missions all over the world were discussing the question of whether the missionaries should immediately withdraw from foreign countries so that the young churches would have the opportunity to develop on their own and find their identity without Western influence. The slogan rang out: "Missionary, go home!"

Gudina was of the opinion that such a moratorium was not actually a theological question but an economic one. Obviously, it is the goal of each church to stand on its own two feet, but such autonomy would not be achieved by sending missionaries home. A church would not find its own identity by canceling financial help from elsewhere.

Gudina suggested another alternative in its place: external help should be reduced over the course of twenty years, bit by bit. Meanwhile, the Mekane Yesus Church should try to increase its own income.[6]

Gudina's speeches stirred things up the most when he sketched out in very practical ways the cost of living as a Christian. For him, to be a Christian meant sacrifice and suffering. Consequently, he required church workers who made more money to submit to a lowering of their wages for the sake of their coworkers who earned less. He asked the employees of the Mekane Yesus Church to renounce luxury; the situation in the country required a drastic alteration in the level of wages.

---

6. Trans. note: See section 10 in part 1 of this volume, "The Moratorium Debate and the ECMY."

Gudina took the first step of reducing his own salary. The church employees reacted cantankerously, though.

The concluding sentences of his speech have not lost any of their relevance.

> The gospel of Jesus Christ is God's power to save everyone who believes it. It is the power that saves from eternal damnation, from economic exploitation, from political oppression, and so on. Because of its eternal dimension, the gospel could never be replaced by any of the ideologies invented by men throughout the centuries. It is the only voice telling about a loving Father who gave his Son as a ransom for many. It tells about the forgiveness of sins and the resurrection of the body. It is the good news to sinful man, the only power to save mankind from its sinfulness. It is too powerful to be compromised by any social system. It is too dear a treasure to be given up (Matthew 13:44). Nationalism has its own place, but it can never replace the gospel of Jesus Christ.[7]

From that point on, the regime tried to muzzle Gudina, because his speeches were being heard by the whole world. Dawit Wolde Giorgis, a Derg official who later defected to the United States, ordered Gudina to appear before him. But suspecting that he would be abducted, Gudina chose not to go.

Our Own Home

Meanwhile Gudina had borrowed money from the church to buy a house of his own off of Asmara Road on the edge of the city. He wanted to protect his family.

I still remember this time well—it was a beautiful time. The Norwegian mission station lay close nearby, and we took active part in the congregational life at Urael Mekane Yesus Church. I worked with Mrs. Magerøy from Norway in the Women's Association. Once a year, we organized a church bazaar to sell handicrafts and food we had prepared ahead of time. We took in four thousand Birr! Our whole family was actively involved in the congregation's life, not least of all our children, and above all the two young ones.

But then came the political upheaval, and Gudina had to be extremely careful. It was very important for him to have all his affairs in order. He made a point of not being in debt so that nobody could put pressure

---

7. Trans. note: See the complete text of Gudina's essay in section 9 in part 1, "Memorandum: Some Issues Requiring Discussions and Decisions."

on him that way. For this reason, he sold the house so he could pay the church back. For the family, this was a hard time, but for Gudina independence was important. And the church needed the money.

Gudina and his family moved to a newly built apartment belonging to the Mekane Yesus Church, in which the central office of the church was also to be located. The old office had become much too small for all the church activities.

We moved into the sixth floor. The apartment was beautiful, and we almost always had guests. There were only three of us in the household by now, so we had enough room for others.

Then we bought ourselves a car. Sometime before, during a trip abroad, Gudina had been offered a car by some potential donors.

"No, thank you!" he said. "If you want to give something, give it to the church."

So it was a long time before we could buy a car ourselves. Our money didn't reach that far, but when we sold the house we got back our equity ratio from the sale of the house in Nekemte.

And so we could afford a little car.

For Gudina, offers such as the car were such a lovely temptation. But he remained adamant. He didn't want to take advantage of his position. He'd been hired to serve the church.

"I am only a poor servant. I am only a sinner. I am allowed in my work to serve a great Lord. Everything belongs to him. He cares for us with what we need."

He stood unwavering. For me, it was naturally also a temptation, and I would have liked to persuade him to think otherwise. But that would not have been right. In these things we had to be very exacting and live blamelessly. We are the children of humanity but also the children of God, and we should live like children of God. If we live according to our human will and personal wishes, not much good will come of it.

Gudina also quit smoking. He had begun smoking while overseas, when a doctor recommended it to him as a way to reduce stress. Smoking was supposed to calm the nerves. But the stress never got any less—with the result that he was smoking more and more.

But one day he said suddenly that to continue smoking was not right. He was setting a bad example for others. On that day he decided to quit. And one week later he threw away all his smoking stuff. It was not good for his health anyway, since by the end he was smoking so many cigarettes a day. Other doctors had already told him as much.

Youth Service

Soon after the revolution, all the youth of the country were drafted into the so-called "development campaign." The real goal was to indoctrinate them into the nation's new ideology. It was to make communists out of them. Big camps for youth were organized in many places across the country, and several of these places were concentration camps, plain and simple.

The situation was especially bad for young Christians. They couldn't consent to the motto of the revolution: to honor Ethiopia as their reason for living and to deny the existence of God. Many, many Christian youth didn't want to put anything in the place of God, including Ethiopia. They could not renounce God.

In the attempt to force young Christian people to reject their faith, terrible things happened in many of these camps. The persecutions were pitiless and cruel.

But these measures had the opposite effect of what they intended. Naturally, some youth yielded to pressure—it's always that way. Some betrayed other Christians, which didn't make things any easier. But many, even the majority of youth, withstood the pressure and confessed their faith quite openly.

That made a great impression. In spite of the terrible pressure under which all Ethiopian youth lived, many became Christians, and Christians grew to be numerically huge. They were truly conscious Christians, no longer Christians in name only. The Christian faith proved its ability to see them through oppressive circumstances.

Naturally, the children of Gudina and Tsehay got drafted too. First the three oldest were drafted. The fact that they were the children of the general secretary of the Mekane Yesus Church and would not submit to the ideology being propagated by the Marxist regime didn't make things any easier for them. After some time, the oldest daughter, Kulani, was detained while the oldest son, Amanti, had it incredibly hard. He was beaten and mistreated and some of his friends were killed.

The Oldest Son

Gudina and Tsehay's oldest son, Amanti, was sent to Akaki on the outskirts of Addis Ababa. There was so much resistance from young people in the camp that he, along with many other students, ended up in prison. A little later, he was released and sent farther away to a camp in Najo. In that youth camp a big riot broke out shortly after his arrival. In the midst of the turmoil he managed to run away. He fought his way through to Addis Ababa and his family.

Suddenly there stood our son in front of us. But he couldn't stay with us because they would immediately look for him here. But where in the world could he go? They would find him no matter where we hid him—and they would not hesitate to kill him.

Gudina had to find a solution. In the strictest secrecy, he made contact with some Norwegian missionaries. A plan was arranged: our son would be taken in the transport vehicle of Church Emergency Aid to the south, in the direction of the border with Kenya. Everything would be arranged so he could be discreetly hidden in the car.

His heart was in his throat when he climbed into the truck. On the way south, they'd have to pass through a number of control posts—but God performed a miracle. No one recognized Gudina's son. When the car arrived near the border, he climbed out and fled to Kenya.

He was just sixteen years old, and already alone in the world. I can only guess what was going on inside of him—hopelessness, despair, fear.

Where could he go? How would he get by? What should he do? Many emotions moved us. We had only God; he was our refuge, our only hope. In prayer, we told God everything that was burning in our hearts.

I know that he arrived in a foreign land, and with the help of our friends he made it to Germany. There he got help from German missionaries and could begin his education. But his experiences and worries over his parents and siblings left deep scars on him. To live with these things was not easy, and the following years were very difficult for him, even though he was living in freedom. And it was not going to get any easier.

The Youngest Son

Latera was a lovely boy, an enthusiastic Christian, active in congregational work. He was afraid to participate in anything that might be wrong and lead him away from God. At home, he was always a source of great joy to us because he had a great sense of humor.

One day, our seventeen-year-old had a bad experience. Some of his acquaintances wanted to talk him into joining an anti-government youth party who ambushed and killed pro-government youth, which he refused to do. They beat him up and stoned him until he fell to the ground.

Luckily—or by God's direction—a policeman came by. He delivered a warning shot, the mob fled, and the boy was saved. Later, I visited the policeman and thanked him for saving our boy's life.

Three months later, Latera suddenly became ill. On the Thursday previous he'd been at a youth meeting in church. The youth leader, Tsigge, led a Bible study. During the meeting it was asked, "Who would like to accept Jesus today?"

Our son raised his hand. He wanted once again to be quite certain that his relationship with God was in order.

That was already remarkable. Then when he came home, he straightened up his room and decorated it as if for a holiday. His clothing had to be clean, everything had to be beautiful, as if he were preparing for something special. We only puzzled at it and understood nothing.

On Saturday he suddenly got sick, and his illness lasted only three days. What was actually wrong with him I still don't know, but we assumed it had something to do with the stoning several months earlier. No diagnosis was ever made.

On Sunday evening he had pains. Once he said, "Mama, it hurts so much here," touching his head. He was in a lot of pain, that was clear.

And later he said, "Mama, don't you see the great white host up above?"

I saw nothing.

He pointed to the ceiling and said, "Look, they stand there all together, with bright white clothes. Tomorrow I will die."

We were all terribly frightened. "What are you saying?" I cried.

"Oh," he mused, "if only you could see what I see. That would be so nice for you."

"Come on, what's wrong with you?" we asked.

"Don't worry, nothing is confused in my head," was his answer. "But pray for me!"

We knelt down and prayed intensely for our son. Then he could say nothing more. "Pray for me" was the last thing he ever said.

We were deeply upset. His words rang in my mind afterward: "Mama, if you could only see what I see. That would be so nice for you."

On Monday, the third day, he died.

For seventeen years, this boy was a gift of God to us. Then God took him home.

On Tuesday was the burial, and Gudina himself gave the sermon. He preached about the hope of the resurrection. His words were like rain in a dry land. They were comfort for many others who were also affected by deep mourning in that terrible time.

A man who was at the burial remarked after Gudina's impressive sermon: "When I die, I would like to be buried just like Gudina's son."

That was, as mentioned, on a Tuesday. After the burial, this man went to the doctor to have a vitamin injection. As it turned out, the injection was contaminated.

On Wednesday the man became very sick, and on Thursday he died. On Friday he was buried—just like Gudina's son had been.

We all missed our boy very much. It was especially hard for his sister Aster, our middle daughter. Grief and despair hit her so hard that for half a year she suffered under a deep depression.

What a hard time that was. To lose my son was bad enough. But he had been a gift from God, and I knew that God had taken him back to himself again.

I had peace about it, even though I missed him terribly—not least of all because our oldest son had also gone away. In spite of that, I was at peace. And for me it was always a comfort that he had not died at the hands of another. God had called him home in peace. We were allowed to give him an honorable burial. So many people came to our house of mourning, and so many had been at the burial, including many youths. His burial was a powerful witness to faith in God that affected a wide circle of people.

But on top of that, to endure the suffering of my daughter was incredibly hard. Finally, after six months, she came through.

At that time I learned—and often again since then—that nothing is so hard that God cannot help us through it.

I am reminded of the book of Daniel. In it, God allows three young men to be thrown into the fiery furnace. But the fire did not burn them. So many times, I myself have been "thrown into the fiery furnace," but God's hand was always there protecting me. That was also the case during all those bad years when I didn't know what had happened to my husband—whether he was alive or dead or what he might be suffering.

God's loving hand alone carried me through all of it. So many tears I cried! So many prayers I brought before God! So many nights I could not sleep because my heart threatened to shatter with grief! There were days when I was in agony. But I could always pray, and God was there.

Two of our girls competed and won scholarships to travel to socialist countries for further education. That was one strategy to get them out of harm's way, as many youths who had to stay home were subjected to beatings, imprisonment, and brainwashing. Kulani, our oldest, was sent to Czechoslovakia, and our second-oldest girl, Aster, was sent to East Germany.

Neither of them had it easy. Aster was always hearing in East Germany, "There is no God!"

"No!" she always replied, "there is a God!"

Her passport was withdrawn so she had to do without it for two years, which was not without its dangers. She got help from a devout pastor, who organized her escape to West Germany.

Later, Kulani, our oldest daughter, found out that the Ethiopian embassy was having her followed with the intention of assassinating her. She was still Gudina's daughter. But God kept his hand upon her. She also was able to escape from Czechoslovakia to West Germany.

Now we had only Lensa, our youngest daughter, at home. We had once been sixteen people in the house—and now we were down to three.

Darker Horizons

Gudina knew harder times were coming. He was always anticipating something of that sort. He said to me that persecutions were awaiting us, and also death. He told me all that.

I pressed him to go to Europe instead of staying here to die.

"I can't do that," Gudina answered. "Christ is there, and Christ is here. But I must be where Christ wants me to be."

He also predicted, "No one will be allowed to go into another part of the city without permission anymore. We will be banned from proclaiming the gospel."

He was right. It turned out exactly like that. The Bible was banned. Many, many people were thrown into prison for the Bible's sake.

"Husband and wife will be turned against one another," said Gudina. "Children will betray their parents. That's what's coming to our country."

He proved to be right again. Many children denounced their parents and sent them to their deaths. Fathers betrayed their children. Mother against father, and father against mother. In the Bible, it says it will be so "in the last days." In our country, it happened.

On the day Gudina prophesied all that to me, I got furious. I protested. That never would be allowed to happen! When I thought it over later in prison, I was shocked. He'd been right about every single detail!

Gudina's closest coworkers in the church office report a story from around this time:

> Very early one morning—it was just getting light—somebody rang at the door. Gudina and Tsehay had come. It was unusually early, but the past night the two of them had hardly slept because they'd been praying. God

had shown them that persecution and death threatened if they continued in their lives as Christians so openly and obviously as before. If they did not leave off, their own family would be ripped apart and destroyed. They were putting not only themselves but also their children in great danger, as long as they continued on the same path.

Was that right? Was that their way?

That night, the whole family spoke and prayed together. Now Gudina and Tsehay came at dawn to friends to tell them that they had no choice. It was an either-or for them. To follow Christ was the only thing that they could do in good conscience—even if it meant the destruction of the whole family.

What a choice! It was a portentous decision that they had reached in prayer. Come what may, their Savior could not and would not lose them.

The missionary friend listened quietly. It was a holy hour together with these two great servants of the Lord, filled with the Holy Spirit.

In Prison

One day, the very thing so long finally happened. Government officials—the secret police of the Derg—arrested Gudina. They took him from the church office and drove away with him. He witnessed several other people being seized in various places. The mood in the car must have been despondent.

The people were brought to the Third Police Station, which was notorious on account of its prisons. They locked Gudina up together with thieves and bandits. For two weeks, they kept him locked up in a little cell that was nearly jam-packed with people. Gudina reported later how little room there was. They had to take turns sleeping; some slept while others stood.

Early the next morning we began to look for him. That was a difficult undertaking. He was not at the First Police Station; he was also not at the Second Police Station. So we drove on to the Third. There we met a man who hinted that Gudina was in there. A desperate situation. How was he surviving in that horrible place?

We drove back home and packed up a woolen blanket and food in the hopes that we would be allowed to give them to him. The nights in Addis Ababa are often ice cold, and without a blanket they're hard to get through. The things we brought were taken from us at the prison gate, but we weren't allowed to see him. After that, we begged many times to see just his hand—could he just wave at us? That was all we asked for.

What could we do to get him out of there? I sent a friend to the authorities to ask about the charge against Gudina. The person in charge said only, "I got an order by telephone to lock him up."

We never learned anything more about it.

Each day, I drove to the prison with food. After a week, someone secretly gave us news from Gudina. He'd asked us to smuggle a Bible in along with the food because he was eager to teach the prisoners and preach the gospel. That doing such a thing was forbidden and could endanger his life Gudina cared not a bit.

After two weeks, we found out that he had been transferred from Addis Ababa to Asella, a small town in the southeastern part of the country. We inferred from this that they wanted to have him killed there in secrecy.

To prevent that from happening, I myself drove to Asella. The first night, I slept in a hotel that was swarming with rats. The next night I preferred to spend in my car. The following day I went to buy some food from a woman in a nearby house. I told her of my troubles.

"You can stay with me," she said. It turned out that she and her husband worked for the Security Force, the secret police, but neither of them could say anything to me about it. But they helped Gudina and established contact between the two of us.

Fourteen days passed. Then my landlady informed me that Gudina was going to be brought to Addis Ababa by car. She advised me to have a car come from Addis Ababa to fetch him. In other words, she had a suspicion that Gudina was going to be killed along the way.

I called Addis Ababa, and two cars came immediately from the church office. I was able to ride along in one of them with Gudina and the police.

The police were ruthless. Gudina had gotten nothing to drink in the scorching heat, and we were not allowed to speak with each other.

When we arrived in Addis Ababa, they brought Gudina directly to Tesfaye Wolde Selassie, a high official of the military government, who lived in the vicinity of the Tikur Anbessa Hospital.

"I know all about you," he said, and sent Gudina on to the Second Police Station.

"We don't want him here," they said. "We'll have nothing to do with him." He was then brought to the office of the Derg in the old imperial palace. Interrogations took place in that notorious place where there was also a prison, as was well known.

I'd spent the whole day waiting for him at each stop along the way. Now I had to let him go because he had to spend the night in the prison in the palace compound. I slipped him some things that I'd already had along in Asella—a woolen blanket and a towel—so that he had something for the night. Later I heard that he gave the woolen blanket to a severely tortured man. He took the small towel for himself, hardly sufficient for such a tall man.

And I could only go back home—in despair. "They're going to kill him," I thought. I didn't sleep a wink all night.

On the next day, Gudina was taken again to the Second Police Station, and soon thereafter they let him go free. Ato Asfaw, who worked in the church office, had to give a guarantee that Gudina would be at the police's disposal at all times.

Many people gathered at our place when Gudina came home again. There were so many that the neighbors had to lend us extra chairs.

Gudina said, "I've learned something. You sit there behind locked doors. The people you love—your wife and your children—can't be near you. But Jesus is there. Even locked doors can't keep him out."

That was for him a very powerful experience.

We'd been worried about his health because he had always needed to take medicine for his severe allergies. The prison director in Asella didn't allow us to bring Gudina the medicine he urgently needed. At home, everything always had to be dust-free. If he came in contact with the smallest mote of dust, he began to sneeze. How would it be for him in a filthy prison? We were very worried.

But during his time in prison, Gudina had almost no allergic reactions at all. There was only one time in his whole life when was he was freed of his allergic plague: during that imprisonment. A great miracle of God!

Gudina had not been arrested for committing a crime. What they really wanted was to get him to make a deal with the government. If they could bring Gudina around, get him to work as a representative of the Ethiopian government, it would amount to a huge victory for public relations abroad.

The Mekane Yesus Church was, furthermore, in a favorable position to pass on significant amounts of money for emergency aid in the country. Gudina was the man who was in contact with the people abroad. He had a good name with them.

That was what the new powers-that-be in Ethiopia wanted to exploit. "Go abroad and collect money for us!" they demanded. They needed money for the enforcement of the communist system in the country.

But Gudina replied, "Go abroad to ask for money for you? No, I can't do that. My task is to look after the duties and needs of the church."

It wasn't really about emergency aid anyway; it was about military armament. That was a different matter entirely. Gudina didn't want to gain governmental favor that way.

"Since you're only making trouble for the Mekane Yesus Church anyway, why should I do anything for you?" Gudina asked them.

The motto we were supposed to greet each other with, and to which all of us were to submit, was: "Ethiopia first! Ethiopia above all!"

"Never!" said Gudina. "God comes first. God should be honored above everything else!"

From his release in August till the next May, Gudina did not keep quiet, not in the slightest. He traveled around and preached the gospel. And his allergies bothered him just as badly as before.

Imprisoned Again

In May, Gudina preached at a big meeting in the town of Woliso in front of several thousand people. I noticed that he had observed something during the sermon, but he kept on leading the event up to its close as if everything were just fine.

Afterwards we met up. "What's wrong?" I asked.

"They're going to take me now," Gudina answered. He had seen something in the crowd. "Tsehay," he said, "tonight we're going to spend the night in a hotel instead of driving home, because tomorrow I will be taken to jail."

I was completely miserable, but what could I do? Only Gudina knew! So we spent the night in Woliso.

Early the next morning, we heard calls and shouts outside. A man burst into our room and warned us that the police had come to arrest Gudina.

"Drive fast to Addis Ababa!" he recommended. He also told us that the police had been at the gathering the evening before and wanted to take Gudina into custody there. For some reason or another, they didn't succeed.

So God granted us that one extra night to be able to pray together and prepare ourselves for what was coming. We went outside and got into the car and tried to drive off. But the car didn't start. We had to get a push. Somehow we came to the next small town, even though it took a lot of time. Meanwhile Francis Stefanos from the church office had caught up with us. "They're coming from the Derg office to arrest you," he said, letting us climb into his car and driving us to Addis Ababa and the office of the Mekane Yesus Church.

From there Gudina went directly to the office of the Derg.

Again he was charged: "You are preaching against the goals of the nation, the new ideals of the nation," they said. "You speak against the revolution. You

are leading the youth astray so they don't follow the ideals of the revolution,"
they said. Then they locked him up in prison.

One week later, our youngest daughter Lensa was arrested, too. Someone
had denounced her. This time she was stuck in a private house. Many private
houses were confiscated during that time, because the jails weren't big enough
to hold all the people under arrest—they were overflowing. This particular
house had been the property of a rich man whose fortune had been confiscated.
Gudina was brought into the house along with several other men, and Lensa
was alone in a second house that stood out in the country.

At night, the Security Force came to Lensa's jail, and she had to watch how
the men tortured other prisoners before her very eyes.

Tsehay sat at home and agonized about her sixteen-year-old daughter.
A young woman under the control of thieves, bandits, and unpre-
dictable wardens. A miracle from God was needed to protect her. And
God performed the miracle!

Lensa reports:

I could see my father from far off. He and I tried to speak to one another
secretly through the fence. He always got up early and went with the ket-
tle to the tap. I knew the approximate meeting time and made sure that I
was also there then. So we got a chance to speak with one another briefly.

In addition to this, a small Oromo boy lived in the jail. I don't know why
he was in prison. But he could speak only in Oromo. My father liked the
boy and looked after him. The boy could go where he wanted, so he was
able to carry lots of messages between us.

My father sent the boy to me with a message that he would be collecting
water the next morning at eight. When it was eight, I sat outside and
waited for him. When he came, he talked loudly with the others so I could
hear everything. Then he stuck his tongue out at me to make me laugh.
That was a great comfort.

When they interrogated me, they made me afraid by saying that everything I told them they would tell my father. Maybe that was to make it
more difficult for me. I spent sleepless nights out of fear.

I slept in the same room with male soldiers. As the torture chamber
was right across from my room, I watched people being taken in and coming out, unable to walk because of hard beatings and the wounds resulting from torture. One day I was called in for interrogation where eight
men surrounded me and threatened to torture my father in front of me. I
wanted to die so badly, rather than seeing my father being beaten. Then
they resolved to torture me first. As was customary, they went to a nearby
local bar that evening to get drunk and get ready for the torture. I stayed
up the whole night waiting to be taken but none of them showed up.

Early in the morning I saw the head cadre walking in with bloodshot eyes, uncombed hair, and wrinkled clothing. Later on, a lady who worked for them told me that they had gotten so drunk that they all fell asleep in the bar. God saved me from their hands miraculously. So young and vulnerable, I don't think I would have survived such an act of violence. Never again did they dare to speak to me about torture.

My father worried a great deal about me and about the hours of school that I was missing. He implored me to ask the prison administration if I couldn't be allowed to go to school as a free person but in the evening come back to the prison. Naturally, that was impossible; they wouldn't allow it.

There was so much international pressure exerted on the government to set us free that they let me go first, and a week later my father was also released. After that all the terrible times seemed to be over.

Tsehay continues:

I have heard that the ambassador to Sweden—Kassa, Mengistu's brother—called up Mengistu. He had learned in Sweden that Mengistu had had a churchman by the name of Gudina Tumsa arrested. He said Mengistu ought to let him go immediately or else Ethiopia would have no chance of getting financial assistance from Sweden.

On that evening, I was already driving to the prison with food for Gudina. It was about 9:30 p.m. There the police told me that they would let Gudina go free if I could provide the bail. I drove again to Asfaw Ayele, who had bailed him out last time. Asfaw came with me, signed the document, and later in the evening we picked up Gudina.

Safe and sound we arrived back home, and Gudina said, "Tsehay, at some point it's going to happen. Maybe it will happen in the street, maybe at home. But I can't quit going out and about. God is here. If it is God's will that something should happen to me, then I will accept it."

I forbade him to go out again, but he couldn't live that way. If he drove somewhere, I accompanied him. I was so afraid that something would happen to him.

Red Terror

Gudina had problems, certainly. But "our home is not in this world," and we wanted to live for God's kingdom. I always think about what my son said shortly before his death: "Oh, Mama, if only you could see what I see. That would be so nice for you."

I didn't see it, but his vision got me through a lot of things. It is God's king-

dom. That's what we're living for. Nothing else matters. We are willing to pay the cost, whatever it may be.

It was the time of red terror, a time of fear. Almost every family was affected: everyone lived in constant fear for their loved ones. If someone came home late from work, the family was terribly worried. The regime struck like lightning out of a clear sky.

People used the new system to get rid of people they hated. You could just denounce someone as an enemy of the revolution. No one had to prove anything. Most of the executions took place without any sentencing.

Day and night, the people lived in uncertainty and excruciating fear. You couldn't say anything about it, because such speech qualified you as an enemy of the revolution. You would have practically been signing your own death warrant.

Countless people, young and old alike, disappeared and were never found again. Others were discovered to have been executed in beastly ways—they were trying to save on gunpowder, since it was expensive.

Luckily, I hadn't found my son as a corpse in the street. But there were many others who did. They discovered their sons and daughters butchered somewhere in a street grave. At most, there was a note attached to their chests, announcing that the person had been an enemy of the revolution and gotten their well-deserved punishment.

And you were not allowed to mourn the dead! In that way, they would have proven that you supported an enemy of the revolution and thus were yourself against the revolution. I don't know whether I could have survived such an experience.

But God carried us through all these trials. He never promised us an easy life. Quite the contrary, he said that we must reckon with persecutions and problems. They are constant companions for God's people. But it is unbelievable how much power God gives us so we can bear it. We can only thank him and praise his name.

It is not easy to speak about that extreme time. It is a burden that weighs on me. But if I can give encouragement to other Christians, I will gladly talk about it. No matter what happens, there is nothing that can keep God from being near to us. This certainty makes the burden bearable.

When things were at their worst, I saw Jesus before me. He said, "Have no fear! I am here! I will never leave you."

Sometimes I think, "Why did Gudina have to go through all that? Why did all that have to happen?"

But those are not good thoughts. I know that. When we lost our house, this thought came to me also: "Why do we have to lose it? Weren't you able to help us, God?"

I ask God forgiveness for these thoughts. For I know better now: everything that happens is in accord with his good will, is of value for his kingdom.

The Warning

One day Pastor Yadessa was arrested. On the way to the jail they asked him his name. He said, "My name is Yadessa."

"Not Gudina Tumsa?" They had mistaken him for my husband. Immediately they came to a stop and let him go free. Pastor Yadessa came right to Gudina and warned him.

"They took me prisoner and drove around with me for a while before they asked my name," Yadessa reported. He recommended that Gudina go into hiding as soon as possible.

Many others warned Gudina. Many came also to me.

"Don't go into the church at night. It's dangerous. On a path like that you can disappear so quickly," they said.

But Gudina answered: "No, I'm going to act as I have always done. I am in God's hands. I am safe."

The people argued that it was getting more dangerous from day to day. We spoke about it a lot. And the people proved to be right.

On July 28, 1979, there was a lot to do. Gudina had spoken at the youth conference in Makanisa in front of two hundred young people. From there he came directly back home, because in the afternoon he had to preach at the Urael church. There is a Bible study there every Saturday.

It was his turn that day. In addition, he was supposed to preach at the Sunday service the next day. At home, he sat right down to make his final preparations. Time was pressing. He only got around to changing his clothes after a bath before he plunged into his work.

Our daughter Lensa reports:

> He came to me when he was getting ready and read out the preaching text to me. Then he asked, "Do you believe that they are going to take you prisoner again?"
>
> "No," I answered, "they will never take me again."
>
> He asked back, "How do you know that?"
>
> I answered that I was completely certain of it. "Don't you feel the same way?" I asked.

188

But he was not certain at all. "You see, tonight I'm preaching on the same text as on that day in Woliso when I was taken."

That made him think the same thing might happen to him today.

His text was Luke 14:26-33:

> *If anyone comes to me and does not hate his own father and mother and wife and children and brothers and sisters, yes, and even his own life, he cannot be my disciple. Whoever does not bear his own cross and come after me cannot be my disciple. For which of you, desiring to build a tower, does not first sit down and count the cost, whether he has enough to complete it? Otherwise, when he has laid a foundation and is not able to finish, all who see it begin to mock him, saying, "This man began to build and was not able to finish." Or what king, going out to encounter another king in war, will not sit down first and deliberate whether he is able with ten thousand to meet him who comes against him with twenty thousand? And if not, while the other is yet a great way off, he sends a delegation and asks for terms of peace. So therefore, any one of you who does not renounce all that he has cannot be my disciple.*

Kidnapped

I drove to the Merkato—the central market—to go shopping. Exactly at six in the evening I came back. At this hour, it starts to get dark, and it was wise to be home by then. Gudina had to go to church, and Lensa had to go to the mandatory Marxism lesson all youth were required to attend every Saturday night. There had been loud complaints that Lensa was not engaged enough in neighborhood meetings. It was forced work that often took place at the same time as congregational events. If you didn't participate diligently enough in neighborhood meetings, it would be taken as anti-revolutionary behavior. And that was dangerous.

So this afternoon Lensa had to go to her neighborhood meeting. She wanted to be home again early to prepare supper before our return from the church gathering. I drove Lensa first to her meeting and then started for church with Gudina.

The Bible study was supposed to get done at about 7:30. But today the participants asked Gudina to go on a bit longer, and he did.

After the gathering, we got into our car and drove off. We turned on to a little feeder road toward the main street. Then we saw it. Cars, jeeps, and police squad cars were parked across the whole street. At the same time, we realized that two cars had followed us. We were trapped! There was no way to escape either forward or backward.

189

"Stop!" they shouted at Gudina. We had to stop and they were upon us at once.

They forced out a woman we had brought along in the car. Then they took our bags and all our belongings out of the car. They forced me to climb into a police car while Gudina went into another. From that moment on, I never saw him or heard his voice ever again.

Lensa waited at home with the food. But nobody came. She waited and waited. It was late and she got worried. Then the woman that had been in the car turned up crying. She cried and cried, and it was almost impossible to get a coherent sentence out of her. Finally, Lensa grasped that her father and mother had disappeared.

Lensa reports:

I no longer remember exactly what we said. It was so terrible. I know that I was screaming in despair. One of our neighbors, also a Christian, came and asked what was wrong. After we had told him, he said, "Aren't you a Christian? Then why are you screaming so?"

I was so ashamed that I didn't say anything more.

Soon the president of the Urael church council appeared. He opened the Bible and we read a section of it together. Then we prayed together on our knees. Suddenly the whole house shook. An earthquake rocked our city at exactly that moment.

I remember praying that the earthquake would bring everything to an end because I couldn't imagine life without my father! I wanted to die. The future looked so grim!

Meanwhile, the soldiers proceeded with Tsehay.

They weren't interested in me this time, so they didn't take me prisoner but drove on a ways and then just tossed me out into the dark street.

Where was I? What should I do? Where should I go? I had not a single cent on me. They'd kept my bag. I set off walking and came to a gas station.

"Could you please give me fifteen cents for the bus?" I begged.

The people stared at me. "What on earth happened to you?" asked the attendant.

"I can't talk about it," I answered. Then he gave me one Birr. I gave him a look so he understood that something terrible had happened. In the street I caught a taxi-bus. The car stopped, picked me up, and set me down again at home.

I came just as the earthquake was ending. There sat the church council president. "What should I do?" I asked in tears. "They took Gudina away."

"We must immediately go in search of him," said the president.

"The car is also gone."

"Then we'll at least go to the church office first and report what's happened."

Next, we went to the police station. No one there knew anything about it. They strongly encouraged me to go home and wait.

We searched aimlessly around the city. Then I went back to our apartment. But I had not a moment of peace. Everything in me cramped up from worrying. Sleep was unthinkable.

The next day, I began first thing in the morning to call all our acquaintances and friends. I asked them for their help. We were all convinced that Gudina was dead, so we went searching for his body. We scoured the whole neighborhood, looked in every cave and hole, went to any place we could think of.

Then we called up the office of the Derg, the national government. No, they knew nothing about him either.

Gudina was nowhere to be found. During this period, many people simply disappeared because they'd been killed. It happened all the time. People were taken and killed.

Later on, I would look out from the prison in which I was being held and see a house in which people were shot. A quick process. For everyone who came there, it was the end.

What a terrible day! I cannot express in words how much it hurt. But God let it happen. Even in such cases he should be honored. Everything great and small is in his hands.

Six months went by. I was still living with Lensa, our youngest daughter, in our apartment. I was staying at home—in case Gudina should turn up. People asked me why I wouldn't wear black clothing according to the Ethiopian mourning custom. "Your husband is certainly dead," they said. "No, he is not dead," we answered. But the truth is that we just didn't know.

Arrested and Tortured

The day they arrested me—I remember it well. It was February 2, 1980, on a Saturday afternoon at five o'clock. I was coming home from a congregational event. Not long before, the big General Assembly of the Mekane Yesus Church had taken place, as it does every four years. It was a beautiful event with intensive prayer meetings. It lasted from January 23 to 31 in the pastoral training center in Makanisa.

On Thursday, a bishop from overseas had spoken to us as a guest lecturer. He invited me to lunch the following day in order to discuss an urgent matter.

He believed that it was dangerous for me to remain in Ethiopia. The same thing could happen to me that had happened to Gudina. Therefore, he wanted to help me leave Ethiopia.

But my departure couldn't take place before Saturday, and as I said, the arrest happened on Saturday.

So there I was that Saturday, February 2, at five o'clock. My daughter wasn't with me. I was alone at home.

Suddenly a car stopped in front of the door, and a number of people stormed up the stairs. "Come along!" they commanded. "The Derg wants to see you!"

"Yes sir," I said, and they took me with them to the office of the Derg. When I got there, they began with the interrogation.

"Let's go, Tsehay. Tell us where your husband is!"

"How should I know?" I answered. "We came out of church one evening, and suddenly some people came and grabbed him and took him away in their car."

"Well, don't you have anything else to say? Something about the work of the synod?"

"What am I supposed to say about that?" I retorted. "I know that I have nothing to tell."

"Then give us the money that you got when you sold your house."

"I can't do that. We borrowed the money from the Mekane Yesus Church. That's the reason we sold the house and paid back what we owed. There is nothing left over." From then on, they rained down only swear words and curses on me. It was awful to listen to.

I thought of Lensa. She didn't know what was going on. She must be despondent, coming home to an empty house. Her father was missing, her mother was gone. The house was empty. I saw my girl weeping before me.

About eight o'clock they brought me to another location. I was there until the morning. At six o'clock the next day they barked through the door, "We want to see Tsehay!"

And again: "Cough up the money!"

I explained everything all over again. All the money had been paid back to the Mekane Yesus Church.

Now they seized my hands, forced them under my knees, and bound them together. Then they stuck a pole through this construction and hung me up, with my head hanging down.

A terrible position to be in! I could only move my little finger. My mouth was stuffed full of filthy scraps of cloth so I couldn't make a sound. I was on the point of suffocating, and I was quite sure that my last hour had come.

Now they began to beat me. They hit and hit and struck me all over. My col-

larbone broke. I didn't foresee at the time that ten years would pass before I could get medical attention for it.

My skin came off of my body in long shreds. The worse they treated me, the louder they laughed and mocked me. The wounds hurt horribly. Oh, such pain! It was all so cruel.

They didn't take me down until Sunday evening. I couldn't stand on my own legs: they had been beaten to a pulp. I was the very picture of misery, lying there on the ground.

"Up with you! Go!" They forced me on my bleeding legs along a path lined with sharp pointy stones. My whole body was one gigantic wound. It was worse than the most terrible nightmare.

When a car pulled up outside, they opened the door, grabbed me by the legs, and threw me like a wet sack into the car. I went down in a fog and, in a total stupor, felt nothing more.

At the Third Police Station

Now they drove me to the Third Police Station, a place known throughout the city for the suffering that went on there. The torturers were animals. No one who was brought there could realistically expect to come out alive. Death hovered over everything. It surely was the most terrible place in the whole world.

They brought me into a small room. There were sixty-two of us crammed in there, one up against another. We could only stand, there was nowhere to sit, no room for sleeping. And all that with my battered bones!

We lived day and night in the dark. Without air. In extremely primitive conditions. It was just horrible there.

When you live in such darkness and try to move, your head starts to spin. I lived that way for a year and one month.

Conditions like that should just not exist! No getting out, all locked up, no chance to go outside for a breath of fresh air. Just inside, inside, inside, all the time. Even now when I think of it, I almost get sick. People were treated like animals, not like human beings. Actually, no one would ever treat an animal so cruelly.

At night not everyone could sleep at the same time since it was so narrow in there. And everyone was pressed up so tightly against one another. So in order for some of us to sleep, the others had to stand all crammed together. We took turns through the night. Even when we were lying down, we couldn't turn, it was so tight. If we had to turn, we actually had to stand up first and then lie down on the other side.

We could only lie on our sides, not on our backs or stomachs. There was just no room for that. We all lay with our heads next to our neighbors' feet. Every inch counted.

And all that with my painful legs! The pain was present constantly. They had completely shattered my bones. I could not even draw my leg up to my body, it was so narrow. When the cold set in, my legs swelled up.

The whole time a gloomy darkness dominated in the room. Only a little ray of light under the corrugated iron roof showed us that it was daytime.

All this time in the darkness wrecked my eyesight. Afterwards they never again were back in full working order.

We had nothing to lie on, and we had nothing to cover us unless relatives or friends brought something for us. However, if a family brought a mattress, the guards soon took it away again. They simply ripped it out of our hands. They were stronger. We had no power at all to hang on to our things.

At the same time, the strongest prisoners stole from the weak ones. They took clothing. They took blankets. And if someone like me lay with open wounds on the bare floor, there's no hope of healing. The nightmare was indescribable. We were like animals in a stall. That I even survived is a miracle of God's.

Only much later did I get a mattress to lie on.

In a small adjacent room, there was a hole set in the floor. It was the only toilet for everybody, both men and women. Whoever wanted to go to the toilet had to be very careful. Soldiers guarded the passage to the toilet room with loaded weapons. If we wanted to go to the toilet, we had to stick our heads out of our corral and snap our fingers. If the wardens gave us the sign, we were allowed to go. If they refused, we had to go back in again. We were carefully observed even while we were sitting on the toilet.

But how was I even supposed to get there? Each movement was torture. I tried to move around with the help of a broomstick that paradoxically had been left in the prisoners' hall.

There was no fresh air. We didn't have so much as a peephole to open. Our salvation was that the roof didn't fit closely against the wall and some air blew in through the opening. How can I find the words to describe our suffering? It is unbelievable what people can endure.

In February I had been taken prisoner. It was three months before I started to improve at all. My wounds were never tended; there was no medicine. There was no relief.

I hardly dared to drink water, because it was nearly hopeless trying to get to the toilet. I could not walk on my own feet. My hands were one solid wound. I couldn't hold anything, not even a cup. The problem went on and on. If one wound healed, another broke open again, so that over the course of several weeks I didn't manage to move at all. Fellow prisoners combed my hair; others came with water and tended to me.

But it wasn't only me who went through that. We were all abused. And the nighttime cold touched everyone's skin and caused new pains in old wounds.

New Sufferings

I believe it was in May when they took me and tortured me for the second time. The previous night I'd had a dream. I saw myself with a smashed-up face, with my teeth showing through my skin. In the morning, after this dream, I was downright despondent. I don't normally believe in dreams. But I definitely got some kind of forewarning from this one.

Then they came. "Tsehay, come! Quick! Quick!"

I had no time to dress myself properly. I only had time to grab my cardigan.

This time they threw me on the ground and bound my hands behind my back. They tied up my feet as well and hung me up again. They shouted, "Tsehay, go ahead and pray to your Jesus!"

But I had already been doing that for quite some time.

Then they whipped me. They beat and battered me like savages. This time it was even worse than before. The skin that had healed split open again and shredded. The nightmare began anew.

"Won't he come and help you, your little Jesus?" they taunted. The pain was unendurable. Finally I heard someone say, "Now she's dead."

They let me down again.

I lay in a pool of blood. They drove up again with a car to the entrance and threw me inside like a wet sack. The whole time they insulted and cursed me. Once again, I believed that I would not survive. It was simply harrowing.

I got nothing to clean myself up with. My body burned as if I had a fever. Again the others cried when they saw me. For a long, long time I was afraid to drink anything in case I'd have to go to the toilet, because I never would have made it! Once again I couldn't walk.

After the first time, I was sick for three months. After the second, I never recovered—even years after. Since the torture, my kidneys have never worked properly.

I never would have thought that people could be so cruel to others. They absolutely rejoiced in our sufferings. The worse the pain was, the better it seemed to please them.

In the midst of all the suffering, though, I experienced Jesus near to me the whole time, so close, so close. During the day after they had beaten me so badly,

I tried with the help of the broomstick to stand up. The women wailed over my hopeless attempt. They wept.

"Lie down and rest," they said. But the wounds hurt so much that it did no good. Even the men wept.

Just yesterday I met up with a man who knew me then. "Is it really you? You didn't die? How long were you imprisoned? Ten years? Is that possible? All those beatings, and here you are ten years later!"

But God's hand is great; it reaches so far. It is there even where no friends can reach, no neighbors, no family. But he still comes in. In the midst of filth, he is there, in humiliation, in blood, in stench. Through everything, he went along with me, so close by me. I felt his nearness the whole way.

And I would always remember the word of God, the Scripture, which I had listened to so many times before. One verse especially gave me strength: "Behold, the lamb of God who takes away the sin of the world!"

And the songs that I knew came into my mind. "What a Friend We Have in Jesus." He accompanied me while I lived under the shadow of power.

After the second torture, the nightmare lasted several months. I had given myself up and despaired. I begged God to let me die.

One day when I was on the toilet, I saw a bottle of chlorine. The temptation to drink its contents down was great. That would bring everything to a swift end. But it was as if God stood near me.

"The one who made you, that's me. I have made you by my hand. You do not have the right to end your own life."

In this way, he drew me back from the brink.

On that day, I poured my heart out to God. I prayed the whole day.

But it wasn't over with that. Again and again the soldiers took me for interrogation in the old palace of the Derg.

"Up! Up! Hurry! Hurry!" they shouted again and again. Again they beat me, again they whipped me. Again and again they asked me the same questions:

"Where are Gudina's books?"

"What has Gudina written?"

"Who did Gudina meet with regularly?"

"Who did he work with?"

How was I supposed to answer?

Between the interrogations, we were locked up in a small cell. The circumstances there were horrible. Everyone who'd been taken into custody was hungry and sick; everyone had been tortured.

They brought us a kind of food. Two men carried it in the way you'd carry a stone. They were the leftovers from the Derg office. Gnawed-on bones and the leftovers from their plates. The guards stood at the door and emptied the revolting mess onto the floor. Then they pushed the swill into several piles, each of which was supposed to feed eight prisoners. We were supposed to crawl up to the piles and try to grab something to eat. You can't imagine it; I can't describe it.

"You piece of shit, don't you want to eat?" they mocked.

"Give me some water," I begged. "I need only water!"

One woman who'd been taken for interrogation and torture by the Derg used the opportunity to cut her own carotid artery. Then she wrapped her towel around her throat. She was only discovered when she was already dead.

Another woman drowned herself in the toilet hole, shortly before I was arrested. That's the reason the guards followed us to the toilet.

Like in Hell

Fear tormented us the whole time. If one of us was taken, we never knew if he was headed for some kind of bestial torture or was just going to be killed. Prisoners disappeared daily. Men came back from the torture missing a hand, a foot, both, or other body parts. The guards knew no mercy at all!

They beat strong men into broken ones. In other cases, we could see the tips of their bones sticking out of their feet. After torture, the soles of my own feet had a hole in them. And all this happened amidst the most awful jeering! They were animals. They laughed at us and enjoyed inflicting pain on us. The whole time we were under supervision, they held their weapons with the bayonet sticking out at us. Many, many people died quickly. Death and pain were everywhere.

Not many survived of those who were with me at the Third Police Station. In most cases, the guards came to the door and called out a name. Everyone cringed in a state of panic.

"Come out of there!"

And who can even imagine the despair of those who were called?

Some came back, abused almost to the point of death; others were never seen again. To be called meant to be under the sentence of death. If I tried to report all of the suffering that took place in that prison, this would have to be a thick, thick book.

One woman came back after they had cut off her breast with a knife. She suffered the most appalling pain. Later on, they just let her go free.

Another woman, after the torture, couldn't urinate anymore because they had beaten her so cruelly in the lower abdomen. She suffered terrible pains. Her wounded uterus was cut out in the hospital. After the operation, she was paralyzed from the waist down. In this condition, they brought her back to the *prison for seven more years. She couldn't make it to the toilet; she just lay there. When a bowel movement came, she remained lying in her own feces and stench. It's unbelievable that she didn't die.*

And what could I do? I prayed to God. I prayed ceaselessly to God. But even when I kneeled down to pray, they were always right there again. "Get up!" they bellowed. "Go ahead and call out to your little Jesus!"

But I knew. I knew he was my Lord who helped me through all of it.

Without his help, I never would have survived that bitter, dark night. They could only injure my body. My soul they couldn't touch. My soul was in the hands of the Lord. And that enraged them.

They accused me not only because of my Christian faith. I was also accused of having worked to undermine the government.

They could call it what they wanted. Before I came to jail, I didn't know what politics was. But I had tried to live as a Christian. And as a Christian I had to try to help everyone. As Christians, we believed that all people were equal, whether they were Amhara or Oromo. If everyone is equal before God, then our duty was to help people, no matter which ethnic group they belonged to. It was the same for Gudina. Actually, that should have fit perfectly with the ideals of the revolution, but in practice it wasn't so.

Our faith had to become effective in our lives. We tried always to work for what was right. We couldn't just look on while people got thinner and thinner due to poverty while others were always getting richer and richer at the expense of the hungry. Already under the monarchy Gudina had, for those reasons, as a pastor, refused to pray for the emperor and his house. He said we should think instead of the people who were going hungry in Wollo while the emperor was tossing bread out of his expensive car onto the side of the road.

To be a Christian has consequences in everyday life. And they can use the name of "Christian" to label you as a criminal. My sin against the government was basically only that I was a Christian and accountable to God alone, not to human beings.

I know that they killed many Christians solely because they were Christians. Even more were arrested for that reason.

To be a Christian was a crime. "Politics and Christianity is the same for us," they said. "There is no difference."

On this basis, they sentenced many people to death. Me too. For nine months, I lived under the death sentence. A political prisoner because I was a Christian.

After nine months, they said that the matter would be investigated again. They came for me again. "Now things should start getting better for you," they said. "You can go ahead and tell us everything with an easy mind."

But what else did I have to tell them?

"You know that what you told us before led to the death sentence. You know that very well."

"I don't know that," I answered.

"Yes, and now things should be getting better for you. You can talk now."

"I have nothing else to say," I answered. So I went right back to jail. No verdict was returned.

For a year and a month, I lived in the hell of the Third Police Station. And in all that filth and humiliation Christ lived with me under the long shadow of power.

Despite everything, I had good luck. I knew that almost nobody got out of there alive. That I survived it is a divine miracle.

God sent friends who brought me food. If neither relatives nor friends came with food, people simply starved. Hunger is cruel! It is a grim experience to live together with people who are so hungry. All the food that was brought to us we assembled together and divided up equally. But what was that for so many people?

Once they locked up a sorcerer in the prison. A lot of people brought him food. He shared it with everybody else. As long as he was there, there was enough food. But after a short time they killed him. Then there was only a little bit of food again. I can't tell how often despair gripped us when someone was going to be killed.

In addition to this, all the prisoners suffered from, among other things, toothache. Our teeth decayed and fell out. Tuberculosis, gum disease, and infectious diseases spread and killed. I didn't realize then that it was malnutrition that was hurting our teeth. Now I do.

Someone brought me a Bible that I wrapped up inside my clothes. In unobserved moments, I opened my dress a little so I could read some of those precious words to myself. I had most success doing that on the toilet. Reading was impossible in the room where we slept.

We crouched on the ground. Often other women came up to me and sat down near me. Then I hurried to tell them what I had read. We had to be very careful. We couldn't let anyone notice what we were doing. We would have been harshly punished.

Many people decided to become Christians.

With the Lord as Our Hope

To live as a Christian is to be destined for suffering. Christ suffered for us. If the master must suffer, his disciples could not expect anything better. I only followed after him.

Naturally, you start to think about those who live in peace and joy without any troubles at all. David also thought about it, as he said in Psalm 73. He saw how well things went for people who lived without God. They had no problems. But then he saw the truth of their whole existence. After that he didn't want to exchange places with them anymore.

That is the perspective we can live with. One day our Lord wants to give us a heavenly home. He has paid off our debt. And it is his plan that we should join him there someday.

He wants to have everyone near to him. He loves everyone. Whether we are black or white, it makes no difference. Whether we are children or adults, it makes no difference. I like this children's song so much:

Jesus loves the little children,
All the children of the world,
Red, brown, yellow, black, and white,
They are precious in His sight,
Jesus loves the little children of the world.

God loves everyone. His goodness is so great. He loves the little ones. He loves the big ones. And he loves us. He alone is our God. Even when parents scold or punish their children to make them learn something, it's never long until they show their love for them clearly again.

Children who are not brought up in this way have a bad or perhaps hardly any relationship at all with their parents. You have to speak with children. They have to hear what is right and wrong. They will not always understand why their parents treat them so.

We also have times when we cry out to God: "Why, Lord?" He gives us an answer, but we don't understand it. But we can thank God that we know him. For what hope do we have without the Lord? There is only darkness and death.

In the end, that's what it's all about. That is more important than everything else.

Here's a person who was alive yesterday. Today he is no more. What remains?

I have experienced, and I know, that this world means nothing to me anymore. I live for eternal life. Everything revolves around that. The Lord alone is our hope.

I have experienced good times. I had a good husband, I had many good children. I had a nice home. I had everything that a person could wish for. But we can't take anything in this world with us. And when all that was gone, I still had the Lord.

I wanted to die. I begged God to let me die. To come home to him was all that I wanted.

Pain and despair tormented me. My home, my husband, my children, I had lost everything! That hurt. Death would have been a liberation.

I groaned at the thought of my husband. Never have I experienced anything like that. Had he been killed? Did he still live but in great suffering? The whole time I hoped that he was dead. But still, it would have been good to know for sure one way or another.

I heard rumors. But how was I to know which one was right? I had heard that the president himself had killed him. Gudina was built so large that it was almost impossible to keep him hidden, unnoticed somewhere for a long period of time. That he should still be alive I took to be impossible.

But all those years in prison I still hoped that I might run into him. I didn't want to give up hope.

When I speak about it, my tongue is almost mute. It is so hard, so hard. One day I will be able to tell it all to my children. That will do us all some good. As long as the old regime stayed in power, I had to keep silent, just keep silent. I couldn't say a single word to anybody. It was like an ulcer inside of me that threatened to explode.

There were many who asked questions, but that wasn't the problem. The problem was what I was supposed to say in response. It was dangerous to talk about it. And I knew: I would not survive losing my freedom again.

In the Big Prison

Of my fellow prisoners at the Third Police Station, only a few survived. That I, along with two other women, got transferred to the big prison was a miracle. God is with us in the darkest valley. He allowed the enemies to lead us into the bitter night, but he himself is with us there, too.

When we arrived at the big prison, they brought my fellow prisoner Marta, whom I loved dearly, into a tiny little room with me. Marta was Kulani's age and her father was among the evangelical pioneers in western Welega. Here we were penned up with sixty other people. They were mostly thieves and murderers. Each morning they drove us out of the cell, and each evening they drove us back into it again.

There were neither beds nor mattresses. They certainly would have been full of vermin anyway. We lay on the ground in our clothes—what was left of them.

It's better not to speak of the fleas and lice; there were hosts of them. But even worse were the bugs on the walls. Oh, how they bit us, and absolutely everywhere! They got stuck in everything! How can I describe it? Typhoid was very widespread among us the whole time because of them.

And then there were the rats. The prison was positively swarming with aggressive rats. They crept along the earth and had absolutely no fear. They climbed high up the wall and along the ceiling. Was I afraid of them? What good would that have done? Many people suffered from sheer terror.

We tried to catch the rats. One day I killed fifty of them! Another day it was only eleven. I took my loaf of bread, the only thing that I had to use for bait, and flung it with all my might toward them. Scoot. . . ! That's how we got rid of them.

Often sleeping was just plain impossible. The rats scrabbled on the roof and peed down on us so that it sprayed all over. It was like it was raining urine! There was no escape route, no way out!

Later we got rat traps. One day I managed to kill fifty-four of them!

Once the rainy season set in, it got worse than ever, because now all the rats from the outside came streaming into the building. When all the prisoners had lain down and it was quiet in the room, the rats crept closer and closer. The floor and walls were downright plastered with rat excrement!

I can't describe it in words. The stink was excruciating. There was no window to open to get fresh air. There was not a single airhole. Oxygen was not to be had.

The one thing that saved us was that the earth in certain places came loose from the clay walls, so the littlest bit of air could seep in.

We also had a corrugated iron roof that the air crept in under. At the same time, though, it made the room ice cold when the rainy season came. Many people were too thinly dressed to keep warm.

If, however, the sun burned down on the roof, the room became like an oven. It is no surprise at all that many people got fevers that quickly turned into lung inflammations. And those were the ideal circumstances for tuberculosis.

The whole day we had to stay outside. Around three o'clock in the afternoon they drove us back behind locked doors again. Then the night began for us.

Despondent

Many distressing things happened. We all lived so close together. Many people slept pressed up against each other. One night a woman came and lay down right by me. She had nothing to cover herself with. It was cold. I took pity and shared my blanket with her. She crept right up next to me and soon fell deep asleep. Suddenly she urinated right in the middle of my bed. Both of us were soaked. The mattress that I'd gotten was sopping wet. Even the blanket was damp. And the stink! I sat up and just began to scream. I had no power anymore over my reactions. It was the last straw. I could throw up even now just thinking about it.

The woman was diabetic so she had no control over her bladder. It was so disheartening that I don't know how to describe it. I was drenched in her urine, my whole body!

A young woman near us came over and comforted me.

"Don't cry, Mama Tsehay, I'll help you," she said. She dragged the mattress outside to let it dry out. She helped me take off my wet, stinking clothes and lent me her shawl. Then she took the clothing, the bedsheet, and my wool blanket and tried as well as she could to wash them out in a puddle.

The diabetic woman lay down on the floor. That wasn't too good for her. But she couldn't do anything about it.

It was a long time before the mattress dried out. In the meanwhile, we found a couple of pieces of plastic that I tried to cover the mattress with when I slept. It was impossible to wash it clean.

After three months, they moved us to another room. But there was actually no room at all for us there. We had to lie down behind the door when it was closed in the evening. But soldiers often came in the night and pushed the door open. Then we had to snatch up our things in a hurry. We always had to take our bags with us, coming and going.

Later a bunch of thieves joined our group. But after a half a year they let them go again.

When they were set free, the soldiers wanted to use our room for something else, so Marta and I were brought into another big cell again. I was still always sick and in a sorry state after the torture during my interrogation. There was no room for us in this room, either, and we were again placed directly behind the door. When the door opened at six o'clock every morning, we had to hurry and roll our things up quick so we wouldn't be trampled underfoot. Everyone had to get out, double time.

Once again, we were brought to yet another cell where there wasn't enough room. We got the command to sleep directly next to the door to the toilet. We collected pieces of plastic to cover the mattresses we'd brought along. People had to take a big step to get over us when they went to the toilet. They splattered us while they were peeing. We had plenty to do to protect ourselves from that.

My legs got worse and worse. People were always stepping on them now. My legs swelled up and I was brought to the clinic for a short while. It was a small room. There I was set down on the floor because I had no advocate to get me a bed in a hospital room.

I had been in jail for three years now. A while later, the men in the barracks were moved to a different one because they needed more room for the women. We moved into the barracks, into a huge hall, with two hundred other women. One little corner was partitioned off with corrugated iron. That turned into a little room for twelve sick people and a few mothers.

Marta and another woman who had always been with us were placed in the big room. Finally we got bunk beds for sleeping—narrow, narrow beds.

The bunks were lined up right next to each other. New prisoners had to sleep on the floor under the beds. People slept stacked up on top of one another. The beds were so narrow that we had to lie on our sides so as not to fall out.

A few prisoners managed to smuggle in some insect repellent, although it was strictly forbidden, since people could have used it to kill themselves. We sprinkled it around carefully in order to have some peace from the vermin. But it didn't help against the rats. Swarms of them were constantly streaming into the hall.

And how we froze! It was worst the first year when we'd had to sleep on the bare earth. But even now the walls were not thick. It was drafty. That gave us air, but at the same time it was ice cold. In Addis Ababa, it often dropped down to freezing during the night, since the city lies almost eight thousand feet above sea level.

The women were housed in one barrack and the men in another. But we met up in the school. Everyone had to attend school. At least we finally had something to do.

The food was something else. Every now and then we got injera of the worst kind for lunch. One single injera was supposed to feed four people. Otherwise we got bread, which were really rolls. We got a dried-up roll for breakfast, one for lunch, and one for dinner. Often it was old and moldy by the time we got it.

Together with the roll we got a cup of tea every evening. A lukewarm drop of tea, a tea of sorts. That was all. For the whole day! That was supposed to be enough for the men, too. Who can survive for long when fed this way?

But my friends from the church were a blessing to many people. They faithfully provided us with extra food. We shared, and God placed his blessing on the sharing. For it was painful to look on those who'd had no food brought to them and so had to go hungry. It was horrible.

And all the illnesses! Many got sick, languished, and struggled. Many lay there for one or two months with nothing to eat, no medicine. Many died in the end.

It was terrible to see how fine people simply died off. I remember one industrious young woman. On Wednesday she got sick. She lived through Thursday and Friday. On Saturday she died. If only she could have gone to the hospital. But she had no chance to.

It was the same with a man that I'd gotten to know. He broke his foot playing soccer while he had a day's parole from the barracks. His foot hurt. He got no help. The foot swelled up and finally he got gangrene.

A mere bandage that held his foot in place while the bones grew back together ended up being his salvation. Finally they took him to have his foot amputated. He was still in jail long after I got out. He was so capable that he taught in the prison school. A nice boy, a Christian from Eritrea.

Again and again, I thought about my beloved husband. Was he alive? Was he dead? What had happened? Was he suffering horribly?

He was in his late forties when he was taken prisoner. It's painful when you don't know what's happening. If a hen disappears or a sheep wanders off, the people say, "The hyenas have taken it." If only I'd had the slightest notion whether he was alive or dead!

No one said anything. I was stuck in prison, and in prison they tell nothing. I had certainly heard rumors. But I could not rely on rumors.

One person said, "He is dead."

Then came another with, "He is not dead."

Which one should I believe?

But even if I'd known for sure that he was dead, I would not have mourned. Gudina loved God. He loved the Lord. I worshipped the Lord, too; he was also my Lord. He doesn't cast us off. So often I have felt his love.

If Gudina was dead, it wouldn't mean that God had cast him off. It would only mean that God had taken him home. It would be painful to acknowledge that he hadn't died of an illness. To die by the hand of another human being is horrible. I have seen so many people who were killed. And two of my children had died, hadn't they? A little one and a big one. But they died in peace.

But to die by a human hand—that is abominable. They don't kill quickly. They torture and play with their victims. There were many among us who had been nearly killed but not quite. The torturers broke their bones and stuffed their mouths so full of bread that they almost suffocated. Then they broke their hands and arms. Finally they either beat them brutally with clubs or stabbed them with bayonets.

If they'd simply wanted to kill them, they would've cut their throats. But it seemed like it was of greatest importance to torture the people. How can I describe our terrible life in prison?

That I was able to maintain my sanity was the grace of God. When I encountered such things, I cried out constantly in my heart to God: "You must help us through here. Help us!"

Life in Prison

Out of nowhere, the sentries arrived wanting to check the rooms. All of a sudden they came and penned us up inside the barracks like sheep. "In here! Go, go! And make it snappy!" they hectored us. "Touch nothing, throw nothing away! Come along!"

Sometimes we had not yet gotten dressed so we grabbed our clothes. "Leave that! Take nothing!" bellowed the soldiers. Others grabbed their food. "No! Leave it!"

We had to go. The door was locked behind us.

Sometimes we spent the whole night that way. Sometimes they came in and took a whole bunch of prisoners. They always came when we least expected it. They bellowed and blustered. They swore and intimidated us. Sometimes it happened early in the morning. They rushed in and bellowed, "Nobody move! Nobody touch your things!"

Then one or the other person was supposed to come out. We all thought, "Is he going to be set free?" or "Will she be killed? What do they want with her?"

They could begin as early as four in the morning and continue until noon. They had all the power.

Why did they act this way? They didn't get anything out of it.

Foreigners also counted among the prisoners—particularly people who had owned businesses. The government had confiscated everything that belonged to them and sent the owners to prison.

I also know that they profited from the emergency aid from abroad that had been donated for hunger relief. Many of the items never got where they were supposed to go, since the government itself was responsible for their distribution. They kept everything for themselves. They either used it for their own private needs or they sold it in order to increase their income. Such wares were sold in the market. The poor, who were supposed to get them, had to buy the wares if they could. Foreigners would hardly believe how bad it was.

Lots of emergency aid was sent to prisoners, too. Wool blankets, shoes, clothing. Most of it never reached us. After the guards and leaders in the prison had taken what they wanted for their own use, the leftovers were delivered to us.

Many prisoners froze dreadfully. It happened that some of my friends were able to bring me a pair of woolen blankets. Frozen young people came to me in hopes of getting something to warm themselves with.

One young woman gave birth in prison. The situation was so terrible for her that she practically went crazy.

The guards would get angry at me when I got clothing for the others. "Why in the world do you do that?" they asked.

In the meanwhile, many children were born in prison, and their mothers didn't have so much as a rag to clothe them in. Because I'd been able to inform my friends of how badly we needed baby clothes, they brought many baby things to me. Some of the officers saw that.

"Such lovely clothes! They're much too nice for these grubby kids. They'd suit my children much better. Hand them over!"

I said to them, "God sees what you are doing. Some day all will be revealed."

What was I supposed to do? I couldn't stop them from doing what they wanted.

None of us prisoners could ever really talk together properly. We never could trust anyone else. Nowhere could we ever be alone. Everything we saw and endured we had to carry alone.

The burden got heavier and heavier and always harder to carry.

The whole time I slept badly. Hardly had I laid myself down before I tried to think of good and beautiful things. I thought of good food, of positive experiences. But that was not easy. From the beginning of the evening until ten, eleven, or twelve midnight, the air was full of quarrels and shouting, brawls and racket. Sometimes it went on the whole night like that.

Nightmare

It was always horrible when they suddenly appeared and called out one name or another. It wasn't long then before that person was killed. One day three dead bodies lay outside our door.

Sometimes they called us in the morning with the words, "Come and see what's going to happen to them! It's what we'll do to you if you try to escape."

And then they killed those people right before our very eyes. Over time, our hearts hardened.

Each soldier that had killed a prisoner got promoted to "Chief over Ten" and received more pay. This perfidious system trained the soldiers to kill blindly so they'd get promoted.

I heard of a woman among the prisoners who were supposed to be brought to the courtroom by a female guard. On the way there, the prisoner was shot. "She tried to escape," claimed the guard. Other guards assured us otherwise. The female guard had only wanted to be "Chief over Ten."

With my own eyes, on the way to a check-up in the hospital, I saw them kill a man in front of the interrogation room.

Another case was of a man who'd had a sheep. When a thief stole his sheep, the man ran after the thief and knocked him down, in order to get his sheep back. The police took the man to jail because he had hit the thief. He was sent to us. But in the middle of the night he wanted to go home and tried to escape. He came to the fence. He hid there but was found and then shot. And all because he had been the victim of a theft!

Another man was caught while trying to escape. They forced him to carry a very heavy rock on his back. He had to walk around and around with the rock while they whipped his legs. We had to watch—and we cried. It was unbelievable, but he survived it.

One big and strong woman that I was in jail with had a husband and children waiting outside the jail. One evening she was called by the guards. "What's wrong?" she said. "Could I come tomorrow morning instead?"

They let her sleep in peace that night. Early the next morning they were there again. They called her and also many others to come out. All their clothes and belongings remained behind. They had to walk out naked in front of the barracks. Then they killed them all.

In light of all these experiences, we were just waiting for our own turn. Once they got started, they'd get around to us soon enough. The despondency in the whole jail was absolutely huge.

It was similar among the men. In the evening they called their names. Once the daughter of one of my friends came and asked the police whether she might come to me. They allowed her to.

"Is your father free and that's why you can come here?" I asked her. Then she drew a finger across her throat and I knew what was supposed to have happened. And it did happen. The next morning, they took him and killed him. The girl wanted a mother after that. She was all alone.

The family members never got the bodies. The soldiers buried them in mass graves and strewed lime over the corpses to get rid of them. It hurts to remember that.

Often we were sitting in complete silence in the prison school when suddenly the soldiers arrived. "Come out! Quick! Come out immediately!" At most it was eleven in the morning. "Okay, you there, go back again!"

Somebody was going to die that day. We knew it immediately. It turned out to be a man who sat next to me in school. For nine years we sat there together. Then, in the ninth year, they came and killed him. Why in the world did they let him live for so long? In the interval he'd suffered days of hunger, fear, and pain. It would have been much better if they'd killed him right away. What were three dried-out rolls a day for a full-grown man? The men pounced on the food when morning came. They weren't able to ration them throughout the day. So they went hungry the rest of the day. That was all the food they got. Just once, each morning. If you didn't have any relatives or friends to bring you food, you starved. You had no chance of survival.

When somebody got food, the hungry people streamed up and asked if they could have some of it. It must have been God's wrath on our country. That is what I honestly think.

Everyday Life

Early on we were not allowed to do any handicrafts because people would kill themselves with knitting needles and pins. If people figured out how to slash their wrists with one of them, they'd go to the toilet and take their own lives. They'd bleed to death in a short period of time.

At first we also had little access to water. Later there was a water pump that we could use. Warm water was unthinkable. We originally had to stand in line to draw up our allocated water ration from the well. When the water pump came, we had to keep it in working order ourselves, and many times that brought us to the brink of despair. For what did we know about repairs, and what tools did we have?

Clean our house? We had only a simple brush for sweeping. There were also fields that belonged to the prison. The men had to work there. And there was a workshop where tables and chairs were constructed. The prisoners had no fun doing that. The things were sold for the state. What did they care about the prisoners? They only wanted to have the labor. We women did a lot of handi-work, sewing and weaving. That also was sold. Many people worked, sort of, but only because they would be beaten if they didn't do anything at all.

I myself sewed to raise money for the congregations of the Mekane Yesus Church. I have already told how we women worked to earn some money. In this way, I got many young women involved who otherwise would have had noth-ing to do.

What Tsehay sent out from the prison made an impression on the Mekane Yesus Church throughout the city. Some of the more kindly guards functioned as messengers and carried baskets filled with hand-icrafts out of the prison. They were beautifully embroidered Ethiopian clothes, knit sweaters, socks, and tablecloths.

They couldn't believe their eyes. Everything was made laboriously out of materials that Tsehay's friends had brought to the prison. Fabric, embroidery floss, and wool. Tsehay used the materials to motivate despairing prisoners to work. In this way, many women learned to do handicrafts and so could fill up their endless days.

The women would have been able to sell these handicrafts and earn a little bit of money off them. Instead, they allowed them to be brought to the congregations in the city so that they could be sold for the congregations. In the middle all of that misery, something was being done for the kingdom of God.

The handicrafts were sold at the parish women's bazaars. They always drew a lot of people who otherwise never came to church. So the handicrafts were also an important means of bringing people near to the gospel.

The handicrafts helped the congregations financially. At the same time, it was an encouragement to the Christians outside prison to witness to their faith even in such difficult times.

The baskets with the handicraft materials were also filled with food. Bibles were hidden between the foodstuffs and yarn so they could be smuggled in to Tsehay.

She always needed new Bibles. Many prisoners wanted to read the word of God. To distribute Bibles was forbidden in all of Ethiopia. No one was allowed to influence anyone else in that way, as it was officially said. So Bibles became extra valuable, especially in prison.

Each time that someone came to the prison during the visiting hours on a Sunday, the basket was searched through exactingly. Often, relatives of the prisoners came with dishes full of beautifully prepared food. The guards poked around in the pepper sauce with filthy sticks in order to check whether something had been hidden in there.

When Tsehay's friends came with Bibles, it was dangerous. If they were discovered, it could have serious consequences for Tsehay as well as for the visitors. But other Christians prayed during the visiting hours, and the remarkable thing is that despite the most careful searches no Bible was ever discovered. Instead, only the baskets without Bibles were specially examined. God performed a miracle. He closed the eyes of the inspectors.

Bible Smuggling

Bit by bit I got many Bibles smuggled into prison. Bibles were strictly forbidden; it was a life-threatening matter. And there lay a heap of Bibles next to me!

Suddenly the guards came to search through everything.

I prayed to God that he would make the guards blind so they would overlook the Bibles. And they found nothing!

Exactly at this time, I had a whole cardboard box full of Bibles that I wanted to distribute. The men also were to get some of them. And the guards saw nothing!

On the same occasion, they discovered everything the others had hidden; not even a notepad was overlooked. They searched through every single mattress. But they didn't see the Bibles. That really was for me evidence of God's hand.

The search was prompted by Mengistu wanting to pay a visit to the prison in three days' time. The entire place was turned upside down. When they came to check us they said, "Everybody out! Come out with your hands over your head! Don't take anything with you!"

Everyone went out.

"One person can stay while we search. Mama Tsehay, come here!"

I knew where all the Bibles were. They turned the clothes inside out. They ripped mattresses to see what had been hidden inside of them. They combed through everything they could find.

But when they came up to my bed, they asked, "Mama Tsehay, why on earth are you locked up in this prison?"

And they didn't touch my things.

"Mama Tsehay," said a guard, "Mama Tsehay, I haven't had breakfast yet today because I had to get here so early."

I found some chocolate in my pocket and gave it to him.

Is God not a God of miracles? He is the one who carries us through.

He led the people of Israel through the Red Sea. He made its water into walls. They passed through. Exactly the same happened with my Bibles. God held his hand before their eyes. Everyone else's stuff, every bit of it, was all messed up. My things were not once touched. God never tires!

If I took time to think of all his blessings, I'd forget everything else. The valley of the shadow of death is here, is it not? Yet he takes us and carries us through. It was hard, all those years in the prison. I heard nothing of what was going on and what was happening to my loved ones. It was strictly forbidden to ask questions. Visitors were allowed to mention only trifles.

We met with them in the visiting area. It was a long, fenced-off corridor where the visitors and prisoners could see one another. The guards walked up and down along the corridor and listened to everything that was being said. Or should I say, everything that was being shouted? For we prisoners stood on one side of the fence and the visitors on the other side. Everyone had to call out so that the other could hear. Those were our visits. If the visitors had a basket along with food or other gifts, the guards first checked through everything thoroughly before passing it on to the guards in the corridor. And those guards often checked everything too before they handed the basket over the fence to the prisoners.

Once it worked out that a card was smuggled to me inside a basket without being found. Otherwise it would have been taken out and I would have been punished. But once a letter from my children got through to me.

"How did that get here?" asked the guards.

"I just got it," I said, "but you can read it if you want. There's nothing special in it." It was only a letter between mother and children. No politics were mentioned in the letter, which had been written in Oromo. Despite this, they got very angry.

"That is not supposed to happen," they said. In the letter, nobody was mentioned by name. There was nothing about the government or the ruling powers. It was only greetings and a few passages from the word of God for me. Despite that, I got an earful. But even so, I got the letter back again after they had read through it carefully.

Punishment

Once at Christmastime, I went together with someone else to the guards and asked whether we could be allowed to send Christmas cards to our friends. I had friends all over the world. I wanted so much to reach them with a Christmas greeting. But it didn't work.

Now and then someone would try to do something secretly. But that was horribly dangerous. However, fortunately, there were differences among the guards. Some treated us well. When the good guards were on duty, we rejoiced. When the vicious guards were there, we were afraid.

For some time, a young woman was with us who had nothing to eat. I gave her some of my food. We had to share to save those who were hungry. Then came one of the cruel guards. "It's not your job to give this bad person something to eat!" screamed the guard. He snatched the food away from the girl and threw it out. Afterwards he locked the girl up for two weeks.

Not long afterwards, this girl was sent to the terrible Police Station. They seized me too and informed me that they wanted to whip me for my behavior. The others around me wept. "She won't survive," they said. "She's used up all her strength. She is old and sick."

If they had killed that sadistic sentry, it would have been a great joy for everybody. He tormented all of us as much as he could. Then he took me to be whipped. But fortunately the other soldiers let me go. It was only a matter of food, after all. What a relief! You are gripped by an icy fear when the long shadow of power falls on you.

When I came back about half an hour later, my fellow prisoners wept for joy, all of them together. But I noticed how in such moments the fear that had been thrust aside and suppressed suddenly filled everyone completely up again. Death would have been a liberation.

When this happened, it was probably 1986.

Right after I had arrived in the big prison, I got a stool. With the terrible pains in my legs, it was a torment always to be squatting on the ground. Pastor Tasgara brought me a traditional stool. That did me good, since for many years we'd had not even the edge of a bed to sit on. Day and night we had to spend on the floor.

Now, in the daytime after that bitter night, I praise God. I had a good husband, I had lovely children, I had a nice home, and I had many good friends. But when I came to prison, I no longer had husband nor children. And most of my friends forgot all about me.

"She is certainly dead," they said. But God helped me to forget about that. He sent me new friends from the other side of the ocean. From many countries, he sent me friends who cared for me and kept me alive. Marie Myrhen, Marit Bakke from Norway, Schonherr from Germany, and all my Christian friends from Holland. There were many others I never saw or whose names I never knew but whose rewards are with the Lord.

You came with food to the prison so that I wouldn't have to go hungry. You brought yarn so I had something to do. You came with clothing so I wouldn't be cold. You were the hand of God for me; did you know that? Oh, God's hand is longer than the long shadow of power! It reaches as far as God wants it to. What would I have had to eat if you had not brought me food?

Here in prison I saw many children grow up. I could help them out with the things I got. God helped so that what I received served the needs of many. You were my sisters, my brothers, my friends. When you came to the prison, the others called to me, "Mama Tsehay, your relatives have come! Mama Tsehay, your relative has come. She is standing outside. Hurry! Hurry!"

In this way, I got salt, pepper, flour, bread, and even money now and then. I got onions. They were gifts from God. I thank him for that. When one of you had to go back home, I cried. I was so despondent. But then God sent me still other people. Many I hadn't even known before. Nevertheless you came. You were my family, God's gift.

God allowed the three young men to go into the fire. But he was with them and rescued them from it. He let Daniel get thrown into the lion's den, but he was there and shut the mouths of the lions.

New Christians

Despite this, we were afraid. When someone dies, you are afraid. When they seize your neighbor, you start to fear. When they take your home, you start to fear. Fear comes and you tremble.

I saw how people around me couldn't sleep. They were doubled up with fear. But God's people, even when they cannot sleep, perceive that God stands by them and gives them his peace in the midst of all the fear.

That is the unbelievable difference between those who believe in God and those who don't. We live differently. We talk differently. We act differently. The others don't always understand it. They simply don't believe that someone would like to do them a good turn, that we want to do them good because we believe in God. They refuse to accept it from us.

But I have seen how they observe us, and how, by and by, they realize that it really is so. Finally they listen to our words. After a certain time, they ask for a Bible to read. They want to become Christians. "You were a Christian all along in the way you conducted yourself. We want to be Christians too," they say.

I proclaimed the gospel the whole time I was in prison. That was forbidden. But they saw that I prayed to God anyway.

Then came the other prisoners and said, "Pray for us."

When we got the Bibles that we distributed in secret, I told them where they could start reading. We hid ourselves in all secrecy in a certain place. Each evening, I was asked to read aloud from the Bible. They came again and again. They could never get enough of it.

On Sundays, I had contact with the emperor's family, as they were imprisoned there in a room of their own. I prayed for them. We sang together. Before they were thrown in prison, they hadn't cared much for the gospel. But three of them prayed to God a lot; I should especially mention the oldest princess. They still belonged to the Orthodox church, but they wanted to pray with an evangelical Christian. They believed in God. They prayed in his name. "That is the only thing that matters," they said.

For a long time, they had prayed to God for a Bible, and now we could give them one. They sang chorales and they sent me a message: "Come, Mama Tsehay, we want to pray together."

Later they requested, "Come, Mama Tsehay, now again it is the time to pray."

Now that we have been set free, I visit them often. At such times we pray together. We do not ask only that God would make us healthy and strong again, but that he would preserve our soul and spirit and faith in him. That alone is what's important.

Prison life brought me together with all kinds of people. I will never forget a certain sorceress. She had been arrested with her children. I loved children and gave her some of the children's clothes that I had gotten in prison. She had an unusual kind of clothing on and did many peculiar things when she called upon her spirits.

"Oh, what will become of me?" she often wailed while she read her incantations.

After a year she came to me. "Mama Tsehay," she said, "I've had enough of all this. Nothing helps. I would like to throw it all away now. I want to believe like you do."

Together we took her instruments of sorcery and threw them all away. We burned the incantation ingredients to ashes in a garbage can.

She had some money and wanted to get a new dress. She didn't want even to look at the old one anymore. Away with this costume!

I asked Marie Myrhen to buy fabric for a new dress. Marie came with some magnificent thick fabric. I sewed the dress for the former sorceress.

She became a Christian. She began to pray to God. She became a truly new person. Later they brought her and her children to Godjam. When they took her away, the woman wept.

They were still in the prison in Godjam when I was released.

Another woman who made her living from sorcery was also in prison with her children. I tried to help her as well. It is not good to be a sorceress. "Now you must believe in Jesus," several people had said to her. "That is much better."

She came to me and said, "I want to believe in Jesus now." Then she tore off all of her amulets and threw all of her incantation ingredients into the river and accepted Jesus Christ with her whole heart.

Another woman in our group had killed her own three children and another woman. That's why she was imprisoned. One day she also came to me.

"Mama Tsehay," she said, "can I also hear the gospel?"

"Yes," I said, "it is for you also." I began to explain the message of the Bible to her.

God works. He works long before we do. He is the one who acts.

The Communion of Saints

Sometimes we were punished for singing. The singing of Christian songs was strictly forbidden. Over time, however, we noticed that other prisoners also came over when we gathered around my bed to sing softly together. But we had to be careful because there were also non-Christian prisoners who would give us away to the guards.

Some of the guards liked us and tried to help us Christians. Others went berserk over the smallest thing and beat us.

One time I prepared a small meal that I invited the others to. "Come, everybody," I said, "let's meet. Hurry and call the guards over." The guards came and drank tea with us.

Finally we got to the point where no guards scolded us when I was around. But when I went to the hospital, I heard that afterwards the Christians drifted apart. They were not allowed to sing together anymore.

I could pray in my bed. At Christmastime I got some lovely Christmas cards and had some candles brought to the prison. I decorated my bed with the Christmas cards, burning candles, and a small green twig. It was beautiful. The ones who didn't know the gospel sat there and marveled. They had never seen anything like it before.

I baked some bread from the flour I had gotten. In the later years, there was a little coal oven we could use during the day for warming our food up. During the first few years, such a thing would have been unthinkable. But in the meanwhile so many children had come to live in the women's barracks that they had to grant us women a favor.

In our barracks there were always many children. They grew up there. Some of them became quite tall while I was there. One girl lived in the prison from birth to seventh grade. She was finally released from custody, but her mother had to stay in prison. They wouldn't let her go free. The girl went to live with her relatives.

Many people in prison were there even longer than I was. Four women from the northern part of the country came there before me. Their hair had grown gray there. When they came, they didn't believe in God. But here they became Christians. Now they pray to God. While they were free they had said that there was no God. Now they believe in him.

When I pray, I think especially of those who are all alone, who have nobody to think of them, who have no children, no relatives, no food, who have nothing. There are many people like that.

A Visit from Mengistu

One day the president himself, Mengistu Haile Mariam, came for a visit to the prison.

"Why have you been imprisoned?" he asked.

"I don't know," I answered.

"How many years have you been here?"

"Six and a half years," I answered. "And I have never been sentenced."

"You've never been sentenced?"

"No," I answered. Then he left.

Later my fellow prisoners asked me, "Why in the world didn't you throw yourself at his feet and beg him for mercy?"

"No. I bow down before God alone," I said. "God will take me out of here when he wants to. He will open the door for me, and on that day it will stand wide open."

In the Hospital

Shortly before I was set free, I finally got into the hospital. I had been begging and praying for that for a long time. But the prison administration didn't want to let anyone go there too easily. I had pains particularly in my shoulders. My collarbone was definitely broken and could not grow together again correctly.

I went to the leprosy hospital in Addis Ababa, called the Armauer Hansen Research Institute. The hospital is named after the Norwegian Gerhard Henrik Armauer Hansen, who discovered the leprosy pathogen.

It was marvelous to finally go to the hospital. My sick body would actually get treatment here. But after everything that had happened, it was for me above all a restoration of the soul. I was completely exhausted and at my wit's end.

Friends from far-off lands also came to the hospital to visit me. Many others did not come. They were afraid, since a visit to me under such circumstances was not without its dangers. But toward the end of these terrible times in our country, God sent me friends from other countries. They were his gifts to me. The God who blesses!

"O Lord, I must thank you and praise you for your unending care and good will toward me!"

Finally Free

Before important events, I find that I cannot rest or sleep. It is a kind of forewarning, although most of the time I don't know what's going to happen. That's how it was when my first child died. That's how it was when they took my husband. That's how it was when they took me prisoner. That's how it was when the other son died. And so it was this time, too. I believe that I have experienced it five times. Each time I was very dull because sleep had proven impossible.

On that Friday morning I had just finished my prayers.

Exactly at six o'clock in the morning, I had just gotten up off my knees when a largish group of people came running into our barracks in a big hurry. Many residents of the barracks went out to see what was up. But I stayed inside and warmed up some water to wash my hair with.

I had just finished with that when the loudspeaker boomed out. "What on earth is that all about, at this time of day?" I thought. But I didn't worry any more about it, for we were used to the loudspeaker filling the air with trivial notifications. And it was not easy to understand what exactly was being said anyway.

Then they began to call out names. I heard the name of a woman with whom I'd been imprisoned all these years now. She had first been sentenced to death, then to twenty-five years for murder.

When her name was called out now, I began to tremble. She shook too. What if they were going to kill her at last?

"Don't be afraid!" I comforted her despondently. "Maybe they will let you go free."

"Yes, maybe," she said and went out.

I grabbed her most important things and went with her to the door. Then the call-outs began. Many people had assembled. Certainly almost all the prisoners were outside by then. They cheered with the old Ethiopian call, "Il, il, il, il, il, il, il, il . . ."

Something especially joyous must be happening. What in the world could it be? I turned around to go back inside. Then they called, "Mama Tsehay, you have been set free!"

"What's wrong?" I asked back.

They shouted it out from all sides at me: "They called your name!"

"It isn't true!" I said. "You must have made a mistake."

There I stood with wet hair, a towel wrapped around my head.

"You are supposed to go free. Get dressed!" they called. I was still standing there in my nightgown.

"No, I don't believe it," I retorted. Then they began to cry, many soldiers and prisoners. They cried so loud.

"Now we are losing Mama Tsehay. What are we going to do? How are we supposed to carry on without her?" they lamented.

"Cut it out!" I said. "It's better if you go out there and find out what is actually going on. This howling won't help anybody."

I now tried to understand the announcement myself.

Then I heard my name, loud and clear. And what did I do? I knelt down and thanked God. God had remembered me. He had thought of me.

"To you praise and thanks are due," I prayed. Then I began to get dressed, quite slowly.

They shouted from outside, "Come out now, they are calling you for the last time!"

"Yes, I'm coming," I called back and appeared in the doorway.

Everyone was standing outside already like a convoy. "Mama Tsehay is free! Mama Tsehay is free!"

Some of them wailed, "What am I supposed to do now? Mama Tsehay was my helper. She gave me food when I was hungry. She helped me in all my need."

What was I supposed to say? What was I supposed to do? I went up the hill in the direction of the gate. There the soldiers stood all crowded together.

"This isn't true. It's just a trap. Here comes death." I was completely convinced of it.

They had just driven three grandsons of Prince Makonnen out. They called many names, always new names.

Then I heard, "Has she come yet?"

"Yes, she is here." And so I was driven onward.

Then I really got scared.

A big bus came driving up to the site. That had never been seen before. At the same time several trucks came up. Countless prisoners were being called.

I thought, "Where are they bringing us now? Where are we supposed to go?"

Everyone was in a state of panic, for we were going in the direction of the Third Police Station. Fear chilled us all.

Then the truck suddenly turned and drove in another direction. "Maybe they have another place where they kill people," we thought, completely stiff with fear. We were all certain that we were going to die.

We drove just a little bit farther, then the truck stopped.

"Go, get out!" called the soldiers. "Come down! Go! Over here! No talking!"

Everyone was silent. Everyone stood still. From the truck we heard the radio rattling and whistling, always spitting out new orders. Now even more cars were arriving. "Come over here! Come here!"

"Rrrrrrrrrr," crackled the radio.

Then they began to call everyone who came from the Tigray region together. Then I was even more certain. "They just want to torture us specially," I thought. But I was ready to meet my God.

"Now you must forgive us for the many years that you were locked up," they announced. Many people had spent twelve or thirteen years or even more in detention. "Now go and work for our ideals!"

On that day, they let nine hundred and seven prisoners go free.

So there I stood. I had no idea where I was. People began to walk away. Some were picked up by relatives. There were no taxis. No buses came by. There was nobody there to ask for help.

I stayed there almost completely alone to the very end.

Marta, my fellow prisoner, came over to me. There were only three of us now, a man and her and me.

Suddenly a car pulled up. "Mama Tsehay, come here, come here!" called the driver. Another car came and took Marta along. What else could we do?

The second son of Prince Makonnen was dead but they brought us to his grandchildren. They had been jailed together with us for many years. They invited us to have lunch with them, although there was a huge group of people already gathered together there, almost two hundred former prisoners. How were they going to carry it off, unprepared as they were to serve a meal to so many people? No one had anticipated this.

"No," I said. "No need of that. Be so kind and help me to get to the Norwegian mission station."

A small Volkswagen was able to take me along. It went straight across the city to the mission station in Urael. When I arrived, it was maybe four-thirty in the afternoon.

The car drove into the area and stopped in front of the office. I got out. The people there did know my name, but no one had ever seen me. One of the missionary ladies asked me, "Aren't you Gudina's wife?"

"Yes," I responded simply.

"But where are you coming from just now?" she asked in surprise.

"I've been set free," I said.

"Is that a police car over there? Aren't those police officers in the car?"

"No," I answered, "there are no policemen here. I really have been set free."

There was a guest house on the mission property, but at the moment all the rooms were occupied.

"Is there no room?"

"Hmm, the whole place is fully occupied." But by now many women were standing all around us.

"We have prayed for this in all of our prayer meetings. She is free! We must call up Marit Bakke in Makanisa immediately."

Marit wanted to come get me at once.

"But I'm not alone," I said. "There are two of us." Marta was still with me. Marit answered that there was enough room for her, too. Whoever wanted to come could.

About an hour later we were in Makanisa. Marit received us. Now it got going: Marit telephoned all over the world. She called Norway, she called Germany. She spent the whole evening on the phone, with only short breaks, calling every corner of the earth. The news went out to everybody.

Marit tried to reach my children in Germany. Late in the evening she finally got through.

"It can't be true," they said. They couldn't believe it. Aster even said, "Mama isn't free. She is only in the hospital, and you are calling us from there."

"Yes, but think about it, in Ethiopia it's the middle of the night right now," I said. Then I began to cry.

"Oh," she said, "is it really true then?"

The next morning, we got up right at six in the morning. Marta and I. Neither of us had been able to sleep. When we stood up, we looked around. We were completely alone; no soldiers were here with us.

A little bit later Marta's relatives came and took her.

On Sunday morning I went up to the church that lay on a little hill near the apartment. To take part in a worship service was the most important thing for me. Imagine being allowed to go to God's house again and be able to join in the worship. That is what I promised him all the years I was praying for my release.

The church was completely full. When people heard that I was there, they all began to weep. In my report, I praised and extolled God again and again for his help. "Yesterday I had no future, but today the future stands open for me."

I thanked and thanked God the Lord. There was nothing in particular that I had to thank him for. It was simply that he had helped me. It was God, he alone, who had helped me. The others had given up, hadn't they? They had gotten tired. From overseas they had again and again begged the government for information. But they got no answer. Finally almost all of them gave up.

But when God's hour had come, then it happened. I have been born twice. It was like I had risen from the dead—from all these cruelties—risen from all these people who had died around me.

Many people were still sitting in prison. Many were still being killed. It wasn't over yet.

I still have problems when I sit. Walking is not so easy for me either. My hips were beaten till crooked and lame, my arms and back too. My feet are disabled. To walk with them doesn't come easily. But no one can see that when I have shoes on. Otherwise my health is improving, even if it is not as good as before. At home I just crawl around, since that's easier.

I waited for change to come to this country. Only God can intervene and make a change. I said that often in jail.

"Only God can take me out of here," I said. I just had to wait until he came and intervened.

It is my firm belief that he can change even the situations that seem impossible. Nothing is too difficult for him, if it is his will, if his hour has come.

But often he has us wait for him. Oh, how long those years were! Long! Long!

Long! And we human beings are weak. We often think that what he has allowed to happen to us is too hard. He knows how we suffer.

God's thoughts are a mystery. No one knows God's thoughts. I don't understand his thoughts. No, we will never understand the mystery of God.

It is also a mystery of God why all this horror had to happen in Ethiopia. Here and there we get a glimpse of light, a brief illumination of his thoughts. He sees everything. He is over all!

God in heaven! You are Lord over all things, Lord over everything! You are God for those who have everything. You are God for the poor. You are the Lord of the rulers.

You can do everything. All mysteries lie in your hands. No one knows them. No one is over you. And you need no one under you. No human being can understand your thoughts.

Only you can help us. Only you can carry us through. Lord, we praise you and thank you for all things, for grief, for joy, for the things that make us cry, for the things that make us laugh.

You, Lord, are our Father. You have mercy on us. You care for us, Lord. You seek the lost. You comfort the grieving. We praise you for that. In our grief or in our joy, we have only thanksgiving to offer you. You require no blood. You accept no gold. You don't want any money. Lord, be praised!

You gave us our Lord Jesus Christ, who could not be bought, not with gold and not with power. You gave him to us. He paid for our guilt. He ransomed us with neither gold nor weapons. He ransomed us with his own blood—through his suffering on the cross and facing damnation for us. On the third day, he rose from the dead because he had conquered death. It was in this way that he ransomed us. You have given us his inheritance. We have heard it. We have been able to receive it.

Praise to you, David's God and mine, you, God, who were with me through the whole bitter night, you who were with me in the fiery furnace!

What Happened to Gudina Tumsa?

During all those long years that Tsehay spent in prison, Gudina's brother Negasa Tumsa went all over Ethiopia trying to find out what had happened to his brother. He explains:

We searched for him in all the prisons of Addis Ababa, in the city jail and in every conceivable hiding place. We looked for him in the outlying regions as well, because there were all kinds of rumors going around. We heard that he was in Arsi, in Harar, in Dembidolo.

An official search was, of course, impossible. The military government never informed us whether he was serving a jail sentence or whether he was dead. We pleaded with some friends in influential positions for their help. Each time we got the same answer: "Just be patient. A decision will soon be reached on this matter."

We kept searching until the military government was overthrown in 1991.

In the meantime, Gudina's children appealed to sister churches abroad and to prisoner's aid associations, asking for their support in making an investigation. The Mekane Yesus Church was encouraged in the many letters it received to undertake further measures toward the discovery of his whereabouts. But it was all unsuccessful.

After the fall of the military regime, a merger of assorted liberation fronts took over the government. A colonel by the name of Asrat Ayele and Konea Ebsa gave an interview on Ethiopian TV in which the long-guarded secret was finally aired.

Colonel Asrat Ayele had served a sentence in prison himself for a while under the military regime and knew Tsehay Tolessa from this period. After his release he had gone to fight on the war front in the north. He moved back to the capital city again with a liberation movement called the Ethiopian People's Revolutionary Democratic Front.

Several weeks after that, the Colonel gave the TV interview along with Konea Ebsa, a former nurse of the Security Force. According to their statement, many people had been taken from prison and killed. They identified Gudina Tumsa by name along with the archbishop of the Orthodox church, Abuna Theophilos, who had also been kidnapped since he refused to work with the communist system. Some other missing persons were also identified by name.

When I heard the news, I got in touch with these people myself. But when I talked to them, it soon became evident that they could only testify to the fact that the prisoners had been taken from the prison. They didn't know where the people had been brought or what had happened to them after, whether they were being kept in another location as prisoners or whether they were dead and possibly also buried. They had no usable information at all. So we got no further.

Later I turned to the Mekane Yesus Church with a request that they designate a representative who, together with me and another friend, could set up a committee to collect information about Gudina Tumsa's case.

First of all, we asked the Mekane Yesus Church for a letter to the new head of the government. He was supposed to assist and support our search through the Ministry of the Interior.

Again we turned to Colonel Asrat. He suggested we meet once a week. We arranged Friday morning as a convenient time to exchange thoughts and the information we had collected in the course of each week.

We were always on the lookout for people who might know something, and we especially searched for people who had been in prison or who had played a leadership role under Mengistu's regime. We traveled throughout the whole country to speak with them. They even let us speak with Tesfaye Wolde Selassie, who had been the Minister of Security during that time. He led us to the palace of Prince Asrate Kassa to show us where they had buried the religious leaders.

He went all around the whole area. "I know that they were killed," he said, "but it is already so long ago that I can no longer say exactly where they buried them."

We had the same experience with former Security officers. One after another, the former employees of the State Security Service, including the official who had had the authority to issue the death sentence, refused to cooperate with us in any way.

Then, at the end of April 1992, a soldier turned up who had been born in Welega, raised in Sidamo, and known Pastor Gudina personally. He had served during that time as a sentry in the gate guard when the murders were taking place, he told us. When Gudina Tumsa was killed, he was standing on watch.

After the fall of the military regime and the establishment of the new government, he heard the testimony on TV. He waited for continuing reports but none came.

After a while, he traveled to the capital city. Since he knew nothing of Gudina's family, he went directly to the Security division of the newly set-up government and told them there that he knew the burial place.

That happened on a Monday. They had our telephone number and called us on that same evening. On Tuesday morning we gathered in the Security Division. There they informed us that Kebbede Amare had voluntarily come from Dessie. "He would like to explain exactly what happened, how and where Gudina was killed."

At first we didn't believe it. This man was just an ordinary soldier. The people in the Security Division didn't believe him either, but in order to be sure we drove to the palace with him. There he led us slowly to the fencing around the premises. During the dictatorship, the fence all the way around the property had been sunk into deep holes in the ground as protection against enemy intrusions. The soldier said that most of the murdered had been buried along there. The dead of one day would all be buried together at the same time, always three or four to a hole. Thirty-eight people had been murdered on that particular night. Pastor Gudina, however, they killed alone, and he was buried in a separate place.

When he led us to the first hole, he said, "Here you'll find the body of Abuna Theophilos."

He mentioned by name the famous politician Haile Fida, saying his corpse would also be found there. He showed us where we could find all thirty-eight victims from that night.

Then he went with us in the direction of the palace. About five meters away from the castle path, he showed us the place where Pastor Gudina Tumsa lay buried.

Afterwards we went back to the place where the thirty-eight were buried and began to dig. First the corpses of some soldiers came to light, which we recognized by their uniforms. Their family members were not there, so we were hesitant as to what we should do with them. An official from the authorities oversaw the exhumation until something was found to put the bodies into.

During the afternoon, I went again with Kebbede Amare to the place where Pastor Gudina was supposed to be buried. This time he specified the location more exactly, about a meter away from the place where he had pointed in the morning. Then we began to dig. We dug down about one meter before we found him. We recognized him by the skull. The size of the body permitted no doubts about his identity. He even still had his socks on.

I filled in the grave again and hurried to the house in order to inform Gudina's oldest daughter, Kulani, who was living in Germany, by phone. I reported to her that I had found the remains and identified them. I would not have risked saying anything to her about it unless I was absolutely certain. Otherwise the disappointment would have been too great.

Kulani asked me to wait an hour. In the meanwhile she communicated with her mother, brother, and sisters. In the evening she called me up and said that she would arrive in Ethiopia on June 27, and she asked me to plan the burial service for that day.

Immediately I got in contact with the Mekane Yesus Church and reported my discovery to them. Then I told them about my plan to invite the media to be witnesses to the exhumation. I asked whether a coffin with the remains could be laid out in a Mekane Yesus Church until the burial. In turn they asked only that we hurry to get the corpse into a coffin as quickly as possible after the opening of the grave. They were glad to do what I asked.

That happened on Wednesday. On Wednesday afternoon, I got in touch with Ethiopian television and the Security Service and asked them to announce the news in all the media. On Thursday at about nine o'clock, all the preparations with the coffin were ready. In the presence of several hundred people and with TV cameras reporting live for Ethiopian TV, the remains of Pastor Gudina Tumsa were exhumed and laid in a coffin. The coffin was placed in a Mekane Yesus Church in preparation for a memorial worship service for the beloved church leader.

We discovered then that all thirty-eight of the murdered—among them also Abuna Theophilos—were killed on the evening before the capture of Gudina. All of them were buried far from the palace. Pastor Gudina was murdered one day later, on the same evening as his kidnapping.

Our informant told us that he had overheard the State Security officers talking about how they had not found Gudina the same evening they'd taken the others prisoner. They had been outside and were looking for him. But on the following day they realized that he would be teaching in the Urael church that evening. There they arrested him, as was well known, around seven o'clock in the evening.

They brought him to the prison and immediately began to interrogate him. Then they stripped off his clothing and left him wearing only his underclothes. Because of the cold he had been wearing white long underwear. They brought him to the palace of Prince Asrate Kassa.

The sentry then demonstrated how the assassination took place. Directly behind the house entrance there was a kind of waiting room. From there it opened onto a very long passageway that led to a room whose door stood open. Immediately before that room there was a door on either side. A soldier would call the name of a prisoner from the room in back, and the prisoner was supposed to go directly toward him. The prisoner saw only the man who was standing in that doorway and walked directly toward him. Suddenly, just before the prisoner entered the room at the other end of the passageway, two soldiers leaped forward from behind the doorways on the left and right, each with one end of the same cord in their upraised hands. They jumped over the prisoner and crossed paths in back of him in order to disappear again into the dark doorways on each side. The cord was wrapped around the prisoner's neck. Then they pulled tight and strangled the victim.

That is the report of Negasa Tumsa, the brother of the murdered man.

At the same time, another description of the events surrounding Gudina's death was going around Addis Ababa, one that is even more barbaric and is based on testimony from witnesses who are known by name. If this version is correct, Gudina suffered a truly terrible death. The matter needs to be researched further so that the whole truth comes to light. The witnesses who were present at the exhumation did see that the neck of the victim had been broken.

According to this report by a fellow prisoner, who told it to a soldier, Gudina was actually murdered on the third day after his capture.

The soldier added that on the same evening, Mengistu Haile Mariam was in the palace together with some highly placed persons within the government. They were standing in one of the castle's two second-floor apartments. This came to be the custom: they would personally watch the execution of prominent persons to be sure they were really dead. They watched until the person was killed and buried. After a murder, Mengistu and the other functionaries present would celebrate with a party in the castle.

The castle was used equally for the removal of prominent persons as

226

well as for the festive reception of guests from abroad. The location is indeed a peaceful place, about ten kilometers from the center of Addis Ababa.

Naturally the question arose as to why they imprisoned Tsehay and kept her in prison almost ten years if they already knew that Gudina was dead. Were the authorities of that regime of terror just full of burning hatred because Gudina had refused to work with them?

The Burial

The afternoon of June 27, 1992, is sunny in Addis Ababa, but dark rainclouds threaten from afar. The bougainvilleas trail from the veranda posts of the houses. They shine in a bright red, lilac, and orange blaze of color, and the birds chirp cheerfully all around them.

In the middle of the square stands the massive old Mekane Yesus Church, right in the place where the first Lutheran missionary in Ethiopia, Cederquist from the Swedish Evangelical Mission, had taken up residence at the beginning of the twentieth century when he finally received permission to enter the country.

It is a square full of memories of both good times and hard times for Christians. Several times a week the old church is full. It is an active congregation. The stone walls are hard and gray, but inside this church the Spirit of God blows.

It is a special day. The body of Gudina Tumsa, which has finally been found after thirteen years of uncertainty and questions, is to be laid to rest today. Already very early people start gathering on the church's front steps to be sure to get a spot at the celebration. In the last few days, numerous guests from faraway lands have traveled to take part in the burial service and to bear witness in honor of Gudina's memory. Once again, they will remember with great respect this man who so bravely turned down the opportunity for a high position in the communist regime and followed the call of his Lord and Master instead, placing his life totally in God's service, even if it would bring him distress and death.

Around eleven o'clock, the church doors finally open and the people stream inside. Immediately all the seats are taken and the church is filled up to its maximum capacity.

The church is adorned only with flowers, candles, and a brass Ethiopian cross on the altar. Now the organ plays, and about forty pastors of the Mekane Yesus Church, wearing their white robes and black-patterned stoles, march into the church with the coffin. They place the coffin in its prepared place. They take their seats with the family in the first row, followed by many guests from Ethiopia and abroad. Tsehay Tolessa is finally at home again in freedom, surrounded by her daughters.

The church choir, dressed in beautiful robes, begins to sing, and the congregation joins in powerfully. Deep emotion moves through the mourning congregation.

Song and sermon point to a deep faith in eternal life. Walter Meyer-Roscher, the district superintendent from Hannover in Germany, preaches on Jesus's words in John 5:24–29. "Truly, truly, I say to you, whoever hears my word and believes Him Who sent me has eternal life. He does not come into judgment, but has passed from death to life" (5:24).

This pastor from Lower Saxony compares Gudina Tumsa to Dietrich Bonhoeffer, who remained steadfast in his faith and in the truth while under the Nazi regime, and who also had to pay for it with his life. He quotes Bonhoeffer:

> It's not having high-flown thoughts that matters; what matters is doing what is right. Only in this way can freedom come. God's command is the plumb line, and faith in Him is the only possible protection. Whoever goes out into the storm and deals with it will discover for himself what freedom is, even if he is subjected to violence, persecution, and chains. Freedom from fear, from hopelessness, and from resignation. Freedom from the power of death.

Emmanuel Abraham, who was the president of the Mekane Yesus Church for many years, stands and reports on Gudina Tumsa's life and works. Emmanuel compares Gudina with the evangelist Stephen and describes him as a great active supporter of the church who burned with the desire to help all people suffering under oppression, hunger, and distress, and who was convinced that all people should have a share in the gospel. "Gudina departed from this life just as he lived it, and we believe that God knew what he was doing when he allowed it to happen. That's why today is not a time for great mourning but rather an opportunity to thank God for what Gudina was."

The leader of the Mekane Yesus Church who took Gudina's place, Francis Stefanos, gives an impressive eulogy in which he speaks of that last Bible study on the evening Gudina was arrested. Francis was present at the gathering and heard Gudina's passionate speech about what it could cost to follow Jesus. "Today Ethiopia has more and more great problems. The famine is horrible. For this reason, God's people must now proceed in the spirit of Gudina and work for peace and reconciliation."

Gunnar Stålsett, the general secretary of the Lutheran World Federation who, in those long and difficult years, so often helped with the pressing demands on Gudina and Tsehay, has traveled directly from Brazil to be present at the memorial service. He speaks of Gudina as a friend of many years and quotes Gudina's own words: "As Jesus himself was, the church must always be the voice of the voiceless and the support of the poor. However, first and foremost, it must make Christ known through the proclamation of the gospel."

And he continues: "God does not want Gudina to die forgotten but wants his death to be a witness of love, hope, and the future. Gudina Tumsa was a peacemaker, a child of God. With his impressive stature he was an impressive witness and an impressive spirit."

Bishop Desmond Tutu, the leader of the African Conference of Churches, sent a representative, who recalls the Bible verse: "Blessed are those who are persecuted for righteousness' sake, for theirs is the kingdom of heaven." The prophets of old were also persecuted, just as Gudina experienced in our own time. "May God, who bestows the resurrection, be honored through this!"

A representative from the World Council of Churches highlights how Gudina has become one of the great African leaders of our time through his tireless concern for human rights. He stood for truth and righteousness.

Then the song of the choir and congregation swells, singing about eternal life, which is a reality for the people of God, the church.

Now everyone departs for St. Paul Cemetery, where Gudina will find his final resting place alongside former missionaries and previous church leaders.

In the meanwhile, the dark rain clouds reach the square and change the hill into a mud puddle. Amidst the great crowd of people that have gathered, many umbrellas can be seen. But nothing can dampen the peaceful song here—the song about heaven, our hope. It belongs to all who have received Jesus Christ.

And the words resound impressively in Amharic: "Oh, how blessed it is to travel home to our Father's hand. Soon the wandering in the wilderness will be over, and we will come into Canaan's land."

For several days, the family holds an open house of mourning, as is customary in Ethiopia. Friends come and go and show their sympathy.

An older man sits there quietly. He is rather poorly dressed, but his eyes gleam. When he leaves the house, he tells me simply: "It was Gudina who showed me the way to life. He told my wife and me about Jesus when he was a young evangelist in Welega. And now we are on the way to heaven. Whether we have black or white skin here on the earth, whether we are rich or poor, we all belong together in God's family, and we will live together in eternity. There will be no more divisions there. Then we will all be God's people."

Conclusion:
The Reception and Expansion of Gudina Tumsa's Legacy in Ethiopia, Africa, and Beyond

Samuel Yonas Deressa

On every continent, there are theologians and church leaders remembered through the generations for their unparalleled contributions to the local and global Christian community. Among these leaders and theologians, those who were martyred for no other reason than their call to live for Christ and others are especially honored. Gudina Tumsa, the late general secretary of the Ethiopian Evangelical Church Mekane Yesus (EECMY), is one among a small number of Africans commemorated in this way.

A leader, pastor, and theologian, Gudina suffered for many years under the military government until he was abducted and murdered by its soldiers on July 28, 1979. Before his death, Tumsa wrote papers of global significance while leading an exemplary life. Studying the life and ministry of Gudina has become a major part of Ethiopian theological training and is growing among a global audience. As one church leader from Scandinavia put it, Tumsa was "a great example of a church leader, theologian, prophet, and friend" to many.[1] Those who knew the depth of his religious convictions regard him as a martyr whose life was cut short by an ungodly tyrant.

Documenting Gudina's Life

Over the last few decades, the Gudina Tumsa Foundation (GTF), which was founded in 1992 and is still operated by Gudina's daughters Lensa Gudina and Aster Gudina, has been collecting papers written by him along with other materials that were produced under his leadership. The GTF has also assembled pertinent documents of the EECMY and its sister churches in Europe and America during the period of Gudina's leadership, from 1959 to 1979.

After finishing my initial theological studies at Mekane Yesus Seminary (MYS) in 2007, my first job was to work as research advisor at the GTF, where my primary task was to organize missiological seminars on Gudina Tumsa's life and ministry and to serve as editor for the Gudina Tumsa book series. As coordinator of the Gudina Tumsa legacy project from 2007 to 2011, I was able to collect materials from Ethiopia, Germany, Sweden, and Norway, a project I have continued since coming to America to study at Luther Seminary in 2011. These resources are stored in the GTF archive for those interested in studying Gudina's legacy and, more broadly, the life of the churches in Ethiopia at the time of the Communist revolution.

GTF's active role in collecting these documents was the result of the consensus reached among leaders of the EECMY and its sister churches during the first missiological seminar held at MYS in 2001. At this seminar, participants urged leaders of both the GTF and MYS to cooperate in establishing a Gudina Tumsa professorship at MYS to "carry on research, study, and seminars on the continuing significance of the issues raised by [Gudina's] life, ministry, and thought."[2]

I was called to teach at MYS in this capacity from 2007 to 2011. During those years, I learned the significance of Gudina's thinking for the development of theology in Africa and in Ethiopia in particular. It helped me realize the importance of Gudina's thinking and leadership role for the present ministry of the EECMY and, in addition, for the EECMY's contribution to global theological discussions in the last few decades, especially with the Lutheran World Federation and the All-

---

1. Cited in Debela Birri, "Gudina Tumsa and Ecumenical Movement of the 1970s: The Ethiopia Case," in *The Life and Ministry of Gudina Tumsa: Lectures and Discussions: Missiological Seminar 2001*, ed. Paul E. Hoffman, 2nd ed. (Hamburg: WDL-Publishers, 2007), 129.
2. "The Communiqué from the Seminar," in Hoffman, *Life and Ministry of Gudina Tumsa*, 2.

Africa Conference of Churches. Here I would like to begin exploring in more detail what Gudina's life, work, and witness mean for Ethiopian Christians as well as the whole Christian family.

An Overview of Gudina's Life

Gudina Tumsa was born on May 5, 1929, to Tumsa Silga and Nasisse Chiracho in the town of Boji in the province of Welega in the western part of Ethiopia. His parents were poor farmers who were members of the Ethiopian Orthodox Church (EOC), which had been established in the fourth century when the Ethiopian king, Ezana, converted to Christianity. At the age of ten, Gudina was admitted to the Protestant "Reading School" in Boji that had been founded by two Ethiopian missionaries, Daniel Debela and Gebre Ewostatiwos.[3] Here he encountered the Oromo translation of the Bible and experienced for himself the power of the gospel in the lives of those who worship Jesus Christ, transforming his entire life.

Gudina stayed at the Reading School through sixth grade, when he transferred to the Swedish Evangelical Mission school in the town of Najo for the next two and half years. He was then employed by the Nekemte Mission Hospital as a gardener and interpreter from 1946 to 1951 and later as a surgeon's assistant from 1952 to 1955 after attending the Nursing School at Teferi Mekonen Hospital. Gudina married Tsehay Tolessa in 1951, and eventually they became the parents of three daughters and three sons, one of whom died in childhood.

With his people, Gudina chafed under the oppressive nature of Ethiopia's feudal system and the particular discrimination suffered by his own Oromo people. Besides working at the hospital, Gudina was committed to preaching the good news to the local community with a perception that only the gospel of Jesus Christ could bring transformation to the economic, social, and political life of his society.[4] Influenced by the holistic ministry of the missionaries, he spent weekends traveling throughout the region, telling the story of Jesus and listening to the needs of the people. It was this commitment that earned him respect from the members and leaders of the congregation in Nekemte, who invited him to be their first indigenous Ethiopian pastor. Gudina studied at Najo Bible School from 1955 to 1958. He was ordained on April

3. Habtamu Bula, *"The Church Should Be a Voice of the Voiceless": A Short Biography of the Reverend Gudina Tumsa* (BTh diss., Mekane Yesus Seminary, Addis Ababa), 2.
4. Ibid., 10.

20, 1958, and served as pastor at Nekemte Evangelical Church Mekane Yesus from 1958 to 1962.

At the request of the EECMY leaders, Gudina went to the Kambata and Hadiya regions of Ethiopia in 1963 to coordinate and help the congregations form a synod, leading to their recognition by the EECMY General Assembly. From there he went to study at Luther Seminary in Saint Paul, Minnesota, from 1963 to 1966, where he earned a bachelor of divinity degree. There he became acquainted with the life and thought of German theologian Dietrich Bonhoeffer and the theology and social thought of Reinhold Niebuhr. He also got caught up in the movement to gain civil rights for African-Americans led by Martin Luther King Jr. Gudina was impressed with the movement's nonviolent nature as well as with its deep roots in the Christian faith. At this time, Gudina became convinced that racial, economic, and political oppression were incompatible with the gospel.

It was while he was studying at Luther Seminary that he received a call from the EECMY to become its general secretary. On his return, on September 13, 1966, he took over this position, which he held until his abduction and murder in 1979. The thirteen years that he held this role can be considered the most fruitful period in the history of the EECMY and indeed of the other Ethiopian Protestant churches as well. During this period, the EECMY experienced phenomenal growth in membership that still has not stopped. Gudina became a well-known leader in the ecumenical movement in Ethiopia, where he helped to found the Council for Cooperation of Churches in Ethiopia (CCCE)—he was its first chair, elected in 1976—and the All-Africa Council of Churches (AACC), as well as participating in the work of the Lutheran World Federation (LWF) and the World Council of Churches (WCC).

Gudina led his church through the difficult transition from feudalism to socialism as the initial high hopes for justice and equality were ruthlessly dashed by the Marxist-Leninist government. His commitment to human rights, democratic structures in church and society, economic justice for the poor, and cultural and political self-determination of the various ethnic groups brought him into a confrontation with the government. He faced the persecution of Christians, the closing down of churches, and the pressure to misuse the church for government ideology. He was executed by order of the country's Marxist dictatorship on or about July 28, 1979, for refusing to endorse state policies, in particular the state's policies against religious freedom.

Gudina's Importance and Impact

Gudina's faithful witness and discipleship were exceptional. In the face of political adversity and dictatorship, he knew that being a disciple of Jesus Christ would eventually mean facing suffering and even death. His witness to the gospel in the political context of his time meant being ready to pay the highest cost of discipleship. His martyrdom adds the depth of personal witness to his prophetic message of faith.

On the national level, Gudina's legacy has been a challenge to his own church, to the missions, to churches and church organizations in partnership with the EECMY, to international ecumenical organizations, and to the Ethiopian government and society. On the broader African level, Gudina invested enormous effort in laying the groundwork to allow Africans to think theologically and produce a theology relevant both to their own communities and to the worldwide church. According to Rev. Dr. Debela Birri, "there was no stone he had not turned to safeguard and develop the theology of this church, the Ethiopian Evangelical Church Mekane Yesus."[5]

For Gudina, the major challenge in the EECMY was a "lack of theological reflection regarding the changes that affect all aspects of the life of our society."[6] He argued that the "lack of a sound theological reflection in the present Ethiopian situation has, in my opinion, affected our work in a negative way, which if allowed to continue uncorrected, will be very harmful to the life of this church to which we have committed ourselves for service."[7] At the same time, he criticized the way in which the Western theology that had been imparted to the EECMY by mission organizations "has lost the this-worldly dimension of human existence."[8] Therefore, he contended, "theology must grow out of concrete daily experiences, from our dealing with the ordinary affairs of life as we experience them in our situation, in our cultural setting, in our economic life, in our political experience, and in our social practice."[9]

In order to address this challenge, Gudina developed a theology relevant to the life and ministry of the EECMY. Based on Gudina's "Report on Church Growth in Ethiopia" presented in Tokyo in 1971, Øyvind M. Eide states that Gudina's theology is drawn from his understand-

5. Birri, "Gudina Tumsa," 129.
6. Gudina Tumsa, "Memorandum"; see p. 89 of this volume.
7. Ibid.
8. Ibid., 101.
9. Ibid., 100.

ing of the gospel as a "religion of love and justice."[10] His report speaks mainly about the "many impulses that were compelling the phenomenal growth of the church"[11] up to the time the EECMY was recognized as a national church in 1959: between 1968 and 1970, the average growth rate was estimated to be 15 percent, and in 1970 alone it was 27 percent. In his report, Gudina argued that "even if the social and political factors [in Ethiopia] cannot be overlooked, one would misunderstand the mass movements if one does not put the main emphasis on the religious aspect. . . . People are tormented with fear of spirits, and they want to accept the new religion of love and justice."[12] Eide explains:

> It is in many ways a contextual interpretation of the meaning of "love and justice" in relation to two crucial phases in the history of the Ethiopian Evangelical Church Mekane Yesus (EECMY) and the history of Ethiopia. Prior to the Ethiopian Revolution the identity and freedom of the church were at stake. Rev. Gudina's papers from this period, before 1974, focus on the power relations between the EECMY and missions/donor agencies. After the Ethiopian Revolution, beginning in 1974, the very survival of the church was in jeopardy. The church-state relationship therefore lay at the centre of his concern. In both situations he argued with a deep sense of compassion and on the basis of an African holistic interpretation of human life and the Gospel.[13]

Gudina was a holistic thinker who did not see human reality as divided into compartments. The 1972 letter of the EECMY to the LWF, "On the Interrelation between Proclamation of the Gospel and Human Development,"[14] reflects the multidimensional theological thinking of Gudina. Despite the shared authorship, the letter is an expression of Gudina's vision of forging a biblically based synthesis between witness and service, proclamation and development, personal piety and social responsibility, self-reliance and interdependence. This was a fierce challenge to the compartmentalization of the dualistic Western worldview and

---

10. Øyvind M. Eide, "Integral Human Development," in Hoffman, *Life and Ministry of Gudina Tumsa*, 38; see Gudina's "Report on Church Growth in Ethiopia," section 4 in part 1 of this volume.

11. Paul E. Hoffman, "'Ministry to the Whole Man' Revisited—A Look Back in Order to Look Ahead," in *Serving the Whole Person: The Practice and Understanding of Diakonia within the Lutheran Communion*, ed. Kjell Nordstokke, with Frederick Schlagenhaft (Minneapolis: Lutheran University Press, 2009), 160.

12. "Report on Church Growth in Ethiopia," p. 37 of this volume.

13. Øyvind M. Eide, "Gudina Tumsa: The Voice of an Ethiopian Prophet," *Swedish Missiological Themes* 89, no. 3 (2001): 291–321, which appears in *Dictionary of African Christian Biography*, accessed March 15, 2015, http://tinyurl.com/j4ma5xr.

14. See pp. 41–53 of this volume.

its resulting organizational structure. As Gudina wrote, "It's impossible for an African to divide the secular from the religious, mind from body, faith from development. Confessio Augustana was relevant to the needs of the reformers. African churches of our time have to develop a 'Confessio Africana,' a confessional stand relevant to African social, political and ideological reality."[15]

In his theology, Gudina was bold enough to challenge the traditional interpretation of the gospel in the EECMY by introducing a revolutionary perspective: that the gospel of Jesus Christ sets us free not only from spiritual bondage or eternal damnation but also from "economic exploitation, from political oppression, and so on."[16] With this confessional position, he challenged a certain Christian opposition to involvement in politics in favor of fulfilling their social responsibilities as citizens.

His theological reflections were related to both internal and global contexts. They were internal in the sense that he addressed the sociopolitical, socioeconomic, and socioreligious issues that Ethiopians were facing in his time. He was also well aware of the global debate on mission and development, which had been taking place among Western missionary organizations from the Edinburgh Missionary Conference of 1910 to the WCC's Nairobi Assembly in 1975. In the global debate, Gudina was critical of the missionaries' patronizing attitudes and even attempts to split the EECMY into the different areas corresponding to different mission agencies. His aim was to strengthen the identity and self-reliance of the EECMY. He advocated for a partnership of equals and for interdependence in a common witness of proclamation and development worldwide.

Extending the Legacy: Gudina Tumsa Seminars

Though EECMY leaders were naturally aware of and indirectly influenced by Gudina's profound contributions to their church, it was only after the first missiological seminar on his life and ministry in 2001 that they began to envision the possibilities for introducing it to the next generation. Paul E. Hoffman of the Berlin Mission played the leading role in organizing this seminar in collaboration with the GTF and MYS. Hoffman came up with the idea while serving as volunteer lecturer at MYS after his retirement in 1994 and hearing students' questions

---

15. Hoffman, *Life and Ministry of Gudina Tumsa*, 37.
16. See p. 106 of this volume.

about the martyred pastor. Hoffman began to realize that Ethiopian students, and probably leaders too, were not well informed about Gudina's legacy despite it being a valuable resource for the development of local theology.

Hoffman had known Gudina personally: they met at the Évian assembly of the LWF in 1970 while Hoffman was working as associate director of the department of studies charged with the responsibility of creating a link to African and Asian centers of theological education. Hoffman joined the MYS faculty in 1973, just a few months before the military government came to power in Ethiopia. At Gudina's request, Hoffman served as a member of the Evangelism Committee of the Addis Ababa Synod and was later involved in a number of study projects dealing with the response of the church to the revolution.[17] During this period, Hoffman was able to observe Gudina's leadership as he led the church through the time of political transition from a feudal system to socialism, and even more so when Emmanuel Abraham, the president of the EECMY, was imprisoned in April 1974 and Gudina had to take up his duties as well. Hoffman left Ethiopia in 1978, a year before Gudina was executed by the military government.

In the early 1990s, upon Hoffman's return to Ethiopia, he became advisor to the GTF and later the editor of a book collecting all of Gudina's extant writings, as well as of other volumes compiling the proceedings of the missiological seminars, which he organized under the auspices of the GTF.[18] His writings and lectures have played an important role in clarifying and uplifting Gudina's character and theology. The late Rev. Dr. Yonas Deressa Tinayo and Lelissa Daniel Gemechu were also instrumental in helping to materialize Hoffman's vision in the years to come. As principal of MYS from 2001 to 2003, Yonas set forth Gudina's legacy as the groundwork for theological studies and conversation within the EECMY. Lelissa invested time and energy as copyeditor of the first two volumes of the Gudina series and coordinated the first missiological seminar, "The Life and Ministry of Gudina Tumsa."

The lectures and discussions dealt with both historical events and the social and religious context. About one hundred people attended, representing EECMY synods, other Protestant churches in Ethiopia, professors from MYS, and colleagues of Gudina's from Finland, Ger-

---

17. Hoffman, "'Ministry to the Whole Man' Revisited," 159.
18. The present volume builds on Hoffman's foundational work.

many, Norway, Sweden, and the United States. The proceedings of this seminar were published in 2008.

One of the primary questions that was raised during this seminar, as well as the seminars to follow, was why Gudina's story remains necessary for the life of the church today. What is its relevance "for the continuing Christian witness and the mission of the Evangelical church in multi-ethnic Ethiopia and for the church worldwide"?[19] Hoffman's own answer was that shining a "light on a particularly challenging and fruitful period in the history of the Mekane Yesus Church, indeed of the churches of Ethiopia . . . [may] stimulate many in Ethiopia and abroad to consider afresh what is involved in Christian, ecumenical mission and ministry *today*."[20]

The second missiological seminar took place in Addis Ababa at MYS in 2003 considering the theme of church and society. Its purpose was "to provide an opportunity for the reflection on the life and ministry of the former general secretary of the EECMY and to consider ways in which the legacy of Gudina Tumsa might continue to inspire and guide the life of the church today."[21] This second seminar was broader in its scope, aiming at identifying the connections between Gudina's life, ministry, and writings and the life of Protestant churches as a whole in multiethnic Ethiopia. Gudina was compared to Dietrich Bonhoeffer and Martin Luther King Jr. This time 250 participants from Ethiopia, Norway, Germany, and the United States attended, including LWF President Christian Krause.

In September 2004, an international seminar took place in Lutherstadt Wittenberg, Germany, entitled "The Life of a Christian Is a Witness to the Risen Lord."[22] Other missiological seminars held in Addis Ababa include "The Role of a Christian in a Given Society" (2006 and 2007), "The Missional Church and the Mission of God" (2008), "The Contribution of Gudina Tumsa's Legacy to African Theology" (2009), "Church and Politics" (2010), and "Holistic Ministry in the EECMY" (2011; also convened in Frankfurt, Germany). Regional seminars were also conducted every year starting in 2006 to inspire and guide young church ministers to bear the cost of discipleship through reflection on Gudina's example.

---

19. Hoffman, *Life and Ministry of Gudina Tumsa*, 2. In this case, "evangelical" has the specific sense of "Lutheran" as well as the broader meaning of "Protestant."
20. Ibid.
21. Paul E. Hoffman, ed., *Church and Society: Lectures and Responses: Second Missiological Seminar 2003 on the Life and Ministry of Gudina Tumsa* (Hamburg: WDL-Publishers, 2010), 11.
22. Publication is expected under the title *Witness to the Risen Lord*.

Extending the Legacy: Gudina Tumsa Theological Forum

In the year 2008, at Hoffman's suggestion, MYS professors and a few other EECMY theologians gathered at Lensa Gudina's house in Addis Ababa under the auspices of the GTF to deliberate on the future of the Ethiopian churches and how these theologians could contribute to their healthy growth. A proposal was put forward to create a theological forum distinct from the missiological seminars to address broader questions of Ethiopian faith and life. The participants enthusiastically endorsed the idea, which was given the name of the Gudina Tumsa Theological Forum (GTTF) and whose proceedings were to be published as the *Journal of Gudina Tumsa Theological Forum*. Thus, while the missiological seminars explore ways and means of learning from Gudina's legacy, the forum aims at dealing with issues of pressing present concern. The context in which the EECMY exists today requires a new ministry approach, developed through theological reflections and scholarly publications. The forum also aims to develop a culture of chronicling and transforming an oral culture into a literary culture better able to engage with the growing global and digital culture.

In 2009, a partnership agreement was signed between MYS and the GTF to carry out the objectives of this forum as agreed in the 2008 meeting. Focusing on relevant issues of the time, seminary professors and pastors created a conversational partnership that has continued to produce relevant materials for Ethiopian churches and sister institutions worldwide.

A further development followed in 2011 when Lutheran University Press agreed to publish the proceedings of the GTTF. The late Rev. Leonard Flachman and Karen Walhof have been instrumental in organizing the forums held at Luther Seminary and publishing their proceedings. Participants in the US forums held in March 2012 and April 2013 have included Ethiopian students at Luther Seminary; the Rev. Gemechu Olana, president of the United Oromo Evangelical Churches; the Rev. Yadessa Dhaba, president emeritus of the EECMY; theologians and pastors of Ethiopian congregations from all over the United States; and former missionaries of the Evangelical Lutheran Church of America.

Topics discussed by the GTTF so far have been: unity and division among Protestant churches, the Bible and human sexuality, African theology, the EECMY's sociopolitical engagement and the present Ethiopian reality, and ecumenism. In addition to the founding event in

Addis Ababa and the two American events, forums have taken place at the Ethiopian Graduate School of Theology in 2009 and Mekane Yesus Seminary in 2010. Thus far, three volumes have been published.[23]

Looking Forward

The issues Gudina raised and the personal witness he made are equally relevant in our time. The church is still trying to define the necessity and boundaries of its self-reliance and ecumenical interdependence, as well as assessing the extent and nature of Christian involvement in political and social affairs, up to and including resistance and martyrdom. Gudina's preaching touched on political, social, and economic issues as well as theological ones. His actions emerged out of his unreserved commitment to defend the rights of all citizens, speak on behalf of the oppressed, and help his church understand its vocation in the midst of all these struggles.

In 2001, Øyvind M. Eide wrote: "[Gudina Tumsa's] murder brought to an end the possibility of creative and visionary theological reflection in the church, which was so much needed in Ethiopia at the time. It was a blow to African theology as well as to the worldwide church. His theology, which grew out of African soil, remains of great interest."[24] Today, Ethiopian theologians are aspiring to fill this gap and help the whole African church become a source of creative thinkers. What is still missing, however, is Gudina's vision of a common voice from the churches speaking to all the burning issues of church and politics, including the concern for human rights. We are still waiting for another to come and boldly take his place in our community.

23. Paul Balisky, ed., *Contemporary Theological Perspectives* (Addis Ababa: Gudina Tumsa Foundation, 2011); Samuel Yonas Deressa, ed., *Emerging Theological Praxis* (Minneapolis: Lutheran University Press, 2012); Samuel Yonas Deressa, ed., *Ecumenical Challenges: Working in Love, Transforming Lives* (Minneapolis: Lutheran University Press, 2014).
24. Eide, "Gudina Tumsa."

Appendix: The Church and Ideologies

Baro Tumsa

After his parents' death, Gudina Tumsa together with his wife Tsehay Tolessa raised Gudina's brother Baro. As an adult, Baro studied law and was at the time of this presentation the leader of a Marxist group called ECHAT (the Amharic acronym for Ethiopian Oppressed People's Revolutionary Struggle). With a strong following among urban Oromo, the ECHAT was a member of the advisory politburo of the Provisional Military Administrative Council ruling Ethiopia under Mengistu. Baro was invited by the ECMY, undoubtedly at Gudina's suggestion, to address the General Assembly, since he had grown up in the Mekane Yesus Church and was evidently considered close enough to the center of power to set forth the new government's policy, and to hear the church's response, regarding the role of religion and church in newly socialist Ethiopia.

In his paper, Baro Tumsa depicts all religion, including Christianity, as "idealism," opposed to "materialist theory, which is Marxism-Leninism." The teachings of Jesus and the rise of Christianity, as well as the movement for Reformation in Europe, were "responses to the [material and economic] transformation constantly taking place in the world." Marxist materialism "asserts that [Christianity] has not kept abreast of the rapid changes that have occurred in man's thinking as a result of technological and scientific developments." A socialist state is a "democratic dictatorship of the working class in alliance with the peasantry and petty bourgeoisie" with a separation of church and state and "religious freedom." But, Baro insists, "the state would expect its

*citizens, as well as the church, not to interfere in its policies and programs."
He states, nevertheless, "I see no contradiction of this program"—a new democratic revolution—"with that of the goals of the church." At most, he supposes,
"Maybe in certain areas the church might have to reorient its methods of work
to the changing situations." But then he adds, with barely a hint of threat:
"And the capability to adapt to new situations becomes imperative for
survival."*

*Baro's paper elicited a strong reaction and opposition from Gudina, who in
his oral rebuttal, according to Gunnar Hasselblatt, retorted that "Marxism-
Leninism and the church can never be friends."*

*By 1977, Baro and other members of the ECHAT had been declared enemies
of the state and were forced to go underground. Baro had also participated in
the founding of the Oromo Liberation Front in the mid-1970s and ultimately
was killed in his activities for that organization in Hararghe in 1978. It is one of
the tragedies of this family's story that these two brothers died so close in time
to one another for very different reasons.*

Before we go into a discussion of this topic, it seems to be appropriate
to clarify the two terms therein.

What Is Church?

Church is a body of people that profess faith in the teachings of Christ.
There are diverse doctrines and sacramental acts practiced by the different church denominations. What is the cause of these trends? The
author of this paper considers these various trends as responses to the
transformation constantly taking place in the world.

What Is Ideology?

Ideology is a world outlook—that is, it is a system of ideas, opinions,
and concepts of nature, society, man, and his place in the world. Ideology does not merely state its principles and try to make people believe
in them but advances logical arguments for these principles. Accordingly, ideology could be equated with philosophy.

There are diverse philosophical doctrines. However, they all,
directly or indirectly, take as their theoretical point of departure the
question of the relationship of consciousness to being (i.e., of the spiritual to the material).

What is the relationship of the spiritual to the material, of consciousness to the objective world? Irrespective of the existence of various philosophical thoughts, there are only two possible answers to be given to this question. One of the answers asserts the primacy of the spirit to nature, whereas the other takes nature as primary and spirit as secondary. All the diverse philosophical schools and trends ultimately fall in either of these two categories: materialism or idealism.

The teachings of all religions, including that of the church, belong to the philosophical or ideological category called idealism.

Materialism holds that social life perpetually undergoes change in a process of development from the lower to the higher. It holds that the motive behind this change is the productive force that continuously develops as man makes an endless effort to control his surroundings, nature. It says that although religion (particularly Christianity) has undergone certain transformations in response to the material transformation of society, just as any other ideologies also change, it has not kept abreast of the rapid changes that have occurred in man's thinking as a result of technological and scientific developments. Below, we will see, very briefly, the origin of Christianity and how the teachings of the church underwent change in response to the socioeconomic transformations known in history.

How the Teachings of the Church Underwent Reforms in Response to Socioeconomic Transformations

According to materialist theory, which is Marxism-Leninism, all social systems are economically motivated, and change is effected as a result of technical and economic changes. The driving force of social change is, therefore, the struggle that the oppressed classes wage to secure a better future. Thus, in the celebrated theory of historical materialism, Karl Marx interpreted history in terms of economics and explained the evolution of society in terms of class struggle. He and Engels systematically explained the transformations of social systems from primitive communism through slave society, the feudal system, capitalism, and ultimately communism. As a new social system is born and grows within the existing one, the ideas, politics, philosophy, and religion are also reformed to conform to the new system. With this brief introduction, we will see how Christianity was brought into being and underwent transformations.

As the Roman Empire declined, the outlines of a new civilization began to form—consistent with Marxism, where the new system is born in the womb of the old, declining society and dialectically grows to replace the old. This process of the decline of the old and the emergence of the new was reflected in the minds of men as a shift of values.

Disruption of the traditional way of life brought with it a sense of insecurity and pessimism in the submerged classes and a sense of apathy in the ruling groups. This led to a search for some relief, and people unable to see a way out of the situation turned to religious faiths that promised a blessed hereafter.

One such religious movement swept through the Jewish communities during the last years of the first century BC and the first years of the first century AD. It was believed and preached that a Messiah was about to come to deliver mankind from sinfulness. Shammaites, Hillelites, and Essenes awaited momentarily some universal fire and the establishment through the Messiah of a kingdom of heaven on earth. St. John the Baptist recognized Jesus as the Messiah.

The Teachings of Christ

Jesus Christ left no writings. His teachings, however, were collected by the authors of the four Gospels. In addition to many other subjects, Christ's message had a lot of teachings on ethics. His sayings are deeply imbued with ethical content. Ethically, his teachings stem from two commandments that he considered primary:

"The Lord God is one God and thou shalt love the Lord thy God with thy whole heart, and with thy whole soul, and with thy whole mind, and with thy whole strength."

"Thou shalt love thy neighbor as thyself."

Positively interpreted, these teachings mean that one must forgive men their offenses. In other words, he demanded mercy, forgiveness, peacemaking, humility, and meekness.

Followers of Marxism assert that this sort of teaching was, at that time, intended to soothe the rebelling slaves against their masters.

Another important aspect of his teachings deals with the law. He condemned those who abided by the strict letter of the law or who paid more mind to outward manifestation than inward purity. He argued that he did not come to destroy the Jewish law, but to fulfill it.

Here again, Marxists maintain that Jesus was trying to save the Superstructure Law then put into question by those advocating change. His teachings proscribed violence.

The Church and Feudalism

During the Middle Ages, the church was a state within a state. Its powers were both temporal (political, economic, and social) and spiritual (religious and moral). It owned vast areas of land. As a land proprietor within the feudal system, the church itself became a feudal overlord. Its properties were made into fiefs, and as fief holders, clergymen swore fealty and homage, collected feudal dues, and produced and marketed goods. Moreover, the church conditioned, and at times even dictated, the roles played by secular governments. In addition to having its own law courts regarding cases that concerned its members, it had a primary guide to the moral life of men and women. In this latter role, it dictated that wealth was a great temptation to sinning, that individual business competition was morally dangerous, and that price manipulation and the charging of interest on loans were outlawed activities. These theoretical rationalizations of the church reflected the feudal tools and tariffs that restricted the flourishing of trade and the concomitant enlightenment of society as a result of exchange of goods and ideas.

All these restrictions were shattered by the defiant spread of new learning, the growth of manufacturing and of trade, and the rise of national states. This is the time of enlightenment, when the feudal system was being corroded by the capitalist system, which is liberal and hence more progressive than the preceding system. The new learning that came in the footsteps of the bourgeoisie and swept Europe did not pass without effecting religious reformation.

The Church and the Capitalist System

Between 1517 and 1648, the dominance of the Roman Catholic Church was shattered beyond repair. Roman Catholicism had then to share its leadership of Christians with a large number of national churches and private sects, each with its dogma and doctrine. The emerging bourgeoisie of the time opposed the Roman Catholic Church and supported the new independent states that would guarantee that the church holdings were immobilized capital, since they thought that the church-held capital, if freed, could be used as a base for a great credit expansion. They, too, resented being deprived of the fluid capital they had in the form of countless payments to the church. Similarly, since the burden of payment was felt more by the peasantry, they, too, echoed the same resentment with bitterness.

In such social upheavals and the political atmosphere thus created, church abuses became the spark of a revolutionary movement to transform it. The movement found its voice in Martin Luther.

After the Reformation, Europe was divided into several sects. For any of the sects to survive, some form of mutual toleration had to exist. And this came into being. Thus Protestantism promoted individualism, and individualism, in turn, accelerated the expansion of popular education. Protestantism accelerated national movements, which resulted in national states. Protestantism encouraged the flourishing of capitalism, thereby contributing to the destruction of the economic power of the medieval church and the system it supported. Later, it influenced and became inextricably linked with the forces of intellectual and religious freedom. This influence became widespread as the capitalist system grew and expanded.

Thus, Protestantism is the religion of the era of capitalism and, hence, being a superstructure of the economic base of the bourgeoisie, is a liberal religion that appealed to those who were revolting against medieval shackles.

But as capitalism grew old and the rule of the bourgeoisie countered the aspirations of the working class, the superstructure that defended the status quo was challenged by a scientific ideology formulated by Marx.

The Role of the Church in a Socialist Society

Marxists hold that religion is the instrument of the propertied class used to hoodwink the oppressed from revolting against the oppressive machinery.

A socialist state is a democratic dictatorship of the working class in alliance with the peasantry and petty bourgeoisie. Since it is a democratic state, it gives and guarantees such freedoms as speech, press, assembly, correspondence, association, domicile, religion, procession, and demonstration, as well as cultural endeavors.

Specially, as regards religious freedom, a socialist state guarantees this freedom of its citizens by separating the church and state and banning religious instructions in schools. It also guarantees the freedom of religious belief by abolishing privileges of any religion and giving protection against persecution.

248

It has to be noted that any right entails a corresponding responsibility. Accordingly, the state would expect its citizens, as well as the church, not to interfere in its policies and programs.

To come to our country, Ethiopia is a developing country. It belongs to the Third World where domesticated backwardness has facilitated for imperialism to plunder the resources of the country and expand its political and social influences, thereby impeding independent development. The masses of the people have to then wage struggle against any systems and forces that impede its liberation. The three enemies known to oppose the liberation of the masses of the Third World countries are: (a) feudalism, (b) bureaucratic capitalism, and (c) imperialism.

The revolution that is going on and is to continue for a long time to come is then going to be a struggle against these enemies of the people. This type of revolution is known as New Democratic or National Democratic Revolution. It is worth pointing out the possibility that the state of New Democracy under the leadership of the proletariat class would ultimately lead to socialism. Ethiopia can only proceed from one revolution to the other, and it is worth pointing out that there is no such thing as accomplishing both in one stroke. It is only a government of democratic centralism that can fully express the will of all the revolutionary people and most powerfully fight the enemies of the revolution.

Thus, the program to be adopted [the National Democratic Revolutionary Program of Ethiopia/NDRPE, April 21, 1976] has the foregoing underlying principles: political, economic, and cultural programs on the basis of New Democracy, which is believed, at this stage of the revolution and in the concrete situation in which we find ourselves today, to be in the best interest of the people's livelihood.

I see no contradiction of this program with that of the goals of the church. Maybe in certain areas the church might have to reorient its methods of work to the changing situations. And the capability to adapt to new situations becomes imperative for survival.

Source: ECMY Ninth General Assembly, Minutes GA-9-37-68, Doc. 4.

Bibliography

Balisky, Paul, ed. *Contemporary Theological Perspectives.* Journal of Gudina Tumsa Theological Forum 1. Addis Ababa: Gudina Tumsa Foundation, 2011.

Bula, Habtamu. *"The Church Should Be a Voice of the Voiceless": A Short Biography of the Reverend Gudina Tumsa.* BTh diss., Mekane Yesus Seminary, Addis Ababa.

Deressa, Samuel Yonas, ed. *Ecumenical Challenges: Working in Love, Transforming Lives.* Journal of Gudina Tumsa Theological Forum 3. Minneapolis: Lutheran University Press, 2014.

_____, ed. *Emerging Theological Praxis.* Journal of Gudina Tumsa Theological Forum 2. Minneapolis: Lutheran University Press, 2012.

_____. "St. Gudina Tumsa." *Lutheran Forum* 46, no. 1 (2012): 36–39.

Eide, Øyvind M. "Gudina Tumsa: The Voice of an Ethiopian Prophet." *Swedish Missiological Themes* 89, no. 3 (2001): 291–321.

_____. *Revolution and Religion in Ethiopia: The Growth and Persecution of the Mekane Yesus Church, 1974-85.* Oxford: J. Currey, 2000.

Hirpo, Tasgara. "The Cost of Discipleship: The Story of Gudina Tumsa." *Word & World* 25, no. 2 (2005): 159–71.

Hasselblatt, Gunnar. *Gespräch mit Gudina.* Edited by Wolfgang Erk. Stuttgart: Radius, 1980.

Hoffman, Paul E., ed. *Church and Society: Lectures and Response: Second Missiological Seminar 2003 on the Life and Ministry of Gudina Tumsa.* Hamburg: WDL-Publishers, 2010.

_____, ed. *The Life and Ministry of Gudina Tumsa: Lectures and Discussions: Missiological Seminar 2001.* 2nd ed. Hamburg: WDL-Publishers, 2007.

Mathewos, Misgana. "Gudina Tumsa's Hermeneutical Interpretation of the Bible from Global and Ethiopian/African Perspectives." *Swedish Missiological Themes* 98, no. 2 (2010): 193–209.

Nordstokke, Kjell, ed. *Serving the Whole Person: The Practice and Understanding of*

Diakonia within the Lutheran Communion. With Frederick Schlagenhaft. Minneapolis: Lutheran University Press, 2009.

Sæverås, Aud. *Der lange Schatten der Macht: Augenzeugenbericht: Die Geschichte von Tsehay Tolessa und Gudina Tumsa, dem ermordeten Generalsekretär der Mekane-Yesus-Kirche in Äthiopien.* Translated by Antje Meier and Ralph Meier. Giessen: Brunnen Verlag, 1993.

_____. *I Ildovnen.* Oslo: Lunde Forlag, 1992.

Tumsa, Gudina. *Witness and Discipleship: Leadership of the Church in Multi-Ethnic Ethiopia in a Time of Revolution: The Essential Writings of Gudina Tumsa.* Edited by the Gudina Tumsa Foundation. 2nd ed. Hamburg: WDL-Publishers, 2008.

Subject Index

Abraham, Ato Emmanuel, 20, 37, 75–76, 228, 238

Africa, xvi, xix, xxi, xxvii, xxxiii, xxxiv, 10, 25, 27, 43–44, 63–66, 67–68, 98, 100, 141, 167, 232, 234

African theology, 62, 87, 249–40

All-Africa Conference of Churches, 10, 65, 97–98, 232, 234

Amhara, Amharic, xxxii, 102, 109, 114, 142, 164–65, 198, 229, 243

animism, 23, 31, 152, 169

assistance, xviii, xxi, 19, 21–24, 28–29, 33, 36–37, 41–45, 50, 55, 71, 79, 99–101, 168, 170, 172, 186

atheism, xviii, xxviii–xxx, 105, 110, 115, 122

atonement, 5, 14

Berlin Mission, xxxii, 237

Bible, xvi, xxvii, xxxi, 7, 11, 28, 29, 32–33, 52, 91, 94, 102, 104, 107–8, 115, 117, 120, 121, 139, 141, 150, 154, 161, 163, 178, 180, 182, 188–90, 199, 210–11, 214–15, 228–29, 233, 240

body of Christ, xxix, 6, 10, 72–73, 102

Bonhoeffer, Dietrich, xvii, xxi, 121, 228, 234, 239

Boru, Tolessa, 142, 148

Buthelezi, Manas, xxxiv, 67, 86

capitalism, 126–27, 245, 248–49

children, xvii, xxviii, xxx, xxxii, 23, 24, 44, 55, 57, 100, 134, 136, 140, 143, 144–49, 151–52, 155–56, 159–62, 164–65, 174–76, 180–81, 183, 189, 200–01, 205, 207–8, 212–16, 220–21, 223

church, xvi, xviii–xxv, xxvii–xxx, xxxii–xxxiv, 3–10, 11–12, 16–17, 20–23, 25–34, 35–46, 47–59, 61–70, 72–73, 75–95, 97–104, 107–8, 113–20, 122, 124–26, 135–36, 139, 140, 151, 158, 161, 163–78, 180–84, 186, 188–92, 204, 209–10, 214, 221, 223, 225–29, 231–41, 243–45, 247–49. *See also* Ethiopian Orthodox Church, Ethiopian Evangelical Church Mekane Yesus, All Africa Conference of Churches, World Council of Churches, congregations

citizenship, 23, 85, 94, 124–25, 129, 237, 241, 244, 248–49

civil rights movement, xvi, xxiv, 234

colonialism, 42–43, 50, 55, 65

Commission on Church Coopera-tion, 25, 35–36, 53

community, xix, xxii, xxix, xxxi, 4–6, 36, 40–41, 43, 52, 64, 67–70, 77, 85, 94, 231, 233, 241

congregations, xviii, xxi, xxvii, 7, 8, 11, 1617, 22, 27, 29, 32–33, 36, 40, 41, 45, 55, 73, 77, 82–83, 85, 87, 91–93, 95, 100, 102–4, 116, 119, 136, 161, 163–64, 167–70, 172, 174, 177, 189, 191, 209–10, 227–29, 233–34, 240

Council for Cooperation of Churches in Ethiopia, xix, xxx, 113, 118–19, 234

creation, xviii–xix, xxiv, 66, 73, 87, 108–9, 117

Creator, 13, 41, 89, 109, 115, 123–25, 127

cross, xxix, 5, 7, 15, 64, 66, 73, 90, 122, 139, 189, 222, 227

Czechoslovakia, xviii, 179–80

Danish Ethiopia Mission, 21

democracy, xxviii, 40, 52, 95, 171, 234, 243, 248–49

demonic powers, xv, xxv, 30, 65, 124, 152

Derg, xxvii–xxviii, xxxi, 113, 121, 140, 174, 181–82, 184, 191–92, 196–97

development, xix, xxviii, 35–46, 47–48, 52, 56–59, 61–67, 69–74, 78, 85, 87–88, 101–2, 168–69, 236–37

discipleship, xxxii, 73, 88, 90, 121, 134, 235, 239

disease, 30, 85, 149–51, 199, 201–2, 217

ecumenism, xvi, xix, xxiii–xxiv, xxx, 3, 9–10, 29, 51–52, 76, 81, 87, 113–20, 234, 239, 241

education, xv, xix, xxiii, xxv, xxviii, 23, 28, 36, 41, 43–44, 72, 75, 91, 102, 149, 154, 158, 162, 170–72, 177, 179, 238, 248

emperor, xviii–xx, xxviii, 168–69, 171, 198. See also Haile Selassie

Ethiopia, xv–xviii, xix, xxiii–xxiv, xxvii–xviii, xxix–xxx, 7, 10, 11, 20–30, 32–33, 37, 45–59, 61, 72–73, 75, 77, 80–81, 85–89, 91, 97–98, 100, 102–5, 109, 113, 118–20, 126, 133–35, 139–42, 145, 148, 150–53, 157–58, 166–68, 170, 176, 183–84, 186, 192, 210, 221–22, 225, 227–30, 232–36, 238–39, 241, 243, 249

Ethiopia Consultation, xxix, 36, 47–59, 61

Ethiopian Evangelical Church Mekane Yesus (EECMY/ECMY), xviii, xxv, xix, xxix, xxx, xxxi, xxxiii, 3, 7–11, 16, 20–23, 25, 32–37, 40, 43–45, 47–59, 61–63, 68–89, 91–105, 113–21, 129, 173, 231–32, 234–40, 243, 249

Ethiopian Evangelical Church Mekane Yesus, Constitution of, 8, 48–56, 80, 91, 99

Ethiopian Evangelical Church Mekane Yesus, Executive Committee Meetings of, 3, 10, 21, 71, 74–77, 83, 92–93, 95, 97, 99, 103–4

Ethiopian Evangelical Church Mekane Yesus, General Assemblies of, 7, 32–33, 36–37, 45, 55, 76, 85, 92, 95–96, 99, 105, 112–13, 118–21, 123, 129, 191, 234, 243

Ethiopian Evangelical Church Mekane Yesus, Integration Policy of, 16, 49–50, 80

Ethiopian Military Regime. See Derg

Ethiopian Orthodox Church, xix, xxxiii, 25–27, 118–19, 233

Evangelical Church Mekane Yesus. See Ethiopian Evangelical Church Mekane Yesus

Evangelisches Missionswerk, 48

evangelism, xv, xxx–xxxi, 11, 15–16, 19–22, 27, 29, 31–33, 35–36, 43, 45, 62, 65, 87–88, 97–98, 100, 102, 104, 161, 164, 170, 238

faith, xvii, xxi–xxiii, xxx, xxxiii, 5, 14, 16, 24, 34, 36, 56, 67, 69, 79, 84, 87, 94, 105, 108, 110–12, 117, 121–22, 124, 126, 129, 139–40, 152–53, 161–62, 176, 179, 198, 210, 214, 228, 234–36, 240, 244

Father, heavenly, 5, 32, 92, 110–11, 117, 122–23, 127–28, 137, 174, 222, 229

feudalism, xvii–xviii, 79, 85, 88, 126–27, 171, 173, 233–34, 238, 245, 247–49

Finnish Missionary Society, 21

forgiveness of sin, xxx, 8, 24, 66, 92, 116, 124, 134, 174, 188, 246

Germany, xviii, xxi, 36, 47–48, 51, 54–55, 59, 61, 100, 166, 170, 172, 177, 179–80, 213, 220–21, 225, 228, 232, 239

God, xvi–xvii, xix–xx, xxii, xxiv–xxv, xxix, 4–8, 10, 13–17, 23–24, 29–31, 38–39, 42, 49, 56, 64, 66–68, 70, 73, 79, 83, 87, 89, 91–92, 94–95, 105–12, 114–17, 122–25, 127–29, 133–34, 136–37, 140–42, 150, 152–54, 156, 158–61, 163–67, 169–71, 173–80, 183–88, 191, 194, 196, 198–201, 204–05, 207, 209–19, 221–22, 227–30, 239, 246

gospel, xvii–xviii, xix, xxix–xxxi, xxxiv, 4, 78, 10–14, 20, 22, 27, 29–30, 32, 36–37, 40–43, 47, 49–50, 52, 56–57, 59, 61, 63–66, 72–73, 76–77, 81–82, 86, 89–90, 92, 94, 100, 114, 122, 124, 127, 153–56, 161–63, 165–66, 168–70, 174, 180, 182, 184, 210, 214–16, 228–29, 233–37, 246

government/state, xvii, xix, xx, xxiv, xxx, xxxiii, 3, 8, 22–24, 26–27, 49, 51–53, 65, 72, 75, 78–80, 84–86, 88–89, 100, 113, 125, 140, 169–70, 177, 181–84, 186, 191, 198, 206, 212, 221–24, 226, 231, 234–35, 238, 243, 247, 249. See also Imperial Ethiopian Government, Derg

grace, 11, 13–15, 116, 123, 134, 205

grassroots action, 40, 58, 79

Greek language and philosophy, 13, 105–8, 127–28

Gudina Tumsa Foundation, xxxii, 17, 136, 232, 241

Gudina, Amanti, xxxiii, 176

Gudina, Aster, xxxii, 179–80, 221, 232

Gudina, Emmanuel, 156–58

Gudina, Kulani, xxxii, 158–60, 176, 179–80, 201, 225

Gudina, Latera, 177–78

Gudina, Lensa, xx, xxxii, 133, 139, 180, 185, 188–92, 232, 240

Hadiya, 165, 234

healing, 30, 66, 194

Hermannsburg Mission (MAH), 47, 49, 51, 54–57, 71

history, 4, 9–10, 24–26, 39, 73, 77, 86–90, 92, 105–6, 109, 118–20, 127–28, 141, 171, 234, 236, 239, 245

Hoffman, Paul E., xxxii, 4, 71, 97, 99, 232, 236–40

holistic theology, xviii, xxix, 87–88, 115, 136, 233, 236, 239

Holy Spirit, 3, 5, 15–16, 91, 111, 124, 127, 154, 166, 170, 181

hospitals, 52, 72, 77, 149–52, 155–57, 170, 182, 197, 203, 205, 207, 216–17, 221, 233

human rights, xxiv, 73, 229, 234, 241

humanism, 39, 93

identity, xvii, 50, 55–56, 70, 82, 86, 97–104, 173, 225, 236–37

ideology, xx, xxiv–xxv, xxx, 73, 90, 92, 96, 100, 109, 174, 176, 234, 243–49

Imperial Ethiopian Government, 8, 23, 26–27, 49, 51–53. See also emperor

imperialism, xxv, 126, 249

integral human development, 36, 39, 67, 69, 236

Islam, 23–24, 27, 31, 151

Italy, 27, 143

Jesus Christ, xxix–xxx, xxxiii, 3–7, 10, 13–16, 20, 24–25, 27–28, 30, 40, 49–50, 56, 59, 65–66, 72–73, 76, 79, 82–83, 86, 89–92, 94, 99–110, 114–15, 117, 120, 122–24, 126–29, 135, 150, 153, 165, 169, 172–74, 178, 183, 187, 195–96, 198, 200, 215, 222, 228–30, 233, 235, 237, 243, 246

justice, xvi, xix, 31, 39, 42, 64, 70, 73, 83–84, 96, 107, 112, 168, 234, 236

justification, 54, 65, 81, 124, 126

Kambata, 21, 29, 32, 164–65, 234

Kenya, xviii, xxvii, 24, 61, 70, 97, 177

King Jr., Martin Luther, xvi, xxiv, 234, 239

kingdom of God, xxv, xxx, 5–6, 73, 123–24, 134, 210

Krause, Christian, xx–xxi, xxvii, 239

laity, 7, 25, 29, 169

land reform, xxviii, 72, 85, 169, 173

law of love, 6, 13, 129

law, national, 51–53, 125, 129, 247

literacy, 22, 44, 79–80, 85

liturgy, 8–9, 110, 169

love, xvii, xxii, xxv, xxix, 6, 13–15, 31, 73, 79, 85–86, 90, 93, 95, 122–23, 129, 134, 137, 151–53, 156–57, 160, 172–73, 175, 177, 183, 187, 200, 205, 207, 211, 213, 215–16, 225, 229, 236, 246

Luther Seminary, xv–xvi, xviii, xxxi, 165, 232, 234, 240

Luther, Martin, 14, 248
Lutheran World Federation, xv, xix, xxxiii, 10–11, 20, 25, 36–37, 57, 61–63, 70–71, 87, 100, 119, 165, 168, 172, 229, 232, 234
Lutheranism, xviii, xxxiii, 4, 8–10, 21, 27, 29, 35, 48–53, 55, 80, 100, 116, 152, 166, 169, 227, 240

martyrdom, xxii, xxviii, xxxi, 126–27, 140, 231–32, 235, 241
Marxism, xviii, xx, xxx, 75, 93, 105, 109–10, 176, 189, 234, 243–46,
materialism, xx, xxix, 38, 105, 107, 109, 243, 245
maturity, xix, 39, 55–57, 69, 81
medical care, xix, xxiii, xxv, 41, 43, 66, 70, 72, 75, 193. *See also* hospitals, disease
Mekane Yesus Seminary, xxxii, 8–9, 71, 75, 103–04, 113, 232, 241
Mengistu Haile Mariam, xxvii, 134, 140, 186, 211, 216, 224, 226, 243
missionaries, xv, xxv, xxix–xxx, 6, 8, 17, 19–24, 28, 32–33, 42, 48, 65–66, 81, 98, 101–3, 128, 140, 149–50, 152–53, 155, 162, 165–66, 170, 173, 177, 181, 220, 227, 229, 233, 237, 240
moratorium, xix, xxx, 70, 81–83, 97–104, 173
music, 28, 102, 150, 199–200, 228–30
Muslims. *See* Islam

nationalism, 43, 92, 174
New Testament, 3–8, 13–14, 88, 117, 126–27
Norway, xix, xxxii, 19–20, 24, 54, 166, 170, 174, 213, 220, 232, 239

Norwegian Lutheran Mission (NLM), 21, 29, 35, 169
Norwegian Missionary Society (NMS), xxix, 19–24

Old Testament, 13, 87–88, 106, 117, 158
oppression, xxxi, 39, 67, 73, 87, 92, 117, 174, 228, 234, 237
Oromo, xvii–xviii, xxxi, 27, 32, 136, 142, 149, 152, 185, 198, 212, 233, 240, 243–44

paganism, 27, 29
polygamy, 9, 23, 116
poverty, 58, 63, 77, 85, 134, 172, 198
prayer, xxix, 6, 28, 73, 114, 117, 119–20, 128, 150, 154, 158, 161, 169, 177, 179, 181, 191, 217, 220
Presbyterian, xviii, xxxiii, 23, 97
presence of God, 111, 158

qaaluu, 152–53, 161. *See also* sorcery

racism, 39
ransom, 92, 124, 126, 174, 222
refugees, xxvii, 24, 134
repentance, 24, 73, 169
resurrection, 5, 10, 15, 56, 66, 86, 92, 111, 117, 129, 174, 178, 229
revival, 27–31, 86, 120
revolution, xviii, xx, xxviii, xxix–xxx, 73, 76–78, 94, 126, 171–72, 176, 185, 187, 189, 198, 232, 236–38, 243–44, 248–49
Roman Catholicism, 10, 44, 108, 113, 119, 172, 247

sacraments, 4, 8, 64, 72, 100, 115, 244

salaries of pastors, xxiii, 3, 88–91, 93, 103, 161, 163, 174

salvation, xxx, 3, 5–7, 13, 16–17, 41–42, 66, 70, 73, 89–90, 122, 126, 148, 194, 205

schools, xv–xvii, 29–30, 52, 72, 77, 79–80, 85, 98, 102, 104–5, 120, 150–51, 153–55, 159, 162, 165, 170, 173, 186, 204–5, 208, 233, 241, 245, 248

Scripture. See Bible

second coming of Christ, 6, 74, 124

secularism, 39, 65, 67, 69, 237, 247

Security Force, 182, 185, 223

service, servanthood, xxii, xxix–xxx, 4, 7, 13, 27–28, 41–44, 72–73, 76–80, 91, 98, 100, 103, 123, 127, 166, 173, 227, 235–36

Shanqellas, 19, 22–24, 85

Silga, Tumsa, 155, 233

sin, xvii, xxx, 8, 12, 14–15, 30, 34, 66, 73, 79, 90, 92, 116–17, 122–24, 127–29, 163, 169, 174, 198, 247

slogans, 26, 98, 126, 173

socialism, xviii, xx, xxiv, 71–72, 75–76, 85, 88, 94–95, 103, 109–10, 113, 119, 172, 179, 234, 238, 243, 248–49

sorcery, 161, 215

stewardship, xxix, 11–17, 20, 91, 95

Sudan, 23–24, 172

suffering, xvii, xxxi, 6, 38, 62, 66, 68, 73, 88, 91, 133, 136, 141, 173, 179, 193–95, 197, 199, 201, 205, 222, 228, 235

Sweden, xix, 27, 54, 61, 100, 169–70, 186, 232, 239

Swedish Evangelical Mission, 35, 49, 54, 57, 150, 153, 227, 233

Tanzania, xx–xxi, xxvii, xxxiv, 24, 53, 67, 100

Theophilos, Abuna, 223

Tolessa, Tsehay: arrest, xxi, xxviii, 191–92, 197; imprisonment, xvii, xxi, xxv, xxviii, xxx, 133–37, 191–217; mother of, xvii, 134–35, 145–49; release from prison, 217–22; torture, 191–97, 205; wedding and marriage, 151–52, 156, 160

torture, xx–xxi, xxviii, xxxi, 133–35, 140, 183, 185–86, 191, 193–97, 203, 205, 219

totalitarianism, xviii, xix, 140

tree, cultic, xv, 30, 141, 153

Trinity, 5, 15, 115, 124

Tumsa, Baro, xxx, 105, 243

Tumsa, Dinadge, 155

Tumsa, Gudina: arrest, xx, xxvii, xxviii, 121, 139–40, 181–86, 195; as general secretary, xviii, xxiii, xxix, xxxi–xxxii, 3, 35, 45, 47, 71, 76, 121, 133, 169, 231, 234, 239; birth, 152, 233; burial, xxi, xxviii, 225, 227–30; execution, xxi, 121, 224–27; wedding and marriage, 151–52, 155–56, 160

Tumsa, Negasa, 155, 222–26

United States of America, xv, xxi–xxv, 22, 33, 45, 100, 166, 174, 239–40

Welega, 142–43, 167, 201, 224, 230, 233

World Council of Churches, xvi, xix, 9–10, 36, 39, 97–98, 113, 119, 229, 234, 237

World War II, xxi, xxv, 25, 27–29, 32, 49, 116, 118

youth, xviii, xx, 40, 105, 109, 120, 163, 176–79, 185, 188–89

Scripture Index

Genesis
1:26–27 111
3:1–6 106
4:8–9 106

Exodus
20:3 125

Deuteronomy
14:2 111

Psalm
135:4 111
14:1 106
14:7 106
46:1, 9 111
53:1 106
53:6 106
66:10–12 133
66:12 136
73 200

Isaiah
29:13 106
29:15 106
42:1–4 88
45 111
50:4–5 94

50:4–8 112
52:13 88
53:1–12 88

Jeremiah
25:8 111

Daniel 133, 157–58, 179, 213

Joel
2:7–11 136

Matthew
13:44 . . . . . . 92, 174
14:13–21 112
15:8 106
16:18 4
17:14–21 112
20:17–19 90
20:28 66
22:23–32 111
22:37–39 . . . . . . 79, 172–73
23:33 83
24:35 135
24:8 31
26:39 128
27:43 111
28:20 . . . . . . 16, 28, 172–73

4 128
4:23 66
6 128
9:35–38 7

Mark
1:15 124
6:31–44 112
7:6 106
9:14–29 112
9:22–24 111

Luke
1:50–55 111
11:20 5
12:19 107
14:26–33 189
14:27 139
15:1–32 66
19:10 66
23:46 111
4 58
4:18–21 66
9:10–17 112
9:58 84

John
1:14 4
12:24–26 137
13:12–17 88
15:5 16
17 10
17:11 114
17:21 114
4:35 6
5:17 110
6:1–13 112
7:44 128
8:59 128

Acts
1:8 15
17:27 110
17:32 111
20:22–24 90
20:28 5
21:1–13 128
23:6–9 128
4:16–20 126
5:29 129
7:59 111

Romans
1:16 12–13
1:17–18 90
12:1–2 . . . . . . 6, 123
13:1–7 125
13:2 125
5:2 13
7:15–20 39
8:35–39 122

1 Corinthians
1:2 4
15 111
15:3–4 . . . . . . 15, 34
15:54 122
15:55 123
3:2 57
9:6–11 112

2 Corinthians
3:4–6 16
5:13–14 . . . . . . xxii, 129
5:15 xxvii
5:7 84
8:9 89

Galatians
2:19 129

Ephesians
1:18 6
2:12 110
2:9 4
3:2 14
5:23 4

Philippians
2:5–11 88
3:20–21 6

Colossians
1:20 15

1 Timothy
2:1–2 127

2 Timothy
3:1–9 95
3:5 111

Titus
2:14 111

Hebrews
13:8 6
6:5 6

1 Peter
2:9 . . . . . . 111, 123
2:13–14 125
3:15 110

1 John
3:2 6

Revelation
2:13 135
21:5–6 110